ASSER International Sports Law Series

Series editors

More information about this series at http://www.springer.com/series/8858

Anastassia Tsoukala · Geoff Pearson
Peter T.M. Coenen (deceased)
Editors

Legal Responses to Football "Hooliganism" in Europe

ASSER PRESS

Springer

Editors
Anastassia Tsoukala
Sport Sciences
University of Paris 11
Orsay
France

Peter T.M. Coenen (deceased)
Faculty of Law
Maastricht University
Maastricht
The Netherlands

Geoff Pearson
Law School
University of Manchester
Manchester
UK

ISSN 1874-6926 ISSN 2215-003X (electronic)
ASSER International Sports Law Series
ISBN 978-94-6265-107-4 ISBN 978-94-6265-108-1 (eBook)
DOI 10.1007/978-94-6265-108-1

Library of Congress Control Number: 2015960412

Published by T.M.C. ASSER PRESS, The Hague, The Netherlands www.asserpress.nl
Produced and distributed for T.M.C. ASSER PRESS by Springer-Verlag Berlin Heidelberg

Printed on acid-free paper

This Springer imprint is published by SpringerNature
The registered company is Springer Science+Business Media B.V. Dordrecht

Series Information

Books in the *ASSER International Sports Law Series* comprehensibly chart and analyse legal and policy developments in the emerging field of European and international sports law. The Series uniquely features contributions from leading sports law scholars and is the most cited in its field. It is a valuable resource for practitioners, academics, sports officials, and anyone interested in or impacted by sports and the law.

The Series is developed, edited, and published by the ASSER International Sports Law Centre in The Hague. The Centre's mission is to advance the study and practice of sports law, in its translational manifestation, through high-quality scholarship, research, education, and consultancy.

Apart from the Series, the Centre also edits and publishes *The International Sports Law Journal.*

Series editors

Prof. Dr. Ben Van Rompuy, *Editor-in-chief*
e-mail: b.van.rompuy@asser.nl

Dr. Antoine Duval
e-mail: a.duval@asser.nl

Marco A. van der Harst, LL.M.
e-mail: m.van.der.harst@asser.nl

Editorial Office

ASSER International Sports Law Centre
T.M.C. Asser Instituut
P.O. Box 30461
2500 GL The Hague
The Netherlands
www.sportslaw.nl
sportslaw@asser.nl

international sports law centre

In Memoriam

Dr. Peter T.M. Coenen (1981–2015)

Shortly before this book was published, one of its editors and authors, Peter Coenen, passed away aged 34. Peter was assistant professor of Constitutional Law at Maastricht University's Department of Public Law. Prior to that he worked at the School of Law at the University of Lucerne.

Peter was passionate about sport, but above all he was an academic. His specialism, legal responses to public disorder at football matches, demanded measured and calm scholarly investigation. Peter provided exactly that.

This book was conceived of by Peter. In bringing together authors from eight European nations, it stands as an important scholarly contribution to the discipline, as it is the first comparative analysis of legal responses to football crowd violence and disorder. Equally, it stands as a fitting tribute to Peter, but also a tragic reminder that the sports law community has lost an outstanding scholar.

At the time of Peter's passing, he was preparing to defend his Ph.D. thesis at Edge Hill University. In his thesis, Peter explored the legislation on football-related disorder in England and Wales and in the Netherlands. He urged caution on the use of football banning orders and argued that the European Union should acknowledge the deficiencies of the English and Dutch approaches before taking action in this area. As Peter had submitted his thesis, the Graduate School Board of Studies at Edge Hill University agreed to continue with the examination process. As his Director of Studies, I am grateful to Peter's examiners for having agreed to this.

The conferral of a posthumous doctorate award is in recognition of Peter's scholarly excellence. It does, however, once again remind us of the loss we have suffered, both personally and professionally. In some small way, I hope this award brings some comfort to Peter's wife Xiaolu and his children Julian and Emily.

October 2015 — Professor Richard Parrish

Contents

Chapter 1
Legal Responses to Football 'Hooliganism' in Europe—Introduction

Peter T.M. Coenen, Geoff Pearson and Anastassia Tsoukala

Abstract In this introduction, the authors explain the subject and the motivations behind this collection. They explain the methodology used, the rationale for the jurisdictions chosen and the value of this contribution to the existing literature on the subject of football crowd regulation and management. They consider the transnational responses to football-related disorder: for example, the European Convention in Spectator Violence and Misbehaviour at Sports Events, and in Particular Football Matches 1985, and the relevant legislative instruments as well as the role of the European Union in the regulation of football-related disorder. The authors explain how the legal regulation of football-related disorder relates to civil rights/liberties and human rights law. Finally, the authors explain the difficulties attached to the use of the term 'football hooliganism'.

Keywords Football hooliganism · Football-related disorder · Crowd management · Transnational regulation · Comparative law · Methodology · Legal regulation · Human rights

---

At the time this chapter was written, Peter Coenen (deceased) was Assistant Professor of Law at Maastricht University in the Netherlands. Dr. Geoff Pearson is Senior Lecturer in Criminal Law at the University of Manchester's Law School. Dr. Anastassia Tsoukala is tenured Associate Professor at the University of Paris XI.

G. Pearson (✉)
School of Law, University of Manchester, Manchester, UK
e-mail: geoff.pearson@manchester.ac.uk

A. Tsoukala
University of Paris XI, Orsay, France
e-mail: tsoukala.anastassia@gmail.com

A. Tsoukala et al. (eds.), *Legal Responses to Football "Hooliganism" in Europe*,
ASSER International Sports Law Series, DOI 10.1007/978-94-6265-108-1_1

Contents

1.1 Introduction

Every week hundreds of thousands of European football supporters attend matches to watch their teams play, often travelling long distances to away matches both domestically and abroad. However, large numbers of spectators—many of whom are visiting fans—intent on engaging in noisy and colourful support of their team pose crowd management challenges for both the football authorities and the police. Football crowds are generally perceived to pose a higher potential for violence and disorder than other sports crowds, and the phenomenon of football crowd disorder and violence has become popularly known across Europe as 'football hooliganism'. This phenomenon has been much debated across Europe, with instances of widespread disorder at tournaments and European fixtures involving both international and club sides[1] in addition to problems in the domestic competitions of European nations. Usually this disorder is limited in both duration and the numbers of individuals involved, but occasionally it has led to widespread damage, injury and even fatalities,[2] keeping the subject high on the political agenda. The phenomenon of 'football hooliganism' has captured the attention of the media and the state since the late 1960s in the UK, and from the 1970s onwards in continental Europe. Images of 'rioting' at or around football matches have been broadly publicised in popular media and incidents are typically followed by a demand for more stringent legal and policing measures against the 'hooligans'.

As a result, football crowds have been the subject of increased regulation across Europe, and even though in many states the problem of football-crowd violence and disorder appears to be on the wane, restrictions of both a criminal and civil nature are becoming tighter. Largely following the 'English model' of confronting 'hooliganism', lawmakers in different states throughout the continent have increasingly viewed football crowds as a legitimate target for new and creative forms of legislation and judicial ingenuity to attempt to solve what is perceived as

[1]International examples include widespread disorder during WC 1998 in Marseilles, in Charleroi at Euro 2000, and Warsaw at Euro 2012 between Russian and Polish fans. Club level examples include a Champions League match between AS Roma and Manchester United in 2007 and a Europa League match between Slovan Bratislava and Sparta Prague in 2014.

[2]E.g. the deaths of Michalis Filopoulos in Athens (2007), police officer Filippo Raciti in Catania (2007), Dejan D. in Novi Sad (2008), Brice Taton in Belgrade (2009), Yann L. in Paris (2010), a 43 year old fan of Djurgardens in Sweden (2014) and Kostas Katsoulis in Crete (2014).

a serious social problem. English laws and strategies have typically been viewed as 'best practice' and have been replicated in the domestic laws of many individual member states. At a pan-European level, the 'English' influence can be seen at three different levels: first, in bilateral relations between states, secondly in the active participation of the English authorities during the drafting of the 1985 European Convention against football-related violence and the correlated UEFA security instructions, and thirdly in the long-term 'lobbying' within EU circles and the ensuing determinant role of the English delegations during the drafting of all relevant EU regulatory texts. Under the influence of the English model of confronting hooliganism, a multi-level governance network has taken shape with respect to football-related disorder in Europe.

However, in an increasingly risk-oriented security landscape, the imposition of many of these responses and the ensuing introduction and legitimisation of police practices and hybrid civil/criminal legal instruments brings into question the security of the civil and human rights of football fans. A number of commentators on the subject have challenged the legality of certain legal responses under domestic law and the rights provided to citizens under the EU Treaties and the European Convention on Human Rights (ECHR), especially against those merely suspected of involvement or potential involvement in football crowd disorder or violence.[3] Regardless of these concerns, the twenty-first century has seen continued use of preventative measures and 'hybrid' law such as football banning orders, and the cross-border progression of such measures.

This edited collection focuses on the legal regulation of football hooliganism in a number of jurisdictions in Europe, combining a human rights angle with a comparative law approach. The domestic legislation on football hooliganism in these states will be identified and analysed by academics and legal professionals from within those jurisdictions. The authors will compare the different approaches and draw together common themes and problems, identifying both good and bad practice in the management of football crowds and those convicted or suspected of engaging in football-related crime or disorder. We conclude with recommendations for how public and sports authorities can respond generally to the challenge of football crowd management, without risking breaches of human and civil rights protected by the Treaty on the Functioning of the European Union (TFEU) or the ECHR.

Two important issues should be clarified from the outset; first, the labels 'football hooliganism' and 'football hooligan' should be used with extreme care. These are labels that were first created by the British media in the mid-1960s,[4] which then seeped into legal responses to the problem,[5] and were later appropriated by those commenting on the phenomenon in non-English-speaking nations.[6] However, there

[3]Armstrong and Hobbs 1994; Greenfield and Osborn 1996; James and Pearson 2006; Pearson 1999, 2005; Stott and Pearson 2007; Tsoukala 2002, 2009a.

[4]Dunning et al. 1988, p. 165; Stott and Pearson 2007, p. 13.

[5]Pearson 1998.

[6]E.g. Bodin 1999; De Biasi 1998; Pilz 1996; Spaaij 2006.

is neither an accepted popular nor legal definition of the labels in England and the terms have been used to describe different phenomena, and in different contexts to demonise, but also to exonerate the behaviour of football spectators,[7] which can have serious implications upon the individuals implicated by creating a 'master-stigma'[8] that can justify disproportionate legal and policing responses. The use of these labels has been subjected to severe academic criticism, described as a 'historical (and hysterical) mass media construction'[9] and is becoming 'increasingly redundant'[10] as a meaningful and useful label to describe the nature of football violence or explain why it occurs (or, indeed, why it is usually absent). Therefore, the editors use the label not to describe a singular phenomenon but to refer to the wider social and socio-legal construction that has developed around the connected problems of (a) 'spontaneous' disorder and violence at and in connection with football matches, and (b) that of gangs who travel to matches with the intention of engaging in violence with rival gangs. The contributors to this edited collection have been invited to be reflexive about their use of the term, or to clarify their own definition for their use thereof. This issue is developed further below.

Secondly, in this collection we have encouraged contributors to consider the impact that laws and policing practices which have been designed to manage football crowds have had upon both civil rights (or liberties) and human rights. It is important to note the difference between civil rights—i.e. those rights, freedoms or liberties granted by the state to its citizens—and human rights—i.e. those rights that are granted by supra and international conventions and declarations to all citizens. The former by their nature are limited because citizens only possess these rights or liberties insofar as the state grants them; states will retain the ability to change or amend even a written constitution or bill of rights in order to legitimise laws that otherwise would have infringed civil rights. Human rights on the other hand are designed to apply equally to all citizens at a supra or international level, and states themselves can be sued for infringing them, even though under their own domestic constitution they may be perfectly entitled to restrict them. Human rights are particularly pertinent here, because with only one current exception, the European Convention of Human Rights binds all European states, including all the states that this collection focuses on.

1.2 Methodology

This edited collection will use a comparative legal methodology. The essence and goal of comparative law is the comparison of different legal systems.[11] This necessarily implies a transnational component to comparative law; comparative law

[7]Pearson 1998.

[8]Salter 1985.

[9]Redhead 1993, p. 3.

[10]Pearson 2012, p. 186.

[11]Zweigert and Kötz 1998, p. 2.

demands a comparison between at least two (national) legal systems. Comparative legal analysis can be done at different levels. Research which compares the spirit and style of the legal systems, and the methods of thought and procedure of those systems, is called macro-comparison.[12] On the other hand, research into a specific problem or issue is called micro-comparison.[13]

Comparative law in the abstract has only one methodology: namely the comparison of laws, norms, institutions and sometimes even entire legal systems.[14] However, there are numerous techniques to carry out such comparison; historical, functional, statistical, thematic or structural.[15] The dominant technique of comparative law is functionalism.[16] By looking to other nations for solutions to certain legal problems, a far greater range of possible solutions can be found than when one looks only at one single nation.[17] The comparative research method looks outward to gain a better understanding of a domestic legal system. By analysing solutions proposed in other jurisdictions, comparative research contributes to a more complete analysis of the domestic system. Comparative law also alleviates the risk that our own system is taken for granted and seen as the 'natural' state of affairs.[18] Comparative law offers guidance to the legislator, and the comparison of various legal systems has been successfully used in the construction and reform of legal systems around the world, and has been an aid in the (international) unification of the law.[19]

The methodology of comparative law is in constant development,[20] but functionalism is the basic feature underlying comparative research. Functionalism ultimately determines which laws to compare, the overall size of the project, the benefits and possibilities of the project, but also its limitations. Kötz in this respect states that, "[i]ncomparables cannot usefully be compared, and in law the only things which are comparable are those which fulfil the same function."[21]

It is important to note that the basic proposition underlying comparative law is that every legal system faces some of the same problems, and that every legal system solves these problems in different manners, but often with similar results.[22] Therefore, it is important to start a comparative legal research project by wording a question in terms that seek to reach a certain neutrality. The problem that the research sets out to investigate should be looked at in as nation- and language-neutral

[12]Ibid., p. 4.

[13]Ibid., p. 5.

[14]Palmer 2005, p. 263.

[15]Ibid.

[16]Ibid.

[17]Zweigert and Kötz 1998, p. 15.

[18]Heringa and Kiiver 2012, p. 1.

[19]Zweigert and Kötz 1998, p. 24.

[20]Ibid., p. 33.

[21]Ibid., p. 34.

[22]Ibid.

a manner as possible, and not be coloured by the language of a certain legal system. In addition to the language used, it is crucial to keep in mind that different legal systems also have fundamentally different structures. In comparative legal research, it is essential that not only the law is looked at, but also other circumstances that can have an impact upon the research questions. It is important to have a basic understanding of the society and the nature of the other legal system to give complete answers to the research questions posed.

An important consideration in a comparative legal research project is which systems to compare. According to Kötz a necessary degree of restraint should be employed in this respect;[23] in any comparative research project, a thorough and objective analysis should be made of each legal system that is researched.[24] This provides the data which can be used to compare the legal systems and look for answers to the research questions. The comparative analysis of the data is the most important phase in any comparative research project.

Any comparative research must be done to achieve a certain goal. When using comparative law, there needs to be an awareness of why this methodology is used.[25] In a comparative analysis it is not sufficient to merely list the similarities and differences between the legal systems researched.[26] In the analysis, it is crucial that there is sufficient attention to the solutions offered by various legal systems, free from the background and the biases from the legal system from which these solutions emanate.[27] The solutions offered in the legal systems that are the subject of the research need to be analysed in as objective and unbiased a manner as is possible.

Once the analysis has yielded possible answers to the research questions posed in the various legal systems researched, and the answers found in the various legal systems are freed from their national contexts, then these solutions need to be grouped in a systematic manner. It is important in this respect that a common vocabulary is used, which covers all the legal systems researched. Different national legal systems use a different vocabulary and the same words can have different meanings. However, comparative law is only possible with a common vocabulary, which fits all the legal systems researched. Finally, the findings need to be critically evaluated. This step necessarily involves a subjective element. However, since the comparative method revolves around finding a suitable solution for a specific legal problem in a number of legal systems, it is necessary that at the end of the project the researcher will come to a solution s/he considers suitable.

In this edited volume, following this introduction, we will have a more in-depth analysis of a number of countries in Europe. There will be an in-depth analysis of Italy, England and Wales, Germany, France, Greece, the Netherlands, Austria and Ukraine. For these analyses, the editors have worked with contributors to produce

---

[23]Ibid., p. 41.

[24]Ibid.

[25]Heringa and Kiiver 2012, p. 2.

[26]Zweigert and Kötz 1998, p. 43.

[27]Ibid.

a thorough understanding of the legal, cultural and social landscape of the countries analysed. Furthermore, the contributors' knowledge of the subject of this book has been gained from different standpoints and backgrounds within the legal systems analysed. The diverse exposure of the contributors to the subject matter of this book enables the reader to view the subject of this collection from a variety of angles, which is intended to aid a better and more thorough understanding and is instrumental in an analysis of 'football hooliganism' that goes beyond mere domestic solutions.

The rationale for the selection of the countries analysed in this book was based on a number of factors. The editors felt it was important to include the major footballing powers in Europe (in terms of on-pitch success and popularity as a spectator sport), and also those nations with a historical reputation for football crowd disorder and violence. These factors put pressure on the state to take action to reduce problems of crowd disorder and turn a blind eye to the rights of fans. The editors also wanted to focus on those nations that had hosted major international competitions following the regulatory response to football crowd problems that started to take place across Europe in the mid to late 1980s. All the nations covered in this collection hosted such tournaments.[28] For these states, the organisation of football mega-events led to legislative activism to try and reduce the risk of crowd disorder and an important question this book poses is in how far the rights of football supporters were taken into account when these regulatory changes took place.

However, pragmatic reasons also saw the exclusion of a number of jurisdictions that we would have liked to have included. Of the major footballing powers Spain is notably absent, and in terms of recent hosting of events, contributions from Portugal and Poland would have been welcome. Some interesting developments in policing in Scandinavia are not covered, nor the arguably worsening problems in the Balkan states. Unfortunately securing English-language contributions from these areas of sufficient quality in terms of legal knowledge and independence led to the unwanted exclusion of some important jurisdictions. As a result of this, we do not claim that this collection provides a totally comprehensive review of European responses to football-crowd disorder. Nevertheless, we are aware that in a number of other European states similar developments to those discussed in these pages have taken, or are taking, place, for example in Scotland, Russia and Turkey, as supposed 'best practice' is rolled out across Europe.

Despite these limitations, we believe the analysis of the various jurisdictions in Europe in this collection provides us with an interesting and important picture of how different European states have approached the same problem in a variety of ways. The analysis of these countries also enables us to understand how the solutions of different countries have cross-influenced each other. The countries covered in this edited volume are from all parts of Europe and include some of the countries that have been most instrumental in shaping European and international policy on the subject of crowd management, football-related violence and human rights. Most are members of the European Union. All are signatories of the ECHR. Through the analysis of the different chapters and countries in this edited volume,

[28]Including the football tournament at the Athens Olympic Games 2004.

the editors hope to identify certain best practices regarding crowd management and the prevention of football-related violence. However, the editors also hope that this edited volume will contribute to a more thorough understanding of the phenomenon of 'football hooliganism', that the reader will gain a better understanding of football supporters in general and will understand that football supporters have human rights, which can be respected and protected while still successfully managing large 'risk' football crowds.

1.3 Pan-European Responses to 'Football Hooliganism'

Although this book does not deal explicitly with transnational responses to football-related disorder, it is appropriate at this point to give some background on the international responses to the phenomenon. Football has become a truly transnational sport, with international fixtures on the agenda almost weekly, and football supporters have benefitted from increased mobility, allowing them to visit football matches all over the world. Football-related disorder also transcends national borders. Therefore, any legal approach to understanding and managing football-related disorder must also have a transnational component.

The Council of Europe (CoE) played an important role in the internationalisation process after the Second World War. The main goal of the CoE is, 'to create a common democratic and legal area throughout the whole of the continent, ensuring respect for its fundamental values: human rights, democracy and the rule of law'.[29] As a result of the events at the 1985 European Cup Final in the Heysel Stadium in Brussels, where 39 supporters were killed following terrace disorder, the CoE adopted the European Convention on Spectator Violence and Misbehaviour at Sports Events and in Particular at Football Matches (the Convention). At present, 41 member states of the CoE have signed and ratified the Convention.[30] The goal of the Convention is the prevention and control of spectator violence and to ensure the safety of spectators at sporting events.[31] The Convention concerns sporting events in general and is not limited to football matches. The Convention focuses on three core areas, prevention (Article 3), international cooperation (Article 4) and the identification and treatment of those who misbehave at sporting events (Article 5). Since 1998, the compliance of the member states with the Convention is actively monitored. Under this programme, consultative and evaluative visits are made to members of the Convention. Members of the Convention furthermore submit an annual report to the standing committee, outlining their implementation of the Convention and the

---

[29] Council of Europe, The Council of Europe in Brief, Our Objectives. http://www.coe.int/aboutCoe/index.asp?page=nosObjectifs&l=en. Accessed 23 October 2014.

[30] Council of Europe, European Convention on Spectator Violence and Misbehaviour at Sports Events and in particular at Football Matches CETS No. 120. http://conventions.coe.int/Treaty/Commun/QueVoulezVous.asp?NT=120&CM=8&DF=26/03/2013&CL=ENG. Accessed 23 October 2014.

[31] Council of Europe, For a Safe and Tolerant Sport. http://www.coe.int/t/dg4/sport/Source/T-RV/livret_violence_en.pdf. Accessed 23 October 2014.

level of safety and security that has been achieved in the member state since joining the Convention.

The Convention has had a marked impact on domestic and international policies addressing football-related disorder. Tsoukala states that, 'the impact of the European Convention on the shaping of European counter-hooliganism policies is undoubtedly distinguishable beneath the many different domestic penalisations of football-related violent behaviour, and most obvious in the development of domestic and international police cooperation'.[32] A particularly striking feature of the Convention is its wide target population and geographical reach.[33] The Convention applies not only to offenders, but also to potential troublemakers and applies to both inside and outside of football stadia.[34] The result of the Convention's broad level of application, under influence of risk-oriented discourses to the control of deviance, was that '[f]rom then onwards, the domestic surveillance and control mechanisms, ranging from CCTV cameras to undercover policing and intelligence gathering and exchange, expanded exponentially, thus routinising the underlying control of deviance in many different European countries'.[35]

The European Union has also long been involved in discussing and regulating transnational football-related disorder. Driven by some of the major international incidents in the 1970s and 1980s (most notably the Heysel tragedy), there has been a constant stream of regulatory instruments in the EU[36] and the regulation of

---

[32]Tsoukala 2009b, p. 3.

[33]Ibid.

[34]Ibid.

[35]Ibid.

[36]Resolution of the European Parliament on the tragedy at the Heysel stadium in Brussels, 13 June 1985;.Resolution of the European Parliament on the violence at the football match in Brussels on 29 May 1985, 13 June 1985; Council Recommendation on guidelines for preventing and restraining disorder connected with football matches, 3 May 1996; Resolution of the European Parliament on hooliganism and the free movement of football supporters, 10 June 1996; Joint Action adopted by the Council on the basis of Article K.3 of the Treaty on European Union with regard to cooperation on law and order and security, 26 May 1997; Council Resolution on preventing and restraining football hooliganism through the exchange of experience, exclusion from stadiums and media policy, 9 June 1997; Council Resolution concerning a handbook for international police cooperation and measures to prevent and control violence and disturbances in connection with international football matches, 21 June 1999; Council Resolution concerning a handbook with recommendations for international police cooperation and measures to prevent and control violence and disturbances in connection with football matches with an international dimension, in which at least one Member State is involved, 6 December 2001; Council Decision concerning security in connection with football matches with an international dimension, 25 April 2002; Council Resolution on the use by Member States of bans on access to venues of football matches with an international dimension, 17 November 2003; Council Resolution concerning an updated handbook with recommendations for international police cooperation and measures to prevent and control violence and disturbances in connection with football matches with an international dimension, in which at least one Member State is involved, 4 December 2006; Council Resolution concerning an updated handbook with recommendations for international police cooperation and measures to prevent and control violence and disturbances in connection with football matches with an international dimension, in which at least one Member State is involved, 3 June 2010.

football-related disorder has remained high on the EU agenda. The majority of the Member States exchange information with other Member States on football supporters before international football matches. There is now an intricate system in place whereby law enforcement authorities and other stakeholders in the various Member States exchange information regarding international football matches. For this end, in each Member State there are National Football Information Points, whose task it is to exchange information with their counterparts.[37] There is an extensive EU handbook on football 'hooliganism', dealing with a variety of topics to streamline the organisation of international football matches and tournaments.[38] Organising a football match or tournament is no longer a matter exclusively for the hosting Member State; there is now a multi-level regulatory framework in the organisation of football matches, in which the visiting and other Member States and various other stakeholders (UEFA, FIFA, national Football Associations, etc.) are intrinsically involved.

1.4 Human Rights

In Europe, human rights have evolved from opposition to feudal rulers in the Middle Ages to a sophisticated catalogue of rights with domestic and international enforcement mechanisms attached to them. The atrocities committed during two world wars in the first half of the twentieth century have shown that powerful and inward-looking states form a threat against (inter)national peace and individual and collective rights. As a counterweight to this threat, a process of internationalisation was accelerated in the mid-twentieth century. This resulted in, among others, the founding of the United Nations and the Universal Declaration of Human Rights, the establishment of the European Union (EU) and the Council of Europe (CoE) and the European Convention on Human Rights (ECHR). One of the unique features of the European regional system for the protection of human rights has been the European Court of Human Rights (ECtHR). The ECtHR has proven itself as a true supranational court, whose judgments have garnered a fair amount of respect and influence throughout Europe.[39] The ECtHR now has rendered a great number of judgments, many of which, when taken into account by governments, have had a fundamental impact on the rights of individuals and the way in which European citizens look at their rights and their societies.

[37]Council Resolution concerning an updated handbook with recommendations for international police cooperation and measures to prevent and control violence and disturbances in connection with football matches with an international dimension, in which at least one Member State is involved, 3 June 2010.

[38]Ibid.

[39]Although it is fair to say that the influence of the ECtHR's judgments also provoke critique and resistance in the Contracting Parties and that the judgments of the ECtHR are not always observed by the Contracting Parties.

There are a number of ECHR rights that are relevant to analysing legal responses for football-related violence and disorder. The ECtHR plays an important role in promoting the rule of law in the Contracting Parties and protects fair trial guarantees, such as the presumption of innocence. In addition to non-derogable human rights,[40] the ECtHR in her judgments balances a greater number of conditional human rights of applicants against the interests of the state and assesses in individual cases whether the state's actions complained of complied with the principle of proportionality. All states (and by implication, all state police forces and local authorities) have a duty not to disproportionately or arbitrarily infringe the rights of citizens to privacy[41] (relevant due to surveillance techniques and retention/sharing of personal data) and liberty[42] (relevant due to arbitrary preventative detention measures). Furthermore, state organs also have a duty to assist citizens in pursuing positive rights, in this case freedom of expression[43] (in expressing support for a team, nation or locality either verbally through chants or through dress/colours/banners) and freedom of assembly and association[44] (in gathering together with other fans of the same team). While these latter freedoms have traditionally been associated with citizens demonstrating their democratic and political rights, recent European Court of Human Rights cases[45] have started to recognise the rights of groups gathering together for cultural and arguably completely social reasons, thus encompassing dominant forms of European football fandom within the umbrella protection of the ECHR. Finally, for those fans convicted of, or suspected of, involvement in football-related violence or disorder, the right to a fair trial[46] becomes relevant. As we will see, this is particularly pertinent when it comes to preventative civil or administrative orders which have a punitive effect placed on those merely suspected of involvement in violence/disorder.

Human rights do not only protect the majority or those considered popular in our societies; they extend to all the people in our constitutional democracies. Human rights are interrelated, interdependent and indivisible.[47] This means that human rights guarantees also extend to those groups considered different or unpopular in our societies, including football supporters. Football supporters can

[40] Non-derogable human rights under the ECHR are the right to life contained in Article 2, the prohibition of torture, inhuman and degrading treatment contained in Article 3, the prohibition of slavery and forced labour contained in Article 4 and the prohibition of retroactive punishment contained in Article 7. These rights cannot be derogated from even in times emergency (Article 15).

[41] Article 8.

[42] Article 5.

[43] Article 10.

[44] Article 11.

[45] Most notably *Friend v. United Kingdom*, App. Nos. 16072/06 & 27808/08, 24 November 2009, para 50.

[46] Article 6.

[47] See Office of the High Commissioner for Human Rights, What are Human Rights? www.ohchr.org/en/issues/pages/whatarehumanrights.aspx. Accessed 23 October 2014. See also Nickel 2008.

be intimidating for the observer unfamiliar with this phenomenon with their boisterous support for their football team. The ritualised carnival of the football supporter is often not understood or is fundamentally misunderstood. There is no evidence to suggest that football supporters—in and of themselves—are either more violent or prone to disorder than other social groups. Indeed, it is a mistake to assume that football supporters even following a particular team are a homogeneous group. Instead they are made up of many different subcultures that attend matches with different aims and objectives.[48] Most football supporters attend matches to enjoy an entertainment experience and support a team they have an emotional connection with. Some attend in order to bond with their families, to see friends, as an excuse to visit new places, to buy merchandise, or take photographs to enhance their online social status. For other fan subcultures in Europe the most important aspect of a match is creating an 'atmosphere' of noise and colour, often associated with a demonstration of belonging to a given territory, be it local or national, or adhering to a given political movement, be it far right or far left, whereas in northern Europe in particular, the 'craic' of social gathering and alcohol consumption dominates spectator objectives. For these latter groups, this often results in boisterous behaviour, singing and chanting and excessive substance abuse. However, this does not mean that disorder will necessary follow. Finally, at some clubs there also exist a small number of fans who attend matches with the primary intention of engaging in violence or disorder with like-minded individuals supporting a rival team. It is managing and controlling these latter subcultures that have dominated the agenda when it comes to the management of football crowds in Europe.

All football supporters (but particularly those who travel away from home) are met with invasive policing and legal measures to a certain extent. In many nations football supporters are viewed by the authorities as a potential danger and the response has been constant police supervision, continuous CCTV control, special travel arrangements, police escorts, the routine wearing by the police of personal protective equipment ('riot gear'), cages inside stadia and body searches. However, it must be remembered that fans should possess the same civil and human rights as those citizens who do not attend matches.

Human (and civil) rights also extend to the latter group often referred to as 'football hooligans', who attend matches with the intention of engaging in violence or disorder. 'Hooligans', whether convicted or merely suspected of involvement in offences, still possess rights, although these may of course be restricted by law (e.g. a custodial sentence for a violent offence that lawfully restricts the right to liberty), or a proportionate policing response to prevent imminent violence (which may limit freedom of expression or assembly). This does not mean that acts of hooliganism and/or violence should go unpunished, merely that in prosecuting and punishing football 'hooligans', certain standards have to be taken into account. It means using legitimate and lawful means to prosecute and punish

[48]Pearson 2012, pp. 2–5; 24–25; 184.

offenders for their unlawful acts, while also observing their rights. This lends credence to the actions of our societies as constitutional democracies built on the foundation of respect for the rights of every citizen.

1.5 'Football Hooliganism'

This collection compares legal responses to football-crowd violence and disorder, often referred to as 'football hooliganism', in a number of jurisdictions in Europe. A common language is an essential element of comparative legal research, which poses problems when a term such as 'football hooliganism' is utilised, which as we have seen lacks a firm social or legal definition in English, even before it is utilised in non-English-speaking environments. There are many different types of disorder and behaviour at and around football matches and/or involving football fans that have been labelled 'football hooliganism'. There is no clear, single legal definition of football hooliganism[49] and instead, lawmakers throughout Europe have chosen to penalise a variety of modes of behaviour under the label 'football hooliganism'.[50]

According to the sociologists of the so-called Leicester School,[51] football hooliganism is 'not so much scientific sociological or social psychological concept as a construct of politicians and the media'.[52] They add that the term football hooliganism as such 'lacks precision and is used to cover a variety of forms of behaviour'.[53] The relation to football and the level of disorder and/or violence involved in these forms of behaviour also varies.[54] The term football hooliganism has become a catch-all phrase for a multitude of behaviours and incidents. Football hooliganism in popular media, however, is sometimes viewed or portrayed as a one-dimensional, single phenomenon, for which an easy solution can be found.[55]

However, 'hooliganism' is not a one-dimensional problem or even a single phenomenon. There are multiple causes and explanations for disorder or violence that occurs in football stadia or involves football supporters, and any analysis must keep the multifaceted nature of the phenomenon in mind. Behaviour labelled 'football hooliganism' covers, for example, fighting, setting off fireworks, throwing missiles, pitch invasions, acts of vandalism and indecent or offensive

---

[49]Pearson 1998; Redhead 1993, p. 3.

[50]Tsoukala 2007, p. 5.

[51]The Leicester School refers to Professor Eric Dunning and a number of colleagues at the University of Leicester Department of Sociology who did extensive research into the sociology of sport in general and football hooliganism in particular.

[52]Dunning et al. 2002, p. 1.

[53]Ibid.

[54]Ibid., p. 2; Pearson 1998.

[55]Stott and Pearson 2007, p. 48.

chanting. Such behaviour may lead to prosecution and possibly a criminal conviction. However, this list is by no means comprehensive. The current use of the label 'football hooliganism' is much more widely interpreted. It encompasses a wide array of vaguely defined behaviours, most of which are deviant, rather than criminal. Much of the behaviour labelled as football hooliganism does not exclusively happen in the stadium at the time of the match, but can also occur in different locations (bars, train stations, etc.) and can happen on any day of the week.

Salter's research of magistrates' courts from the early 1980s found the following to be defined as 'hooliganism' in football contexts:

> [...] looking aggressive; jeering; shouting; jumping up and down; waving fists in the air; running in groups; issuing blood curdling and obscene threats involving baseball bats; invading the pitch; wrecking motorway service stations; taking a supporting crutch from its unfortunate owner and using it as a club; fighting with fists, kicking rival fans who are on the ground, smashing their faces up with hammers, robbing them of their valuables and clothes; ripping up terracing; 'stampeding' around and outside railway stations with the effect of scattering the public; obstructing the road; denting car bonnets and roofs; the vandalising and overturning of local people's cars; assaulting local residents with iron bars and wooden clubs; 'shouting National Front and racist abuse'; racially inspired hospitalising and disabling attacks with bottles and fists on British Rail employees, Pakistani taxi drivers and shopkeepers; and lastly, throwing missiles at each other, local people, oncoming cars and the police.[56]

Spaaij draws attention to the distinction, 'between spontaneous, relatively isolated incidents of spectator violence and the behaviour of socially organised or institutionalised fan (hooligan) groups which engage in competitive violence, principally with other hooligan groups'.[57] He argues that over time there has been a historical shift from the first kind of incident to the second, more organised kind of incident, which represents football hooliganism in its current form and manifestation. In the early days of football, reported incidents at matches were mostly directed at the referee or players on the field and had a direct relation to the events on the playing field,[58] but Pearson and Vamplew both identified frequent instances of violence between rival supporters at football matches at the end of the nineteenth century.[59]

Other research, either explicitly or by implication, criticises the focus on organised 'hooligan' groups of 'firms', arguing that the levels of violence and organisation of the hooligan firms is exaggerated[60] and that the major threat to public order around football matches comes not from organised 'hooligan' gangs but from wider crowd disorder caused predominantly by poor crowd management strategies and tactics.[61] Based on data gathered from a series of projects investigating the

---

[56] Salter 1986.

[57] Spaaij 2005, p. 1.

[58] Dunning et al. 1988, p. 7. See also MacKay 1986.

[59] Pearson 1983, p. 64; Vamplew 1979.

[60] Armstrong 1998; Redhead 2010.

[61] Stott and Pearson 2007.

best practice in policing football crowds, Stott et al. argue that at matches with an international dimension in particular, 'hooligans' typically lack the power and influence to spark widespread disorder and rioting.[62] The predominance of unorganised and spontaneous disorder is a key feature of many other ethnographic and observational studies[63] into British football fan behaviour, suggesting that in the UK at least we should not make the mistake of assuming that 'hooliganism' is predominantly the result of fans travelling to matches with the intention of engaging in disorder or violence.

Spaaij notes the dissimilarity in football hooliganism transnationally;[64] fan cultures throughout the world, throughout Europe and even within different countries are quite different. However, some general conclusions about the characteristics of football 'hooliganism' can be made. More traditional 'English style' hooligan groups can be found mostly in Northern and Central Europe.[65] In Southern and Eastern Europe there is the quite distinctive fan culture of the Ultras.[66] Ultra groups can be characterised by a relatively high degree of (formal) organisation and their expressive and colourful support for their team. There is a great variation in the violent tendencies of different Ultra groups.[67] Furthermore, over the years these different fan cultures have influenced each other, assisted in no small part by social media. Southern and Eastern European fan groups have become influenced by the 'English style' of support, while Northern and Central European fan groups have adopted elements of the Ultra culture. The fact that fan cultures influence each other over national and local boundaries should not detract from the fact that a large proportion of the behaviour of any fan group is influenced by their locality. As Spaaij notes: '[l]ocal historical and cultural traditions and legacies continue to exert a strong influence over patterns of behaviour'.[68] It is therefore important to not only be mindful of variations in fan culture between different cultures, but also look at differences at other levels, whether nationally, regionally, locally or even within different fan groups. A serious problem in terms of good crowd management practice would therefore arise if legal responses to predominantly spontaneous forms of disorder were shaped by states whose 'hooligan' problem was of a more organised nature. It is therefore important for the reader to recognise the ambiguity inherent in the term 'football hooliganism' and to keep in mind the varieties of behaviour that have been categorised as such.

---

[62]Stott et al. 2001; Stott and Pearson 2007; Stott et al. 2012.

[63]Brown 1993; Giulianotti 1991; King 2000; Millward 2009; Pearson 2012.

[64]Spaaij 2005.

[65]Ibid.

[66]Ibid.

[67]Ibid.

[68]Ibid., p. 3.

References

Armstrong G (1998) Football Hooligans: Knowing the Score. Oxford, Berg

Armstrong G, Hobbs D (1994) Tackled from behind. In: Giulianotti R et al (eds) Football, violence and social identity. London, Routledge, pp.191–222

Bodin D (1999) Hooliganisme, vérité et mensonges. ESF, Paris

Brown A (1993) Ratfink reds; Montpellier and Rotterdam in 1991. In: Redhead S (ed) The passion and the fashion: Football fandom in New Europe. Aldershot, Avebury, pp. 33–44

De Biasi R (1998) The policing of hooliganism in Italy. In: Della Porta D, Reiter H (eds) Policing protest. Minneapolis, University of Minnesota Press, pp. 213–227

Dunning E et al (1988) The roots of football hooliganism. London, Routledge

Dunning E et al (eds) (2002) Fighting fans: Football hooliganism as a world phenomenon. University College Dublin Press, Dublin

Giulianotti R (1991) Scotland's Tartan Army in Italy: the case for the carnivalesque. Sociological Review 39:503–527

Greenfield S, Osborn G (1996) After the act: The (re)construction of football fandom. Journal of Civil Liberties 1:7–28

Heringa AW, Kiiver P (2012) Constitutions compared:—An introduction to comparative constitutional law, 3rd edn., Intersentia, Antwerp

James M, Pearson G (2006) Football banning orders: Analysing their use in Court. Journal of Criminal Law 70:509–525

King A (2000) Football fandom and post-national identity in new Europe. British Journal of Sociology 51:419–442

MacKay P (1986) The fall and rise of football hooliganism. Police Journal 59:198–207

Millward P (2009) Glasgow Rangers supporters in the city of Manchester: The degeneration of a 'fan party' into a 'hooligan riot'. International Review for the Sociology of Sport, 44:381–398

Nickel JW (2008) Rethinking indivisibility: Towards a theory of supporting relations between human rights. Human Rights Quarterly 30:984–1001

Palmer VV (2005) From Lerotholi to Lando: Some examples of comparative law methodology. American Journal of Comparative Law 53:261– 290

Pearson, Geoffrey (1983) Hooligan – A history of respectable fears. London: Macmillan

Pearson G (1998) 'The English disease'? The socio-legal construction of football hooliganism. Youth and Policy 60:1–15

Pearson G (1999) 'Legitimate Targets? The Civil Liberties of Football Fans'. In: Journal of Civil Liberties 4/1:28–47

Pearson G (2005) Qualifying for Europe? The legitimacy of football banning orders 'On Complaint' under the principle of proportionality. Entertainment and Sports Law Journal 3

Pearson G (2012) An ethnography of English football fans: Cans, cops and carnivals. Manchester University Press, Manchester

Pilz G (1996) Social factors influencing sport and violence: on the problem of football hooliganism in Germany. International Review for the Sociology of Sport 31:49–68

Redhead S (1993) Always look on the bright side of life. In: The passion and the fashion, Aldershot: Avebury

Redhead S (2010) Little hooliganz: The inside story of glamorous lads, football hooligans and post-dubculturalism. Entertainment and Sports Law Journal 8:33–72

Salter M (1985) The Judges v The Football Fan: A Sporting Contest? Northern Ireland Legal Quarterly 37:351–358

Salter M (1986) Judicial responses to football hooliganism. Northern Ireland Legal Quarterly 37:280–292

Spaaij R. (2005) The prevention of football hooliganism: A transnational perspective. In: Aquesolo J (ed) Actas del X Congreso Internacional de Historia del Deporte, CESH

Spaaij R. (2006) Understanding football hooliganism. Amsterdam University Press, Amsterdam

Stott C, Pearson G (2007) Football hooliganism: Policing and the war on the English disease. Pennant Books, London

Stott C et al (2001) 'Hooligans' abroad? Inter-group dynamics, social identity and participation in collective 'disorder' at the 1998 World Cup Finals. British Journal of Social-Psychology 40:359–384

Stott C, Hoggett J, Pearson G (2012) Keeping the peace: Social identity, procedural justice and the policing of football crowds. British Journal of Criminology 52:381–399

Tsoukala A (2002) Le hooliganisme et la protection de la sécurité intérieure en Europe. Quels enjeux? Revue internationale de criminologie et de police technique et scientifique 55(3):310–322

Tsoukala A (2007) Security Policies & Human Rights in European Football Stadia. CHALLENGE Research Papers No. 5

Tsoukala A (2009a) Football hooliganism in Europe. Security and civil liberties in the balance. Basingstoke, Palgrave Macmillan

Tsoukala A (2009b) Combating football crowd disorder at the European level: an ongoing institutionalisation of the control of deviance. The Entertainment and Sports Law Journal 7

Vamplew W (1979) Ungentlemanly conduct: The control of soccer crowd behaviour in England, 1888-1914. In: Smout T (ed) The search for wealth and stability. London: Macmillan

Zweigert K, Kötz H (1998) An introduction to comparative law. Oxford University Press, Oxford

Chapter 2
Return to 'Radio Nostalgia': Twenty Years of 'Anti-Violence' Legislation in Italian Stadia

Arianna Sale

Abstract This chapter aims to retrace the implementation of counter-hooliganism legislation in Italy over the past 20 years. The perception of threat connected with football disorder has led to the gradual introduction of 'emergency' measures, generally passed in the aftermath of tragic and extreme episodes of violence at football grounds. Most of these are preventive measures, discretionally used by police and aimed mainly at incapacitating the so-called 'potential troublemakers'. The chapter will focus on these measures, analysing them technically and highlighting the main issues in particular with respect to fans' civil rights.

Keywords Football · Italy · Ultra conflict · Emergency legislation · Social control · Civil rights · Police discretion · Situational prevention

Contents

Dr Arianna Sale obtained her PhD in European Urban and Local Studies at the University of Milan Bicocca with a thesis on police management in football conflict in Italy and the UK. The author would like to thank Geoff Pearson and Lorenzo Contucci for their helpful comments, which have improved the quality of the final chapter.

Radio Nostalgia is the station broadcasting Genoa CFC matches. Nostalgia also represents the feeling of many fans and Ultras for their curva experience, which is gradually fading due to 20 years of 'anti-violence' policies (Contucci 2010; Francesio 2008; Marchi 2005; Sale 2010a, b).

A. Sale (✉)
European Urban and Local Studies, University of Milan Bicocca, Genoa, Italy
e-mail: salearianna@gmail.com

A. Tsoukala et al. (eds.), *Legal Responses to Football "Hooliganism" in Europe*,
ASSER International Sports Law Series, DOI 10.1007/978-94-6265-108-1_2

2.1 Introduction

There are two irreconcilable tropes that recur in political and media debate on the conflict in Italian football, and in particular with respect to the Ultra movement. The first refers to a rich vocabulary of 'animal' and barbaric images: violence for violence's sake, the blind force of the pack, irrationality, cruelty, bestiality. This mechanism, which blurs the boundaries between the human and animal world, is a familiar cognitive dynamic that is typically used to deal with all that which fundamentally belongs to the universe of the unknown. The consequences of this are obvious: if the stadium stands are populated by animals, there is no motivation to tread carefully when it comes to public order strategies that go beyond the mere necessity of restraint or incapacitation. It is the same the world over: one of the strategies used in the UK to contain a crowd, when there are no doubts about its 'violent tendencies', is sometimes described as 'corralling'—the procedure used by herders to control their livestock.

A second key interpretation is provided by newspaper reports on violent football-related phenomena, and emerged for the first time in the wake of a notorious story. On 11 November 2007, the death of Gabriele Sandri, a Lazio fan killed by a gunshot fired by a traffic policeman at a motorway service station, unleashed the fury of the Ultra during a night of street fighting in Rome. The next day, two young men were arrested and for the first time, in reference to Ultra violence, the charge of 'terrorist acts' was added to the now-classic charge of 'devastation and looting'.[1] The accusation of terrorism, a powerfully evocative term, was subsequently dismissed. The fact that the charge was legally untenable did not, however, affect the general discussion or political and media debate on the subject.

These tropes, while incompatible, have two things in common; first, the evocative power of the threat, whether it is derived from bestial irrationality or cynical human planning. The concept of a threat belongs to the sphere of subjective perception and its mechanisms of social construction and consolidation will not be detailed here. However, when discussing this perception, we can find little comfort or contradiction in the social research carried out in Italy on the topic of conflict in football. In other words, it seems that there are few cognitive alternatives available to the emotional connotations applied by the media to the spread of football violence and the familiar Sunday clash between fans and police. The fact is that it is extremely difficult to quantify the true extent of the phenomenon. The ministerial body responsible for the data (the National Observatory of Sporting Events) publishes an annual report on football violence in stadia. However, the data is recorded on the eleventh day of every season (and is therefore incomplete), and is

[1]Article 419 Penal Code, Section V (Offences against Public Order). 'Devastation' is the damage to a large number of things, spread over a wide area that threatens public order. 'Looting' is the theft, often accompanied by violence, committed by several individuals, that disturbs the peace and safety of the community.

constantly marred by inconsistencies and oversights.[2] Moreover, even if the methodology was infallible, official crime statistics, such as complaints and arrests, are more likely to record trends associated with the response adopted by the police, rather than directly measuring instances of deviant behaviour in and around stadia. What is more, the little Italian research carried out on the subject agrees that there is a substantial discrepancy between media attention and the actual scope of the problem.[3]

A second aspect that connects the images of bestiality with terrorism is the counter response of the authorities. The only conceivable reactions seem to be tightening the law on the one hand, and police repression on the other: in other words, the imposition of a strict regime of 'law and order'. The theme of police management in football conflict has been addressed in other papers.[4] This contribution will focus on the legal instruments used: analysing them, highlighting the main issues and retracing the history of their gradual introduction and implementation in Italian stadia.

2.2 Legislation 401/89—The 'DASPO' (Prohibition of Access to Sporting Events)

In addition to the evolution of repressive techniques in the field,[5] the history of social control measures in Italian stadia is based on a series of special legislations usually passed in the aftermath of tragic episodes in the history of conflict involving the Ultras. After a period of uncertainty, which mirrored that seen in Britain,[6] legislation started to be broken down into specific 'stadium crimes' in December 1989, when Public Law 401 entitled 'ensuring proper conduct in the execution of sporting contests' was passed. Public Law 401/89 saw the start of a season of 'emergency' measures on safety in sports stadia,[7] reinforcing 'the tendency of the Italian system to use judicial force for all areas that have strong social unrest'.[8]

[2]These are immediately apparent from the documents published at http://www.osservatoriosport.interno.gov.it/pubblicazioni/index.html.

[3]In particular, Dal Lago 1990; De Biasi 2001; Marchi 2005; Salvini 1988; Sale 2010a, b.

[4]Sale 2010a, b.

[5]De Biasi 1998; Marchi 2005; Sale 2010b.

[6]Tsoukala 2009.

[7]In the previous season, two episodes caused a strong emotional reaction: in October 1988, a 32 year-old Ascoli fan was seriously injured during a violent brawl which broke out between rival fans. A few months later, in June of 1989, Antonio De Falchi, an 18 year-old AS Roma supporter, died from a cardiac arrest after an ambush by a group of Milanese Ultras.

[8]Balestri and Cacciari 1998.

Article 6 saw the introduction, for the first time, of the 'diffida', the Italian equivalent of the UK 'banning order':

> The public security authorities can always order the prohibition of access to places where athletic competitions are held to people travelling there with offensive weapons, or who have been convicted of, or who are alleged to have taken an active part in episodes of violence during or due to sporting events, or having incited or encouraged violence either verbally or written thereof.

The legislators intended that the denial of access to sporting events (commonly known by the acronym DASPO) would not be a punitive measure, but a preventive one, and therefore the imposition of formal authority does not come from a judicial court, but the police (the public security authorities). As is clear from the article, this measure can also be used on people who have only been accused of a crime: a conviction is not necessary. It is the police who press charges and it is the police who decide how to apply the law, giving rise to the so-called 'double discretion'.[9]

The generic nature of the 'conditions' required to ban a supporter leads to a further element of discretion in the application of the notice. Anyone who has visited an Italian football stadium can see the practice of 'incitement' to violence or verbal aggression, through the traditional norms of fandom (e.g. chanting and gesturing) without it ever translating into an effective proposal for action or a real threat to public order. Police have full autonomy to evaluate the application of a banning order as a response to established and overt criminal behaviour but they typically use their wide discretion only to impose this power upon visitors of the stadia they believe are 'problematic' in terms of public order.[10] It has been noted that the practical application of DASPO orders against most of the members of the historic Ultra groups, and in particular their leaders,[11] has been increasing in recent years. For example, 500 banning orders were issued in a single season to members of the 'Brigate Autonome Livornesi', which in 2003 led to the dissolution of this historically extreme left-wing group of football supporters and, in May 2012, 152 DASPO orders were served on the Genoa Ultra following the disruption of the Genoa v. Siena fixture.[12]

---

[9]Balestri and Cacciari 1998; Padovano 2005.

[10]It has been observed from the earliest ethnographic studies on the practices of policing in England that often the decision by the police to apply a rule that punishes widespread behaviour (such as drinking in the United Kingdom) is the result of an overall assessment of the situation not necessarily tied to a desire to strictly adhere to the law but more often to the practical need to manage a 'public order' situation: 'Compliance with the law is merely the outward appearance of an intervention that is usually based on altogether different considerations. Thus, it could be said that patrolmen do not really enforce the law, even when they do invoke it, but merely use it as a resource to solve certain pressing practical problems in keeping the peace. […] virtually any set of norms could be used in this manner, provided that they sanction relatively common forms of behaviour' (Bittner 1967, p. 710).

[11]Marchi 2005.

[12]On this occasion the charge of 'psychological violence' against players was introduced for the first time. In a decisive game that Genoa was losing 4-0, the fans, without exerting any physical violence, successfully forced players to take off their shirts because they were considered unworthy wearers of the traditional red and blue colours.

If the introduction of the DASPO order has made any substantial contribution to the decline in violence at stadia, it is only in recent years. The episodes of conflict between opposing groups of fans continued to be a feature of the Sunday matches and filled the pages of the newspapers in the 1990s.[13] However, this initial failure did not lead to a substantial rethink of the foundations of the measure. The logic of rendering incapable subjects identified as problematic, in a measure applied discretionally by the police with no defence possibilities for those affected, continues to be the basis for all subsequent regulatory changes. The legislation was further tightened by subsequent decrees which were converted into laws[14] in the wake of the 'stadium emergency'. The so-called Maroni Decree, ratified by Public Law 45 of 24 February 1995, extended the prohibition of access to facilities where sporting events occur, to include places 'for refreshments, transit or transport of those participating in or attending the events' (para 1). A condition of the DASPO order may also require, 'the appearance in person once or more during the times indicated in the office or station of the police [...] during the day on which are programmed the events for which the prohibition operates' (Article 1, para 2). This is a significant limitation of personal freedom, especially if one takes into account the fact that it also affects people who have only been accused of a crime.

As with UK legislation[15] theoretically it is a preventive and not a punitive measure and therefore not all principles of criminal due process apply. The jurist Ferrajoli, speaking about the 'divergence of the punitive system', notes:

> This is how our legislators have substantially eroded the main criminal and procedural safeguards with simple word games: using names such as measures of prevention, or safety, or supervision, or police for restrictive sanctions or procedural constraints of freedom essentially similar to punishment and subjecting everything to a regime which is not hindered by civil rights.[16]

There is essentially no defensive remedy against such measures; there is no hearing at which the affected person may contest the ruling. It is possible to appeal to the Supreme Court (however, it will not suspend the enforcement of the order, and thus reveals itself to all intents and purposes a useless and expensive recourse), but only against the obligation to report to the police station, since only this condition, rather than the ban on travel to sporting events, is considered a limit on personal freedom.[17]

---

[13]For a reconstruction of the history of football conflict, Marchi 2005; Francesio 2008; Sale 2010b.

[14]Contrary to the legal system, where Parliament is the deliberative body, the decree-law is adopted by the Council of Ministers (the executive power). The Government should present the bill to the House on the same day; if the decree is not ratified within 60 days, it ceases to be effective. According to the prevailing view in law, this is justified by the need to promptly legislate 'extraordinary cases of necessity and urgency'. In the presence of these conditions, the Government acquires the power to temporarily exercise its legislative function.

[15]James and Pearson 2006; Stott and Pearson 2006.

[16]Ferrajoli 1996, p. 796.

[17]Marchi, 2005. For the same reason, the fact that cross examination was not compulsory was considered unconstitutional (Case 144, May 1997) but only with reference to the obligation to report to the police station, not to the banning notice itself, for which no amendments were considered necessary.

As Contucci notes, ‘it cannot be ignored that all Italian football fan groups, which have hundreds of thousands of members, have agreed that the escalation of the conflict between supporters and police has also been determined by the excessive discretion left to local police forces and insufficient defence guarantees for those affected’.[18] The breakdown of the relationship of mutual ‘respect’ between fans and police[19] is attributed by some leaders of the Ultra interviewed by the author during ethnographic research in Genoa, to the application of the DASPO measure:

> Before there was mutual respect, they arrived, they divided you up, maybe they slapped you around a bit too, eh, and there you are… Oh, they were only doing their job… it was about respect… […] Look, honestly, if they caught me doing something they gave me a year in prison without parole. But you must catch me red-handed. But now with this, you’re out for 5 years, you are forced to sign, even if you’ve done fuck all, it just makes the situation worse…[20]

2.3 The ‘Special Legislation’ from 2001 to 2007

The escalation of conflict in football, which was increasingly defined by the line that divided the Ultra from the police, led to a further tightening of the law in the 2000s. From August 2001 to April 2007, the desire of governments to show their strength in the face of situations perceived as being out of control manifested itself in the issuing of four decrees on violence in stadia, and caused many to convert to progressively stricter laws. In 2001, Public Law 377 extended the maximum duration of the DASPO order, increasing it to a maximum of 3 years and establishing custodial sentences for those contravening its conditions. Specific offences relating to football violence were also introduced; the release of ‘hazardous’ material was made punishable with imprisonment from 6 months to 3 years, and pitch invasions were made punishable by fine or imprisonment.

The main innovation introduced by Public Law 88 (24 April 2003) was ‘deferred flagrancy’. When an arrest ‘in flagrante’ (at the moment an offence is committed) is not feasible for reasons of security or public safety, police can arrest a person who, on the basis of video/photographic elements or other objective evidence, is believed to be the perpetrator, within 36 h of the crime being committed. With this provision, the police gained the power to restrict the personal freedom of an individual after a crime has been committed, a power which according to Article 13 of the Italian Constitution should only be within the jurisdiction of a magistrate. Having a possible unconstitutional element makes the measure an interim order: a suspension of the law dictated by the urgency of an emergency

---

[18]Contucci 2010, p. 115.

[19]For a deeper analysis of the concept of ‘mutual respect’ between fans and the police, see Sale 2010b.

[20]Sale 2010b, p. 325.

situation. The deadline for the cessation of this interim order was 30 December 2005, in accordance with legislation passed in 2003. However, with extensions applied after subsequent changes in the law, it was extended indefinitely and became nothing more than the 'normalisation of the state of exception'.[21]

Public Law 88 of 2003 provides mandatory measures for situational prevention in sports facilities with a capacity greater than 10,000; numbered tickets electronically controlled at the entrances, access gates equipped with metal detectors, video surveillance of spectator areas both inside the stadium and within its immediate vicinity, and segregation to prevent contact between rival spectator groups. For the first time, economic costs for the safety of the facilities became 'the responsibility of the organiser of the event'[22] even if they were owned by the council. These measures for 'structural adjustments' of stadia were further expanded through three ministerial decrees issued in June 2005, which dealt with the selling of named tickets, the installation of video surveillance systems, access to sports facilities and structural safety. These measures, which would have caused the closure of the majority of Italian top flight stadia and the application of which would have involved huge expenditure by clubs and councils, have been subject to constant and repeated extensions, the latest of which is a decree from the Ministry of the Interior in September 2006. Italian law is, once again, as a popular Italian saying states, 'strong with the weak and weak with the strong'.

Public Law 210, dated 17 October 2005 (the so-called Pisanu Law) added more restrictive elements to the Italian regulatory framework. DASPO orders were extended to sporting events taking place abroad. It reinforced the obligation for named tickets and the employment of stewards, the staff responsible for the admission and direction of the spectators, basically equating them to 'public officials'.

In the Ministry of the Interior, the law also established the National Observatory on Sports Events (ONMS), although it merely formalised an organisation already in operation since 1995. ONMS became not only responsible for monitoring the phenomena of violence by publishing an annual report,[23] but most importantly evaluating problems related to the specific scheduled matches. In other words, they assign a risk level to sporting events, on which appropriate measures of public order are based, such as the prohibition of away fans or regulation of restrictions on the sale of tickets. Often going beyond its institutional responsibilities, the ONMS advocate these restrictive measures with a punitive intent, applying them for matches that, although not posing a risk in themselves, involve teams whose fans have recently been involved in a disturbance.[24]

[21]Petti 2007.

[22]Massucci 2008.

[23]It should be noted that it has not been deemed necessary to involve any academic opinion in the research.

[24]The most striking example is the season-long ban on away games imposed on Napoli supporters (Ministerial Directive 555/Op/2144/2008/CNIMS), stated after the disturbances at Rome Termini station during the Roma v. Napoli match on September 2nd 2008. This clearly punitive ban included matches with no risk profile, such as Genoa v. Napoli, long-term "twinned" teams.

The 2006/2007 and 2007/2008 seasons marked a period of substantial change to strategies of social control in and around stadia. The decree of February 2007, issued in the aftermath of the clashes in Catania[25] (precisely 6 days later) and ratified in April of the same year (Public Law 41/2007, the so-called Amato Act), introduced 'emergency measures' to combat football violence. The measures adopted are in three different areas, separated into organisational, preventive and repressive measures.

Among the former, there are measures to ensure the safety of spectators and persons inside and outside stadia, to tackle risks that are both 'structural' and 'subjective'—i.e. those related to the suitability of the facilities and those relating to the 'context and organised presence of "dangerous individuals"'.[26] Articles 10 and 11 set out the requirements for structural adjustments and procedures for the ticket staff already sanctioned by the ministerial decrees of 2005, the application of which are denied any additional adjournments. This is supported, not without sarcasm, by a police officer interviewed during the author's research in Genoa:

> After eight extensions, the decree passed two days after the death of Raciti says essentially this, that the law will apply tomorrow: Article 1 says that games will no longer be played in stadiums which are not compliant. And we witnessed the race to install the turnstiles, which by the way, were fake, they did not work, because it is not like you can install turnstiles in two days…[27]

The second package of measures is aimed at making preventive action 'more effective', reinforcing the measures of prohibition of access to facilities to 'those persons "objectively" and "potentially" dangerous to public order and security as well as materials prohibited for their potential to offend'.[28] 'Objective' and 'potential' are clearly oxymoronic and the offensive potential of an object represents a criterion that is far from satisfactory for declaring with certainty the degree of the threat posed by its owner. People (including minors) have been reported for mere possession of (and not for the act of 'launching', as previously established by the 2001 Act) pyrotechnics or blunt objects and objects capable of polluting (for example, an aerosol canister) and can be given a DASPO order. The mere possession of such material has been transformed from a misdemeanour to an offence, and punished with a prison term from 6 months to 3 years.

The decree and subsequent law of 2007 not only toughened the measures already taken, but introduced a series of bans that in fact complicate, if not prevent, the expression of a particular feature of the world of the Italian Ultra, the 'fan choreography'. According to many commentators, the tacit intent was to limit the role played by the fans by making them passive consumers (and not protagonists) of a

---

[25]At the Catania-Palermo Sicilian Derby on February 2nd 2007, Police Inspector Filippo Raciti died in circumstances never completely clarified during clashes between fans and police in Catania. Antonio Speziale, a 17 year-old youth, was accused. Despite ambiguities in the evidence, which emerged during the trial, Speziale was sentenced to 14 years in prison.

[26]Massucci 2008, p. 8.

[27]Sale 2010b, p. 324.

[28]Massucci 2008, p. 9.

spectacle that must only take place on the playing field.[29] In this sense it is possible to interpret it as a ban on accompanying a choir with drums or other musical instruments or a ban on the use of megaphones to coordinate the cheering in the stands. Among the rules discussed within the framework of preventive measures, was the obligation to notify by fax the club hosting the match of the text of a banner to be exposed in the stadium. This fax must then be forwarded to the police station for a kind of modern 'imprimatur' from the police force. This additional measure, in which it is possible to recognise the classic whiff of censorship, kills the creativity and spontaneity of the traditional messages sent from the stands of Italian stadia. It is considered by many to be in conflict with the absolute right of 'freedom of speech and expression', stated in Article 21 of the Italian Constitution: 'Everyone has the right to freely express their thoughts through speech, writing, and every other means of communication'[30] and also raises questions under Article 10 of the European Convention on Human Rights (Freedom of Expression).

As to the tightening of existing measures, the Amato Act, para 1 states that the DASPO order 'can also be used against those whose conduct, on the basis of objective evidence, is believed to be intended for active participation in violence'. The addition of this point is rather obscure: it now appears that a conviction or a formal complaint is no longer necessary to merit a DASPO order: a simple report by the police which refers to 'conduct intended for violence' will suffice, evaluated on the basis of 'objective evidence' which, considering that this term has not been specified, leads to a further discretionary use of the measure.[31] The maximum duration of a DASPO order has been increased from three to 5 years, and the term of deferred flagrancy has been extended from 36 to 48 h. Furthermore, against 'the most dangerous people, the promoters, even if they are not the architects, of violent group actions',[32] the application of measures provided by the so-called 'Anti-Mafia Law' (No. 575, May 31, 1965) can be used, i.e. measures restricting personal freedom (special surveillance, confiscation of property), based on purely circumstantial evidence.[33] This association between stadium violence and the mafia, as well as some aspects of the legislative response and control strategies adopted, seem to follow the concept of 'the enemy within' which, 20 years earlier in Great Britain (under Margaret Thatcher's Government), associated in the same wave of repression, striking miners, terrorists in Northern Ireland and football 'hooligans'.[34]

The target group for preventive control strategies is not, however, comprised of people who have committed a crime, but by a very large group of spectators

---

[29]Among others, Cacciari and Giudici 2010; Sale 2010b.

[30]Following this procedure, a banner that bore the text of that very Article of the Italian Constitution, prepared by the Sampdoria fans for a Sampdoria v. Cagliari match in March 2007 was denied access to the stadium!

[31]Filing an appeal does not suspend the immediate enforcing of the measure, so it is often useless due to the lengthy Italian legal procedures.

[32]Massucci 2008, p. 10.

[33]So far no examples have been encountered in a football context.

[34]Armstrong and Hobbs 1994.

stigmatised as 'potential troublemakers'.[35] The 'anti-violence' legislation seems therefore to trace the characteristics identified by the jurist Ferrajoli in 'Police Law':

> ...which has the function of prevention of crime and more generally of public order disturbance through measures of social defence *ante* or *extra delictum* applied for administrative purposes to "hazardous" or suspicious characters. The general basis of their application is not in fact the committal of a crime, but simply a personal quality determined on a random basis by purely discretional criteria [...]. *Danger and suspicion are inherently incompatible with the forms of strict legality, as they elude a clear legal predetermination and leave blank spaces based on assessments as questionable as they are uncontrollable.*[36]

The third package of legislative measures contained in the decree and Act of 2007 included provisions that were more typically repressive, with the aim of intensifying the deterrent effect. With the explicit intention to incapacitate, it toughened the penalty for stadium crimes, aiming to 'achieve the desired effect of social protection through cautionary measures by putting the author of violence or other types of risky behaviour in a position to do no harm to the community'.[37] It also introduced the crime of aggravated damage committed on a sports facility, formalising, in Italian legislation, the 'spatial criterion' in determining the seriousness of a crime: a criterion which is already found in other European legislative framework for crimes committed at football events:[38] '...the spatial criterion is both a key definitional element of football hooliganism and the ground of new aggravating circumstance as a person committing offences in connection with sports events is punished more severely than are persons committing similar offences in other circumstances'.[39]

The goal of preserving the stadium and the football spectacle from any form of deviance or social conflict has contributed to the potentially unlimited expansion of social control measures in sports facilities, including the diffusion of 'soft surveillance'[40] technologies and a renewed alliance between security needs and commercial interests. In this framework it is possible to place the adoption of the latest measure to curb football violence, the controversial 'fan loyalty card'.

2.4 A Loyalty Card for Fans (The 'Tessera Del Tifoso')

A loyalty card for supporters was introduced with the Administrative Circular No. 555 of 14 August 2009 which announced the 'provisions for the 2009/2010 football season' to the regional authorities. It is not therefore a law in the strictest

---

[35] This is one of the basic principles of the 'new paradigm of control' (among others, Garland 2001; De Giorgi 2000).

[36] Ferrajoli 1996, pp. 797–798, emphasis added.

[37] Massucci 2008, p. 10, emphasis added.

[38] Pearson 1999; Stott and Pearson 2007; Tsoukala 2007, 2009.

[39] Tsoukala 2007, p. 5.

[40] Marx 2007.

sense of the word as it is not based on any law of the State regularly discussed and approved by Parliament. However, this does not undermine its coercive character. The Minister of the Interior, in fact, requires local authorities to consider as non-compliant (and therefore to close) sports facilities where clubs that refuse to adhere to the 'loyalty card' programme play.

According to the aims of the Ministry, the card represents 'an instrument to increase loyalty', through which the football club has the opportunity to create an 'official fan/customer' base.[41] On the one hand, the card is presented as an instrument of an 'ethical' adhesion to values for the benefit of a community of 'real fans' who share a 'genuine' passion for football; passion, that according to the familiar mythical Olympic ideal, is completely free from any form of conflict that goes beyond healthy competition in the field. On the other hand, the commercial nature of the programme is clear to see:

> The relationship established with the sports club is similar to that which the commercial world proposes to its best customers on a daily basis when selling its products. All personal data submitted by fans from football clubs is stored and only used (in accordance with the Privacy Act) to promote activities and facilities offered to its customers (agreements with transport and refreshment companies, dedicated lanes, an electronic wallet and much more).[42]

Even in appearance, 'the card will look like a normal credit card, but should also have the photo of the owner on it'. With this 'normal credit card', the holder will be able to benefit not only from the various business opportunities offered by their club as part of their marketing strategy, but also in the facilitation of normal security measures in stadia. In particular, again from a ministerial source, the card will help in the purchase of tickets, enabling the reading of the buyer's personal information and therefore rendering an identity card or passport unnecessary:[43] the card will help in making the holder exempt from the restrictions that may be imposed for reasons of public security on both home and away games. Moreover, the card will help in streamlining procedures for entering the stadium and in allowing the holder to benefit from preferential access roads and entrances to avoid searches. In this regard, as noted by Gary Marx, 'there is a chilling sense of continued regression that characterises a society in which we are asked to provide an increasing amount of personal information as evidence of not being "worthy" subjects of even more intensive controls'.[44]

The interplay between marketing tool and control measure is inextricable. If it were only a business opportunity, both for the sports clubs that offer it and for customers who decide to subscribe to it, it should, as with all economic activity in a

---

[41] See www.interno.gov.it/mininterno/export/sites/default/it/sezioni/sala_stampa/speciali/Tessera_del_tifoso/FAQ_tessera_del_tifoso.html (link no longer active).

[42] Ibid.

[43] Although only a few lines further down it is stated that Loyalty Card holders are still required to show a valid ID on request of a steward or the police (www.osservatoriosport.interno.gov.it/tessera_del_tifoso/vantaggi.html).

[44] Marx 2007, p. 45.

free market, be voluntary. In other words, it should be a matter of free choice made by the people involved, without the need for a directive from the Ministry of Interior stipulating its mandatory aspect. The ambiguity between opportunity and necessity (evidently oxymoronic concepts) is revealed in the information on the fan loyalty card programme posted on the Ministry's website: 'The card must be seen as an *opportunity*. It will be *required* to apply for a season ticket or go to an away game [...]. By next football season it will not be possible to apply for a season ticket or go to an away game without the card.'[45]

However, not all supporters are eligible for the card. The ministerial decree of 15 August, 2009[46] stipulated that clubs must submit the names of the subscribers to the police headquarters, which will be responsible for verifying the presence of impediments. If the card represents a trade agreement between the sports company and its customers, the transmission of personal data to the police is in itself problematic, even if limited to the verification of the presence of the necessary requirements for the issue of the card. It has been interpreted by the Italian Ultra groups, and many ordinary fans, as an excessive profiling made on the basis of an association between fan and potential criminal, and putting them into the same category of risk. As to the impediments, they are referred to and specified in Article 9 of the Amato Law 41/07, which prohibits associations organising football competitions, 'from issuing, selling or distributing admission tickets to individuals who have been the subject of Article 6 of Public Law dated 13 December 1989, n. 401 (the DASPO order), or to individuals who have been convicted for crimes committed during or because of sporting events, even if the sentence is not definitive'.

If we exclude those who have been convicted of stadium crimes[47] (regardless of the sentence, which could be just a fine) this not only reverses the presumption of innocence,[48] but the presumed guilt is a label that thwarts the purchase of a season ticket (i.e. the signing of a trade agreement between two private parties) even after sentence has been served. In addition to this, as already mentioned, the range of 'stadium crimes' and reasons to issue a DASPO order have been extended greatly over the years, to include behaviour that is not necessarily violent and extremely widespread as it is linked to practices rooted in the subculture and folklore of Italian football fandom, such as the ignition of fireworks or the display of an unauthorised banner. Regardless of the questionable legal grounds for this system of exclusion, the introduction of this card creates an unnecessary duplication in terms of security: the application for a season ticket or individual named ticket

[45]www.interno.it/mininterno/export/sites/default/it/sezioni/sala_stampa/speciali/Tessera_del_tifoso/FAQ_tessera_del_tifoso.html (link no longer active).

[46]Ministerial Decree. 18/08/09 entitled: 'An investigation by police on the conditions of the requisite impediments to the access to places where sporting events take place'. The date itself highlights the urgency of the measure. *Ferragosto* (15 August, a religious festival) is a national bank holiday.

[47]Determination No. 27/2009 from the National Observatory of Sport Events specifies that 'temporarily excluded from the program are those persons convicted of stadium crimes even if the sentence is not definitive, until the completion of five years after the aforementioned conviction'.

[48]Among others, Bigo 2006; Dal Lago 2000; Tsoukala 2009.

already foresees a background check for impediments by the person issuing the tickets, who will only receive a green light from the police if the purchaser's name is not on the blacklist of individuals denied access to sporting facilities.

Furthermore, the effectiveness of the measure in terms of actually improving public order in sports is highly doubtful. Perhaps denying the mandatory aspect of the loyalty card (which, as we have seen, contradicts its commercial façade), a note of clarification[49] from the Ministry of the Interior specifies how the card is not compulsory and therefore the failure to sign up to the programme will not constitute an impediment to the purchase of individual tickets for home matches (the only prerequisite is the purchase of an annual subscription, which allows considerable savings to the buyer). As for away matches, it is possible to buy a normal ticket provided that it is in a different stand to that reserved for visiting supporters. Therein lies a paradox: the 'official' fan, a cardholder, loyal, verified faultless through careful screening by the police, is confined to 'cages' and isolated areas which contain the hyper-controlled 'away end' of Italian stadia. However, a fan without a loyalty card has the opportunity to purchase a regular admission ticket in the home fan areas, and therefore come into close contact with rival supporters.

The response adopted in confronting this evident complication in the management of public order in football stadia is typical of the logic that has always governed Italian law in this area. The National Observatory of Sports Events assesses on a weekly basis the level of risk at matches and therefore imposes restrictive measures to organising companies for the sale of tickets for the home sections of a ground to anyone without a loyalty card who does not reside in the geographic region in which the sporting event takes place, or resides in the region of the visiting team.[50] These measures presume a localisation of football clubs that is not always reflected in the actual geography of the fan base, thus creating difficulties and paradoxes for anyone who supports a different team than that of their city. More alarming is the territorial discrimination regularly operating to the detriment of fans in contradiction of Article 3 of the Italian Constitution (the principle of equality before the law). In season 2010/2011, more than 40 % of the games in Serie A were subjected to stringent restrictions on the sale of tickets, either in the form of prohibiting sales of vouchers to residents in the region of the host team, or as exclusive sales only to residents in the region or province where the match was held.[51] The ease with which this measure is being used goes against the emergency justification given to a discriminatory measure.

At the end of the second season after the loyalty card programme came into force, data published by the Ministry showed a substantial reduction in violent

[49]See www.interno.it/mininterno/export/sites/default/it/sezioni/sala_stampa/speciali/Tessera_del_tifoso/FAQ_tessera_del_tifoso.html (link no longer active).

[50]This means preventing, for example, a Genoa fan without a loyalty card (who lives in Liguria) buying a ticket for the home end of the Meazza Stadium in Milan for the high-risk Milan v. Genoa game.

[51]The data is easily calculated by consulting the archives of the decisions taken by the CASMS and the relative judgements of the ONMS.

episodes and extolled the benefits of the card.[52] In reality it is an extremely difficult phenomenon to quantify. Official statistics on football conflict, available on the ONMS site, are incomplete and the methods used are flawed. They are produced by the same organisation at the Ministry of the Interior that proposes the countermeasures (a clear conflict of interest). It seems that the calming effect of the card has come about in an indirect way: following the refusal to sign up for the loyalty card expressed by all groups of Ultra and the exasperation felt by many ordinary fans by the tightening of security procedures and the increasing difficulties in buying tickets (which have not been simplified by the introduction of the card), there has been a substantial decline in public stadium attendance, and in particular a significant reduction in the number of fans who follow their team to an away game.[53] Contucci argues that the success of the programme can be likened to a reduction in road accidents had the Ministry of Transport decided to close all highways in the Italian territory for safety reasons.[54]

2.5 Conclusions

An analysis of the legislative and administrative measures taken in Italy to combat football violence shows many trends that define the transition towards a 'new paradigm of control': the application of measures for situational prevention. A focus on pacifying a *space* and not the disciplinary treatment of the individual offender. The introduction of preventive measures to neutralise the potential risk and not to punish the criminal act itself. And finally the elevation of 'security' as a top priority and the urgent demand, driven by public opinion, for a zero-tolerance response from the authorities, whatever the cost in terms of respect for individual civil and human rights. It appears, therefore, a contradiction. As observed by Castel:

> If you want a state of law, this pursuit for total security is going to fail, since total security is not compatible with an absolute respect for legal forms [...]. Perhaps it is a contradiction inherent in the practice of modern democracy. It is expressed through the fact that security in a democracy is a right, but that this right cannot certainly be respected in its fullness without putting into motion the means that prove detrimental to this right. It is significant that [...] the security question is immediately translated into a question of authority, which, once prey to the excesses of enthusiasm, can threaten democracy.[55]

Italy has also witnessed what Armstrong and Hobbs (referring to the control of British sports in the 1980s), called 'the normalisation of surveillance and control

[52]By the start of the 2014/15 season no further statistics had been published.

[53]Unfortunately, there is no systematic collection of official statistics on stadia attendance and no data at all on guest supporters' presence. The independent website monitoring on Italian football (www.osservatoriocalcioitaliano.it) compares data related to 2011–2012 and 2008–2009 Serie A seasons, recording a 8.1 % decrease in stadia attendance. Several experienced observers relate this decline to the decrease of guest supporters (among others, Contucci 2010, www.asromaultras.org).

[54]Contucci 2010.

[55]Castel 2003, trans. it. 2004, pp. 20–21.

without a political protest'.[56] The passage of legislation on violence in stadiums by a logic of preventative incapacitation, so worrying for the protection of individual rights and thus the fate of democracy itself, has not in fact provoked reactions of dissent even from the areas of public opinion generally sensitive to these issues. Indeed, the issue of the unlawful nature of DASPO order was only raised when Interior Minister Maroni proposed to extend it to provisionally cover political demonstrations.[57]

'Total security', as well as being incompatible with the observance of legal forms, is in fact a utopian goal, which makes the coveted peace of the stadia destined to remain incomplete and the progressive tightening of legislation never fully conclusive. The reasons are manifold and can only be alluded to in the conclusion of this review. It is sufficient to remember that, as stated by one of the first ethnographers on the police, 'the phrase "law and order" is misleading because it draws attention away from the existing substantial incompatibilities between the two ideas'.[58] The tightening of regulation does not always produce the pacifying effects hoped for: the zero-tolerance approach dictated by political imperatives often results in restricting the areas of mediation between the police and their opponents which are essential to maintain a certain level of 'structured chaos',[59] which seems to be the most desirable and realistic condition once the utopian image of society (and stadium) as completely orderly and free of any form of deviance, is removed. The stadium never becomes as sterile as the legislature demands; the frustration of pockets of unresolved conflict increases while a private or semi-private enjoyment of football at home in front of the television grows. If however you are a Genoa fan, and therefore hopelessly romantic, you can stay tuned to 'Radio Nostalgia' (the name was never more appropriate), the only place where, so far, it is still permitted to be a 'potentially dangerous' subject.

References

Armstrong G, Hobbs D (1994) Tackled from behind. In: Giulianotti R, Bonney N, Hepworth M (eds) Football, violence and social identity. Routledge, London, pp 196–228

Balestri C, Cacciari A (1998) Allo stadio con l'elmetto! Gomorra. Territori e culture della metropoli contemporanea, vol. 3, n° 1, Costa & Nolan, Genova

Bigo D (2006) Security, exception, ban and surveillance. In: Lyon D (ed) Theorizing surveillance. The panopticon and beyond. Willan Publishing, Devon, pp 46–68

Bittner E (1967) The police on skid-row: A study of peace keeping. American Sociological Review 32(5):699–715

Cacciari S, Giudici L (eds) (2010) Stadio Italia. I conflitti del calcio moderno. La Casa Usher, Firenze

Castel R (2003) L'insécurité sociale. Seuil, Paris (trad. it. 2004 L'insicurezza sociale. Che cosa significa essere protetti? Einaudi, Torino)

[56] Armstrong and Hobbs 1994, p. 215.

[57] *Corriere della Sera*, 18/12/2010, *La Repubblica*, 18/12/2010.

[58] Skolnick 1966, p. 9.

[59] De Biasi 2001; Sale 2010b.

Contucci L (2010) L'avvocato del diavolo. Lo stadio di polizia. In: Cacciari S, Giudici L (eds) Stadio Italia. I conflitti del calcio moderno. La Casa Usher, Firenze, pp 111–128
Dal Lago A (1990) Descrizione di una battaglia. I rituali del calcio. Il Mulino, Bologna
Dal Lago A (2000) La produzione della devianza. Teoria sociale e meccanismi di controllo. Ombre Corte, Verona
De Biasi R (1998) The policing of hooliganism in Italy. In: Della Porta D, Reiter H (eds) Policing protest. The control of mass demonstrations in Western democracies. University of Minnesota Press, Minneapolis, pp 213–227
De Biasi R (2001) Liverpool-Genoa, marzo 1992. In: Dal Lago A and Molinari A, Giovani senza tempo. Il mito della giovinezza nella società globale. Ombre Corte, Verona, pp 135–179
De Giorgi A (2000) Zero tolleranza: Strategie e pratiche della società di controllo. DeriveApprodi, Milano
Ferrajoli L (1996) Diritto e ragione. Teoria del garantismo penale. Laterza, Roma
Francesio G (2008) Tifare contro. Una storia degli Ultras italiani. Sperling & Kupfer, Milano
Garland D (2001) The culture of control. Crime and social order in contemporary society. The University of Chicago Press, Chicago
James M, Pearson G (2006) Football banning orders: Analysing their use in court: Journal of Criminal Law 70:509–530
Marchi V (2005) Il derby del bambino morto. Violenza e ordine pubblico nel calcio. DeriveApprodi, Roma
Marx GT (2007) Sorveglianza soft. Come cresce la voglia di regalare informazioni personali. Conflitti globali, n° 5, Mimesis, Milano, pp 37–51
Massucci R (2008) Il codice delle leggi per la sicurezza delle manifestazioni sportive. Leggi, decreti, regolamenti, determinazioni dell'Osservatorio e normativa del Consiglio d'Europa e dell'Unione Europea. Arcadia, Roma
Padovano S (2005) La violenza calcistica come problema di ordine pubblico. Una ricognizione normativa e sanzionatoria. Dignitas. Percorsi di carcere e giustizia 8:16–27
Pearson G (1999) Legitimate targets? The civil liberties of football fans. Journal of Civil Liberties, 4:28–47
Petti A (2007) Arcipelaghi e enclave. Architettura dell'ordinamento spaziale contemporaneo. Bruno Mondadori, Milano
Sale A (2010a) Etnografia di uno spazio conteso. L'ordine pubblico negli stadi tra Italia e Gran Bretagna. Etnografia e Ricerca Qualitativa, 3:61–84
Sale A (2010b) Chaos and order? Etnografia dell'ordinario conflitto tra tifosi e polizia in Italia e Gran Bretagna. Tesi di Dottorato in Studi Europei Urbani e Locali discussa il 19 luglio 2010, Università di Milano Bicocca, Milano
Salvini A (1988) Il rito aggressivo. Dall'aggressività simbolica al comportamento violento: il caso dei tifosi ultras. Giunti, Firenze
Skolnick J H (1966) Justice without trial. Wiley, New York
Stott C, Pearson G (2006) Football banning orders, Proportionality, and public order policing. The Howard Journal, 45:241–254
Stott C, Pearson G (2007) Football "Hooliganism": Policing and the war on the "English Disease". Pennant Books, London
Tsoukala A (2007) Security policies and human rights in European football stadia. Challenge, Research Paper No. 5
Tsoukala A (2009) Football hooliganism in Europe. Security and civil liberties in the balance. Palgave Mcmillan, Basingstoke

Chapter 3
Legal Responses to Football Crowd Disorder and Violence in England and Wales

Mark James and Geoff Pearson

Abstract Legal responses to football crowd disorder in England and Wales are often seen as best-practice by authorities in other European states. This is because so-called 'hooliganism' was considered to be a serious problem in the UK in the 1970s and 1980s but following a series of legislative and police strategy changes, crowd disorder and violence in and around British stadia is now rare. However, while changes in policing strategy have been important in this development, we should not overestimate the impact of legislation and in particular football banning orders. Some laws have not been proven to be effective, some may be counterproductive, and other 'non legal' factors have played an important role in the reduction in violence and disorder. Furthermore, serious questions remain about the proportionality and legality of some policing and legislative measures when assessed against civil libertarian protections and the European Convention on Human Rights.

Keywords Football · Hooliganism · Human rights · Banning orders · Kettling · Policing

---

Dr. Geoff Pearson is Senior Lecturer in Criminal Law at the University of Manchester's Law School. Professor Mark James is Professor of Sports Law at Manchester Metropolitan University.

M. James
Manchester Metropolitan University, Manchester, UK
e-mail: m.james@mmu.ac.uk

G. Pearson (✉)
School of Law, University of Manchester, Manchester, UK
e-mail: geoff.pearson@manchester.ac.uk

A. Tsoukala et al. (eds.), *Legal Responses to Football "Hooliganism" in Europe*,
ASSER International Sports Law Series, DOI 10.1007/978-94-6265-108-1_3

Contents

3.1 Hooliganism and the 'English Disease'

The reputation of English football in terms of domestic 'hooliganism' appears to have undergone something of a renaissance since the 1989 Hillsborough disaster. Until this pivotal moment in both English fan culture and regulatory responses to football crowds, hooliganism was often labelled the 'English Disease'. As far as the English media and many of its politicians were concerned, crowd disorder at and around domestic matches was out of control; stories of vandalised trains and coaches, brawls outside pubs, rioting on the terraces, pitch invasions and missile throwing frequented newspapers in both the sports and news sections.[1] Abroad, English fans were also regularly reported to be involved in disorder and violence when following both the national team and club sides, notably Manchester United, Tottenham Hotspur, Leeds United and Liverpool. To English citizens who did not attend matches regularly, it may have appeared that there was something inherently violent and anarchical about football fans; for those living outside the UK, it might have seemed that the problem was simply with the English.

This focus on the 'English Disease' overlooked crowd disorder in many foreign leagues, the fact that the vast majority of matches involving English teams did not result in disorder, and the frequent instances where English fans travelling abroad were subjected to extreme provocation by local fans and police who were hyped up for the expected confrontation.[2] However, the disruption caused to the 1980 European Championships in Italy, when England fans clashed with the police, and a series of incidents involving English club sides culminating in the 1985 Heysel Stadium disaster when 39 Juventus fans were killed trying to escape a terrace 'charge' by Liverpool supporters, were impossible to ignore. English teams were subsequently banned from European club competitions for 5 years and domestically legislation and a new policing unit were introduced to try and combat the problem. When English clubs sides were reintroduced to European football in 1990, it

[1] See Pratt and Salter 1984.

[2] See, for example, Ward 1989 and Williams et al. 1989.

appeared that many of the problems associated with club football had subsided[3] and the success of English teams in European competitions in the 1990s was largely trouble-free. Domestically the English game was flourishing; the perimeter fencing that had been one of the causes of the 96 fatalities at Hillsborough[4] had been removed without any observable increase in the number of pitch invasions. Attendances increased and from 1993 the new Premier League quickly established large, noisy, but (in terms of unruly behaviour) docile crowds as part of the attraction of the new brand. The 1996 European Championships in England also passed off with virtually no reported instances of disorder in or around stadia.

When England fans travelled abroad, however, problems of disorder continued. In 1995, a friendly match in Dublin was abandoned as England fans fought and threw missiles in the stadium. At the 1998 World Cup they were involved in serious disorder lasting over 24 h, fighting with local youths and police in Marseilles.[5] Two years later, Belgian police used water cannons to disperse England fans from the town square in Charleroi during the 2000 European Championships.[6] Less serious but still notable disorder involving fans of the England national team occurred in Munich (2001), Slovakia (2002), Albufeira (2004), Stuttgart and Cologne (2006) and when English clubs sides played in Copenhagen (2000), Rome, Seville and Athens (all 2007).[7] Despite the enhanced reputation of the UK authorities resulting from the apparently improved crowd behaviour at Premier League and FA Cup matches, fear of the 'English Disease' remained both amongst those hosting English teams and in popular culture more generally.[8]

The discrepancy between the historical and cultural reputation of English fans (highlighted by their occasional engagement in disorder abroad) on the one hand, and their relatively docile nature at even the most keenly contested rivalries in domestic football on the other, is therefore the subject of interest and indeed some envy, from governments and governing bodies that consider themselves to have a 'hooligan problem'. How was it that apparently high-risk matches played out before crowds as large as 75,000 could take place without missile throwing, pitch invasions, racist chanting, flares, smoke bombs or fighting between rival fans? Despite large numbers of away fans, heavy social consumption of alcohol and the lack of physical controls such as perimeter fencing, netting, perspex barriers, moats and large numbers of riot police, English fans predominantly sat and watched the matches without engagement in violence, disorder or protest. How had the English hooligans been tamed and what could other nations learn from

[3]See King 2002 for a discussion of the transformation of English football in the 1990s.

[4]Taylor 1990.

[5]Stott and Pearson 2007.

[6]Crabbe 2003; Stott and Pearson 2007; Weed 2001.

[7]Stott and Pearson 2007.

[8]The apparent decline of hooliganism in the UK was mirrored by an increase in its appearance in popular culture: the 2000s saw a proliferation of published 'memoirs' from self-labelled 'reformed' or 'retired' hooligans, and feature films such as *I.D.*, *Football Factory*, and *Green Street* kept the reputation of the English hooligan alive and kicking (see Redhead 2010).

this experience? This chapter considers the effectiveness of the legal responses to so-called hooliganism that have evolved since the mid-1970s, investigating their effectiveness at managing crowds, and considering the prices that have been paid in terms of the human rights of ordinary fans.

3.2 English Fan Culture

The picture presented to television audiences by the Premier League brand of English fandom reveals only part of a highly complex fan culture. Research carried out in the course of writing 'An Ethnography of English Football Fans'[9] revealed a number of different subcultures of the match-going fan. Whilst these subcultures were identifiable at all the clubs researched, it should be noted that fans would sometimes drift between subcultures depending on the nature of the match in question and occasionally on external regulatory pressures (e.g. corralling subgroups together by police). The presence of some of these subcultures, and the overlap between them, provide significant challenges to British police, who retain the ultimate responsibility for ensuring public order in and around football matches.

At one end of the scale a subculture of what we will tentatively call 'hooligans' remains.[10] These fans attend matches with the primary intention of confronting rival hooligan 'firms' and try to remain separate from the wider match-going support. During the period of our research, the hooligans were typically characterised by being male, aged between their mid-20s and late 50s, and wearing 'casual' fashion.[11] The size and activity of this subculture varied dramatically between clubs and from match to match. Firms could be formed at all clubs for high-profile matches, but numbers were typically small, with 20–50 core members.

A second subculture identified by the ethnographic research was labelled 'carnival fans'. For this group, the primary intention on a match-day was to create a 'carnival' of transgression from the norm: collective gathering, chanting and social drinking. Away matches typically provided the best arena for this activity and as a result 'carnival fans' tended to dominate the travelling support of the English teams observed. Many also adopted the casual style, avoiding colours for reasons of fashion and practicality; not wearing colours made it easier to access pubs and drew less attention from local fans. While the hooligans and the carnival fans largely had different match-day objectives and usually remained separate from

[9]Pearson 2012. See also Rookwood 2009.

[10]It should be noted that the terms 'football hooligan' and 'football hooliganism' do not have accepted definitions either in law or more generally (Pearson 1998). The definition used here is based on the views of fans interviewed for Pearson 2012.

[11]This refers to the avoiding of 'colours' (e.g. scarves and replica shirts in the team's colours) and a preference for branded clothing, such as Stone Island, Burberry, SuperDry and North Face.

each other, at away matches in particular, correctly differentiating these groups often provided a challenge for local police. In particular, both subcultures saw success off the pitch—an exciting confrontation or 'the craic' of carnivalesque expression respectively—as being more important than the result on it, and some carnival fans in particular would attend matches without tickets or any realistic hope of obtaining any.

On match days these two groups were dwarfed by a larger number of match-goers belonging to other fan subcultures. The primary objective of these wider subcultures was to watch the match and, hopefully, witness a successful result for their team. Many fans from these subcultures also engaged in heavy social alcohol consumption, but they were more likely to wear colours, arrive earlier at the stadium and attend with family members. The differing objectives of these subcultures often led to tensions between subgroups supporting the same team in addition to tensions between rival fans. Indeed, during the ethnographic research, violent incidents between different subgroups within a team's support were more common than violence between supporters of rival teams.

3.3 The Regulation of Crowds in the UK—Legislation

Designated football matches are some of the most tightly-regulated social spaces in British society.[12] A series of legislative provisions, supported by sophisticated police strategies and a modern stadium infrastructure, means that football spectators are prohibited from many actions that would be permitted in other social, crowd or sporting situations. However, the precise impact of this regulation upon crowd behaviour is unclear. Observations suggested that an apparent reduction in racist chanting, for example, was more likely to be the result of changing fan attitudes towards the (un)acceptability of racism at football through self-policing by supporters against those who transgressed those new norms of behaviour, rather than the enforcement of the law. Other football-specific laws, such as the restrictions on alcohol consumption and the prohibition on indecent chanting, had little or no observable impact, possibly due to their lack of enforcement by the police.[13]

[12]Football matches are 'designated' for regulation by statutory instrument. For restrictions on alcohol consumption, for example, the Sports Grounds and Sporting Events (Designation) Order 2005 regulates 'Association football matches in which one or both of the participating teams represents a club which is for the time being a member (whether a full or associate member) of the Football League, the Football Association Premier League, the Football Conference National Division, the Scottish Football League or Welsh Premier League, or represents a country or territory.' (schedule 1(1)). Similar provisions with regard to which stadia are included in the Football Banning Order regime are included in the Football Spectators (Prescription) (Amendment) Order 2010 and the Safety at Sports Grounds Act 1975 states that all sports stadia with capacities of over 10,000 (or in the case of football league clubs, 5,000 following The Safety of Sports Grounds (Accommodation of Spectators) Order 1996) need a Safety Certificate in order to admit spectators.

[13]Pearson 2012.

The starting point for legislative responses to football crowd disorder in England and Wales is Section 3(3) of the Safety at Sports Grounds Act 1975, which was introduced following the Ibrox Stadium disaster when 66 fans were killed in a crush that occurred on steps leading from the stands.[14] Although primarily concerned with fan safety, the Act gave police the power to insist upon control centres in stadia, access to public address systems, perimeter fencing and fan segregation, all of which could assist their crowd management. Police requests for such measures, so long as they were agreed by the local authority, would then be conditions of a club's safety certificate,[15] without which spectators are not allowed into the stadium. The Act laid the foundations for the current system by providing the police with overall responsibility for the management of football spectators inside stadia, including the power to impose structural requirements on stadium design.

Further legislation has criminalised other acts that were believed to be contributing to crowd disorder. The Sporting Events (Control of Alcohol) Act 1985 criminalised entering a designated football stadium whilst 'drunk', attempting to bring alcohol into a stadium, consuming alcohol within sight of the pitch, and consuming alcohol on coaches and trains that had the express purpose of transporting fans to matches. The social consumption of alcohol plays a significant role in English fan culture, so preventing drunken supporters from attending matches was an ambitious aim. Indeed, British police often use their discretion not to enforce this part of the Act, regularly allowing drunken fans into matches, whilst many fans do not realise that it is a criminal offence to attempt to enter a stadium when drunk.[16] The impact of the legislation upon fan behaviour and stadium safety appears not to have been anticipated; restricted access to alcohol inside stadia regularly leads to crushes and disturbances at turnstiles (as many fans arrive at the last minute in order to drink in pubs beforehand) and in concourses at half-time where alcohol can usually be purchased and consumed. Research suggested that the legislation is not achieving its aim of reducing drunkenness at matches, but instead might be creating more opportunities for violence and disorder through fan resistance to its restrictions.[17]

The Taylor Report into the Hillsborough Stadium disaster recommended the criminalising of three further activities in stadia; the throwing of missiles, the singing of 'racialist' and 'indecent' chants, and invading the pitch.[18] The Football (Offences) Act 1991 criminalised these types of disorder but has had varied success in achieving its aims. Pitch invasions are rare at matches in England, and where small numbers of fans encroach onto the pitch, arrests are often made.

[14]Wheatley 1972.

[15]All designated football grounds require a safety certificate. See above n. 12.

[16]Pearson and Sale 2011.

[17]Ibid.

[18]Taylor 1990, para 71.

Likewise, missile throwing is not a significant problem at English matches, although there have been sporadic instances of coin throwing between rival supporters and several high-profile instances where coins, bottles and mobile phones have been thrown at players. Several highly publicised arrests and bans of fans identified as being involved in racist chanting[19] may have deterred spectators from engaging in this practice at English football grounds, but it is more likely that self-policing by fans means that spectators with racist views no longer feel comfortable expressing these inside stadia. As with the restrictions on alcohol consumption, the criminalisation of 'indecent' chanting was overly ambitious and the number of arrests for this offence, as opposed to racist chanting, is minimal. Highly indecent and offensive mass chanting remains a fundamental feature of English fan culture and there appears little appetite amongst police to enforce this provision. Finally, Section 166 of the Criminal Justice and Public Order Act 1994 criminalises all unauthorised sales of football tickets ('touting'), even where tickets are being sold at face value.[20] The rationale behind the introduction of this offence was to protect the segregation of rival spectators in stadia.

These football-specific offences are supplemental to generally applicable UK law. Common law offences of being drunk and disorderly, breaching the peace and the Public Order Act 1986 offences of disorderly behaviour, threatening behaviour, affray and violent disorder are frequently used to regulate low-level disorder amongst fans, constituting around half of the football-related arrests made in England and Wales (Table 3.1).

Table 3.1 Football-Related Arrests in England and Wales 2013/14 (UK Home Office Statistics)

Violent disorder	356
Public disorder	705
Missile throwing	57
Racist or indecent chanting	21
Pitch incursion	174
Alcohol offences	572
Ticket touting	104
Possession of offensive weapon	13
Use/possession of fireworks/flares	188
Breach of banning order	42
Offences against property	41
Total	2,273

Categories established by the Home Office: 'Public Disorder' includes Public Order Act 1986 Sections 3–5

[19]E.g. Following a Blackpool v. Preston 'derby' in 2008: http://news.bbc.co.uk/1/hi/england/lancashire/7300326.stm.

[20]James 2010.

3.4 The Regulation of Crowds in the UK—Football Banning Orders

The 'Football Banning Order' (FBO) has become an increasingly important tool in the regulation of fan behaviour in England and Wales. FBOs were originally introduced by the Public Order Act 1986 to prevent fans convicted of 'football-related' offences from attending matches, and were extended to prevent them travelling abroad to matches involving English teams by Section 14A of the Football Spectators Act 1989 (FSA). In 2000, following disorder involving England supporters at the European Championships in Belgium, Section 14B FSA was introduced.[21] S14B enables the police to apply for FBOs on application (or 'complaint') against supporters who have not yet been convicted of a football-related offence, but who the police believe have previously been involved in disorder and who pose a risk of engaging in future violence or disorder in relation to football matches. FBOs (whether on complaint or conviction) normally last for between 3 and 5 years.[22] FBOs make it an offence for a banned fan to attend any regulated football match, and usually impose exclusion zones around stadia and train stations when matches take place. Fans served with FBOs must also surrender their passport when the English national team or specific clubs sides are playing abroad. In September 2014 there were 2,273 banning orders in operation, with 678 new orders imposed in the preceding 12 months,[23] and overall numbers show a slow but gradual decline (which mirrors the decline in arrests).

3.5 The Regulation of Crowds in the UK: Policing Strategies

Football in England and Wales in the 1970s and 1980s was characterised by mass, reactionary policing methods. Large numbers of police attended matches, with their presence particularly noticeable around stadiums and train stations. The numbers of arrests increased perceptibly during this period. Deterrent sentences were imposed by the Crown Courts,[24] though possibly not the lower Magistrates Courts,[25] but there was little evidence that convictions were reducing the problem of disorder at and around matches.

A fundamental change of emphasis occurred with the creation in 1988 of the Football Intelligence Unit (now the UK Football Policing Unit) within the

---

[21]Football (Disorder) Act 2000.

[22]Where a custodial sentence is imposed, which is comparatively rarely, the FBO can be in place for 6–10 years.

[23]Home Office, 'Statistics on football-related arrests: 2012/13'.

[24]Trivizas 1981.

[25]Salter 1986.

National Criminal Intelligence Service. The Unit was primarily concerned with preventing confrontation between hooligan 'firms' and identifying and gathering evidence against their 'ringleaders'. Through use of overt 'spotters', who made themselves known to, and observed groups of, fans, Football Intelligence Officers (FIOs) responsible for specific teams and areas soon had considerable success in identifying, locating and tracking those suspected of engagement in disorder and violence. Communication between spotters attached to the home and visiting teams (and sometimes the British Transport Police), usually enabled the local police force to corral one or both of the rival groups (often in a pub), thereby preventing confrontation. Even if the rival firms came into contact with each other, the presence of spotters, sometimes supported by officers with video cameras or even police helicopters, often acted as a sufficient deterrent.

This strategy has been effective in preventing serious violence, despite the continued presence of identifiable hooligan firms at many matches, and most serious confrontations tend to occur between firms and the police corralling them (although the deterrent effect of spotters and video cameras also make this rare). Indeed, the view amongst many officers is that 'hooligans' actually need the presence of police to add to the excitement of their day whilst also limiting the risk that they will become seriously injured in an unmanaged confrontation.[26]

As FBOs became an increasingly important tool for the police, the emphasis of the Unit changed. Instead of tracking 'ringleaders', FIOs now spend an increasing amount of time gathering evidence on low-level disorder to enable them to apply for FBOs against fans suspected of being on the edge of these groups, but who typically (in the view of the police) do not become involved in serious violence. As a result, spotters are known not only to the firms, but also to the wider body of regular travelling supporters. It is their role in pursuing FBOs 'on complaint' against suspected 'risk supporters' who have not been convicted of any football-related offence that has caused the most concern to fan groups.

3.6 Impact upon Fan Human Rights

Although the UK does not have a written constitution, principles such as equality before the law, the prohibition on retrospective law and the presumption of innocence have long been enshrined in common law, custom and convention through the rule of law and the application of principles of 'natural justice' in the courts. Following the enactment of the 1998 Human Rights Act, from 2000 UK courts were finally granted the ability to apply the European Convention on Human Rights (ECHR), which the UK had ratified in 1953, directly against public authorities and indirectly when interpreting primary legislation. The Act does not grant courts the power to strike down primary legislation, but it does enable them to

[26]O'Neill 2005, p. 127.

challenge actions of the state, including the police, if they infringe Convention rights.

Concerns remain among fan organisations in England and Wales, particularly the Football Supporters Federation, that these human rights are being infringed by policing methods and judicial responses to football crowd disorder. In particular, it is argued that some of the football-specific measures are disproportionate to the threat posed by football 'hooliganism'. Conversely, police and judges occasionally point to these measures as being the very reason why 'hooliganism' is no longer perceived to be a serious problem.

3.6.1 Restrictions on Movement: Kettling, Escorts and Hold-Backs

Many policing responses to the threat of violence and disorder connected with football crowds are based upon temporary restrictions on the right of individuals to move freely, with the common law power enabling police officers to take 'reasonable steps' to prevent a 'breach of the peace' much used in the policing of potentially disorderly crowds. Since the 1970s, a fundamental aspect of football crowd management in England and Wales has been segregating rival fan groups, both within and outside the stadium. Using their common law powers, police managing football crowds have, to varying extents, insisted upon escorts and stadium 'hold backs' for visiting fans, and the corralling and containment of 'risk supporters'. Since the 1998 Human Rights Act, the courts have been forced to consider the balance between police duties to prevent a breach of the peace and the rights under the Convention of citizens in crowds to liberty (Article 5), freedom of expression (Article 10) and freedom of assembly and association (Article 11).

'Kettling'[27] is a crowd management tactic where groups identified as being a potential risk to public order are corralled and have their freedom of movement temporarily curtailed. This tactic has become the focus of much debate in the UK following its use in managing political protesters. The current legal status of kettling in the UK is that because it is a temporary restriction, rather than a deprivation of liberty, Article 5 EHCR is not engaged unless the decision to kettle is made arbitrarily.[28] However, following the decision in *R (Laporte) v. Chief Constable of Gloucestershire*,[29] police powers to prevent a breach of the peace need to be balanced against Article 10 and 11 ECHR rights. As a result, kettles and other similar restrictions on association and expression can only be imposed by a senior police officer who reasonably believes that, based on the evidence available at the time,

[27]Also known as 'bubbling'.

[28]*Austin v. Commissioner of Police of the Metropolis* [2009] 1 AC 564. The UK has not ratified Protocol 4 of the Convention, which provides for liberty of movement within states.

[29][2007] 2 AC 105.

containment of the crowd is the least restrictive way[30] of preventing an 'imminent, immediate and not remote'[31] breach of the peace.

Despite the *Laporte* ruling, there is a rather low threshold placed on the level of belief that the police need before they can kettle a football crowd. For any fixture where violence or disorder has occurred previously, or where there is intelligence of it being planned (e.g. discussion on an Internet forum/social network), it is likely that kettling a group of suspected risk supporters will be seen as lawful. For football fans with no intention of engaging in disorder, this can be problematic. Segregation, kettling, and stadium 'hold-backs' after the final whistle are usually indiscriminate in terms of whose liberty is being restricted; 'carnival' fans are particularly at risk from this type of restriction, with little hope of legal recourse.

One area where fans have had some success in challenging restrictions on their liberty is in the application to football crowds of Section 27 of the Violent Crime Reduction Act 2006. Section 27 (now repealed) provides a uniformed police officer with the power to direct an individual to leave a designated locality for a period not exceeding 48 h if they believe that their presence is likely to cause or contribute to alcohol-related crime or disorder, and that such a direction is necessary to reduce its likelihood.[32] As away fan culture in England and Wales remains dominated by the social consumption of alcohol, several police forces have used Section 27 to disperse suspected risk supporters, as they will almost inevitably have been consuming alcohol or will have congregated in a pub.

In *R (on application of Lyndon) v. Chief Constable of Greater Manchester Police*,[33] a judicial review was successfully brought against Greater Manchester Police after they corralled over 80 Stoke City supporters who had gathered in a pub before a match against Manchester United. The supporters were held in the pub for an hour, video recorded and served with dispersal notices (being threatened with arrest if they did not sign them) directing them to leave the Greater Manchester area because they were 'part of a group of males/football fans with and without tickets causing a disturbance inside the Railway Inn public house'.[34] This was despite the fact there was no evidence of disorder and the landlady of the pub described their behaviour as 'impeccable'. They were then escorted on to a coach and driven back to Stoke-on-Trent, a 90-minute journey without toilet facilities, causing them to miss the match.

---

[30]*The Queen (on the application of McClure and Moos) v. Commissioner of Police* [2012] EWCA Civ 12, para 94.

[31]*Moss v. McLachlan* [1985] IRLR 76, para 27. In *R (Laporte) v. Chief Constable of Gloucestershire* [2007] 2 AC 105, it was made clear that 'imminence' needs to be considered as 'immediacy' if a restriction on liberty is to be considered proportionate when infringing an ECHR right.

[32]Sections 27(2)(a) and (b).

[33]Statement of Facts and Grounds of Claim, 15 Nov 2008, Queen's Bench Division, 15 Nov 2008.

[34]Statement of Facts and Grounds of Claim: *R (on application of Lyndon) v. Chief Constable of Greater Manchester Police*, 15 Nov 2008, Queen's Bench Division: para 11.

The Court held that it was unlawful to use Section 27 against football crowds in this manner because the provision clearly and consistently referred to directions being made to individuals, not groups. Without an individual assessment of the risk posed by each fan and the specific need to direct them away from the locality, the police had acted unlawfully. Further, the direction to leave 'Greater Manchester' was too wide to be considered a 'locality'[35]—the police only possessed the power to direct individuals to leave, not to relocate them forcibly. Thus, forcing the fans back onto a bus and detaining them there for 90 min was a disproportionate breach of Article 5 ECHR.[36] The police subsequently apologised and paid compensation to the fans.[37]

3.6.2 Intelligence Gathering

Further human rights concerns arise from the use of the stop and search provisions of Section 60 of the 1994 Criminal Justice and Public Order Act. As with alcohol dispersal orders, these powers were not introduced specifically to control football crowds, but have been used extensively in their management.[38] Section 60(1) gives a police officer of at least the rank of inspector[39] the right to issue a stop and search notice if they have a reasonable belief that incidents involving serious violence will take place in their police area and that this power will help to locate offensive weapons. Any uniformed police officer then has the power to stop any individual or vehicle and search for offensive weapons and/or dangerous instruments regardless of whether there are any grounds for suspecting that these articles are being carried.

Section 60 has been extensively used to stop and search football supporters and some forces issued notices routinely for certain high-risk matches (although there is evidence that the use of Section 60 stop and search is now reducing). Crowd and court observations carried out by the authors indicated that Section 60 was often used by local police forces to gather information about suspected 'risk supporters',

---

[35]Guidance on the use of s.27 suggested that the *widest* definition of 'locality' in the Act should be the centre of a town or city.

[36]Following *Austin v. Commissioner of Police of the Metropolis* [2009] 1 AC 564, it is likely that this would not now be considered a breach of Article 5, although it is possibly an infringement of Article 11 and Article 8 (due to the collection of personal information on those given the dispersal orders). Regardless, the manner in which s.27 was used in this case would still have been unlawful as the police were acting *ultra vires*.

[37]Consent Order, 9/7/09, Queen's Bench Division. The 80 Stoke supporters received a total of £184,850 compensation (www.bbc.com/news/10412281).

[38]See Greenfield and Osborn 1996.

[39]Home Office guidance in September 2014 raised the level of authorisation for a Section 60 order to above the rank of Chief Superintendent in an attempt to reduce the number of 60 stop and searches.

sometimes on the basis of intelligence from the visiting force, sometimes merely because a group are dressed in a certain way, travelling by a certain mode of transport or arriving at a certain time and place. Those stopped were usually asked to provide their name, age and address to video camera, with the data then kept on file by the police. This information is often the start of a police profile that may be used later as the basis for a FBO application on complaint.

Football disorder in England and Wales, even between organised hooligan firms, rarely involves the premeditated use of weaponry, so it is unclear how the need to search for such weaponry can be justified. Thus, the gathering, storage and sharing of this data raises concerns about whether the police are acting *ultra vires* when using their stop and search powers and whether this may also be breaching the right to privacy under Article 8 ECHR. Furthermore, following the cases of *Wood*[40] and *Catt*[41] (both in relation to political protests), the legality of the retention of this type of data is also in doubt. Unless individuals are suspected of committing specific offences and the retention is necessary in the pursuit of a future criminal charge such data should not be retained, particularly given the type of low-level criminality that is typically committed in relation to football matches.[42]

3.6.3 Banning Orders on Complaint and Identification of 'Risk Supporters'

Applications for FBOs 'on complaint' under Section 14B FSA require the gathering of evidence of patterns of (usually non-criminal) behaviour that indicate an individual might be causing or contributing to football-related disorder or violence. Once a profile has been compiled, the local police force will make an application for an FBO to the Magistrates Court. For the FBO to be imposed, it must be proved that 'the respondent has at any time caused or contributed to any violence or disorder in the United Kingdom or elsewhere'. Usually, the police are able to prove this by a previous conviction for violence or disorder unrelated to football; occasionally they may try to prove this by reference to evidence of engagement in football-related disorder documented in the profile compiled by FIOs but which has not resulted in prosecution. Once this hurdle is passed, the police must satisfy the court that there are reasonable grounds for believing that imposing an FBO would help to prevent violence or disorder at or in connection with any regulated football matches. This requires evidence to be placed before the court from police profiles that the respondent has and will cause or contribute to football-related disorder. It was initially believed that because FBOs are civil orders, the court needed only to be satisfied that they were necessary on a balance of probabilities, rather

[40] *Wood v. Commissioner of Police for the Metropolis* [2009] EWCA Civ 414.

[41] *R (Catt) v. ACPO* [2013] EWCA Civ 192.

[42] *Wood* [2009] EWCA Civ 414, per Dyson LJ at para 86.

than the higher criminal standard of 'proof beyond reasonable doubt'. Further, civil rules of evidence apply, allowing the use of some evidence that would be inadmissible in a criminal trial.[43]

However, in, *Gough & Anor v. Chief Constable of Derbyshire*,[44] the Court of Appeal assessed the legality of Section 14B complaints against Article 6 ECHR (right to a fair trial) and the right to freedom of movement under the EC Treaty. The Court rejected the freedom of movement point by holding that the restrictions were proportionate under EU law. The accuracy of this conclusion is questionable; the Court did not assess of the severity of the problem of football crowd disorder involving English fans, or whether FBOs could reduce this problem.[45] Nor did it consider whether there were less restrictive alternatives that could have been chosen even if the first two legs of the proportionality test[46] were satisfied.[47] In terms of Article 6, Lord Phillips MR ruled that a higher standard of proof needed to be met before an FBO could be imposed under Section 14B: 'While technically the civil standard of proof applies, that standard is flexible and must reflect the consequences that will follow if the case for a banning order is made out. This should lead the Magistrates to apply an exacting standard of proof that will, in practice, be hard to distinguish from the criminal standard'.[48] The requirement of this higher standard of proof should provide an important safeguard against the risk of FBOs being imposed against supporters on the grounds of flimsy evidence and could ensure that the scheme is Article 6 compliant.

However, the extent to which the higher standard of proof is being applied in FBO applications is questionable. Court observations suggested that while Magistrates Courts almost always referred to Lord Phillips' ruling, the actual evidence accepted as being sufficient for imposition of a FBO was often flimsy and based upon little more than guilt by association. Although the courts may have stated that they were satisfied beyond reasonable doubt of both the quality of the

---

[43]The use of civil rules to manage criminal/quasi-criminal behaviour, and supported by criminal law sanctions also exists in the UK in relation to Anti-Social Behaviour Orders (ASBOs), Sexual Offender Orders and Terrorism Control Orders. This type of law is referred to as 'hybrid law' (Ashworth 2006; Duff and Marshall 2006; Gardiner et al. 1998) or 'two-step' provisions (Von Hirsch and Simester 2006) and have received criticism for infringing human rights.

[44][2002] EWCA Civ 351.

[45]The legislation was primarily brought into prevent disorder abroad by England fans following disturbances in Marseilles (1998) and Charleroi (2000). However, evidence from arrest statistics and football intelligence officers suggests that those English fans who engage in disorder abroad are typically not known to the authorities and therefore would not be subjected to a s.14B application in the first place (see Stott and Pearson 2007).

[46]From *de Freitas v. Permanent Secretary of Ministry of Agriculture, Fisheries, Lands and Housing* [1999] 1 AC 69.

[47]This is debated in more detail in Stott and Pearson 2006.

[48]Paragraph 90. His Lordship applied *B v. Chief Constable of Avon and Somerset Constabulary* [2001] 1 WLR 340 at p. 354 and *R (McCann) v. Manchester Crown Court* [2001] 1 WLR 1084 at p. 1102 in making this ruling.

evidence and that the overall test was met, we observed serious inconsistencies between the quality of evidence that was accepted as relevant and the approach taken to the more stringent *Gough* test. At only two observations did we see the test being applied rigorously, which were also the only observations where FBO applications were rejected.[49]

Our court observations suggested that much of the evidence being relied on for the imposition of FBOs on complaint did not show actual engagement in disorder or violence, but was instead evidence of belonging to a certain subculture of English football supporter or of expressing certain modes of behaviour. In particular, many of the profiles the authors reviewed contained evidence that the respondent was *associating* with others identified by the police as 'risk supporters', usually fans whose FBOs had expired or who were also having profiles built against them. Where FBOs were secured on the basis of guilt by association, the process became self-sustaining as the now banned fan could be used as the basis for implicating others with associating with a 'risk supporter'.

Another problem with using association as evidence of a propensity for engaging in disorder is what behaviour was seen as 'association'. In some cases this went no further than being in the same pub or on the same coach or train as the 'risk supporter'. However, at away matches in particular, this type of geographical proximity may not be the same as socially associating with a specific individual; transport options or safe and accessible pubs for away fans were sometimes scarce. Furthermore, if the respondent was a supporter who enjoyed engaging in the traditional English away match-going culture of gathering with fans of the same team, social consumption of alcohol and engagement in chanting, then often they would find themselves proximate to those the police believed to be 'risk supporters' simply because they shared an enjoyment of this type of activity rather than a propensity for violence or disorder. Further, as there is no publically-accessible register of those classified as 'risk supporters', it is difficult for fans to distance themselves from these supporters.

There are clear implications here for the right of free assembly and association guaranteed by Article 11 ECHR. The ECtHR's decision in *Friend v. United Kingdom* (a fox-hunting case) made it clear that although the original purpose of Article 11 was to protect the right of peaceful political demonstration, it would be, '…an unacceptably narrow interpretation of that article to confine it only to that kind of assembly … [Article 11] may extend to the protection of an assembly of an essentially social character'.[50] Gatherings of football supporters are therefore highly likely to trigger Article 11 protections. However, the way that evidence for FBOs is currently gathered by many forces means that being in the company of other supporters carries with it a risk of being considered to be 'associating with

---

[49]James and Pearson 2006. S.14b applications were observed being rejected in *Chief Constable of Avon and Somerset v. Bargh*, Bristol Magistrates Court 27 January 2011 and *Commissioner of the Police for the Metropolis v. Melody*, Tower Bridge Magistrates Court 9 July 2012.

[50](2010) 50 E.H.R.R. SE6, para 50.

risk supporters', which may in turn lead to an application for an FBO under Section 14B FSA. This clearly has the potential to reduce the freedom of supporters to associate with whoever they like.

Finally, again following the decision in *Friend*, there is an argument that the type of evidence gathering engaged in by many forces policing football matches also restricts the right to free expression under Article 10 ECHR. This is a tentative argument and certainly does not apply to all forces, some of whom are increasingly looking to put human rights towards the forefront of their strategic planning. However, where fans are identified as being risk supporters based on non-criminal appearance, such as wearing 'casual' clothes, or expression, such as engaging in certain chants, the compiling of a profile about them for an FBO application may be incompatible with Article 10 ECHR.

3.7 Conclusions

There are a number of dangers in viewing the English experience of managing football crowds as being best practice that should be replicated across the continent. First, the evident decrease in violence and disorder at and around football stadia when compared with the situation of the 1970s and 1980s, or with current domestic competitions elsewhere in Europe, occurred at a time when many changes were occurring in British football in terms of increasing and changing crowds, redevelopment of stadia and changing social attitudes. At the same time, police strategies for managing crowds were radically overhauled and legislative measures were put in place. To try to isolate any of these factors and identify why it was that football disorder in and around stadia in England and Wales reduced over this period is virtually impossible. It may be that some of the legislative provisions identified above played an important role in this development, but if so, it was almost certainly only one of several aspects driving the changes. It is also clear that some of the provisions identified above have had little impact on supporter behaviour and may even have been counterproductive. Likewise, some changes in police strategies would have assisted the management of football crowds, but these changes are not uniform across constabularies, and there is significant evidence of disorder and violence taking place as a result of ill-conceived policing interventions.[51]

As many of the changes to law and policing strategies have challenged the human rights of those attending matches, other nations in Europe need to be careful that before copying them, they are sure that they are a proportionate response to the problem. That means that they should assess whether the measures have actually been influential in reducing football crowd disorder and that they are the least restrictive (in terms of negative impact on human rights) means of achieving that end. Indeed, in the UK itself, there are currently pressures for change from

[51] Stott et al. 2012.

both police and fan groups. The current system of policing domestic football in England and Wales costs in the region of £25 million per year,[52] and of this policing cost, football clubs are only responsible for paying for police services on property that they own, manage or control.[53] As a result, there is pressure from the Association of Chief Police Officers that clubs or governing bodies should foot more of the bill for policing of fans outside stadia, but also a desire amongst many forces to police ‘smarter’ with the resources they have. At the same time there is pressure from fan groups for a change in police attitudes towards supporters. While there is little doubt that most fans in the UK are policed well in comparison with the situation in the 1970s and 1980s, there are still recurring stories of fans (particularly travelling away from home) being subjected to hostile, provocative and occasionally violent policing. Fans also seem to be rebelling more against restrictions inside stadia; ethnographic research combined with anecdotal evidence from other clubs suggests increasing numbers of fans are standing in seated sections along with an increased use of pyrotechnics.[54]

In this context, many police forces in England and Wales are starting to engage with fan groups, even utilising social media such as Twitter in an attempt to engage in a non-threatening way with supporters. Some forces are looking to improve their policing methods in terms of increasing positive interaction with fans, for example by introducing Police Liaison Teams (PLTs) to attempt to reduce conflict between fans and police. All of these changes are based on evidence that less confrontational, but more interactive, forms of policing can enable a gradual scaling down of police resources without this leading to an increase in levels of disorder or violence.[55] It is in the evolution of police methods in England and Wales and the increasingly constructive forms of dialogue between fans and police, combined with improved stadium infrastructure, that most can be learned from nations looking to rid themselves of a perceived ‘hooligan problem’: not the criminalisation of those attending football matches.

References

Ashworth A (2006) Four threats to the presumption of innocence. International Journal of Evidence and Proof 10:241–278

Crabbe T (2003) The Public Gets What the Public Wants: England Football Fans, ‘Truth’ Claims and Mediated Realities. International Review for the Sociology of Sport 38:413–425

Duff R, Marshall S (2006) How offensive can you get? In: Von Hirsch A, Simester A (eds) Incivilities: Regulating offensive behaviour. Hart, Oxford, pp. 57–90

---

[52]Ibid.

[53]*Leeds United Football Club Ltd v. Chief Constable of West Yorkshire Police* [2012] EWHC 2113 (QB). Even then, these services must be reasonable and technically requested by the club (*Chief Constable of Greater Manchester v. Wigan Athletic AFC LTD* [2008] EWCA Civ 1449).

[54]The dramatic increase in the latter is demonstrated in the 2013/14 arrest statistics.

[55]See Stott et al. 2012.

Gardiner J et al. (1998) Clause I – The hybrid law from hell? Criminal Justice Matters 31:25–27
Greenfield S, Osborn G (1996) After the act: The (re)construction of football fandom. Journal of Civil Liberties 1:7–28
James M (2010) Sports Law. Palgrave, MacMillan
James M, Pearson G (2006) Football Banning Orders: Analysing their use in court. Journal of Criminal Law 70:509–525
King A (2002) The end of the terraces: The transformation of English football in the 1990s. Leicester University Press, London
O'Neill M (2005) Policing Football: Social interaction and negotiated disorder. Palgrave, MacMillan
Pearson G (1998) 'The English Disease'? The socio-legal construction of football hooliganism. Youth and Policy 60:1–15
Pearson G (2012) An ethnography of English football fans: Cans, cops and carnivals. Manchester University Press, Manchester
Pearson G, Sale A (2011) On the Lash: Revisiting the effectiveness of alcohol controls at football matches. Journal of Policing and Society 21:1–17
Redhead S (2010) Little hooliganz: The inside story of glamorous lads, football hooligans and post-subculturalism. Entertainment and Sports Law Journal 8:33–72
Rookwood J (2009) Fan perspectives of football hooliganism: Defining, analysing and responding to the British phenomenon. VDM Publishing House, Saarbrücken
Pratt J, Salter M (1984) A fresh look at football hooliganism. Leisure Studies 3:201–230
Salter M (1986) Judicial responses to football hooliganism. Northern Ireland Legal Quarterly 37:280–292
Stott C, Pearson G (2006) Football banning orders, proportionality and public order. Howard Journal of Criminal Justice 45:241–254
Stott C, Pearson G (2007) Football hooliganism: policing and the ear on the English Disease. Pennant Books, London
Stott C, Hoggett J, Pearson G (2012) Keeping the peace: Social identity, procedural justice and the policing of football crowds. British Journal of Criminology 52:381–399
Taylor Lord Justice (1990) Hillsborough Stadium Disaster Final Report. HMSO Cm. 962, London
Trivizas E (1981) Sentencing the football hooligan. British Journal of Criminology 21:342–349
Von Hirsch A, Simester A (2006) Regulating offensive conduct through two-step prohibitions. In: Von Hirsch A, Simester A (eds) Incivilities: Regulating offensive behaviour. Hart, Oxford, pp 173–194
Ward C (1989) Steaming In: The Journal of a Football Fan. Pocket Books, London
Weed M (2001) Ing-Ger-Land at Euro 2000: How 'handbags at 20 paces' was portrayed as a full-scale riot. International Review for the Sociology of Sport 34:407–424
Wheatley Lord (1972) Report of the inquiry into crowd safety at sports grounds. HMSO Cmnd 4962, London
Williams J, Dunning E, Murphy P (1989) Hooligans abroad. Routledge, London

Chapter 4
Legal Measures and Strategies Against Violence at Football Events in Germany

Marco Noli

Abstract This chapter investigates the policing of football supporters in Germany and the legal measures and strategies designed to reduce the problem of football crowd disorder and violence. It argues that football supporters have been made the subject of a number of experimental techniques for the control of groups within German society, which are considered to be problematic. The author analyses a number of such techniques and critiques: some of these are based upon their impact on the civil and human rights of football supporters.

Keywords Football · Supporters · Policing · Germany · Ultras · Pyrotechnics · Fan projects

Contents

Marco Noli is a lawyer at Noli, Seidler, Fischer and van Bracht in Munich, Germany, where he specialises in criminal law. He is also a member of the Fan Lawyers community.

M. Noli (✉)
Noli, Seidler, Fischer and van Bracht, Munich, Germany
e-mail: noli@kanzlei-westend.de

A. Tsoukala et al. (eds.), *Legal Responses to Football "Hooliganism" in Europe*,
ASSER International Sports Law Series, DOI 10.1007/978-94-6265-108-1_4

4.1 The Development of Fan Culture in and Around German Stadia

4.1.1 Development of the Ultra Fan Culture

The phenomenon of football crowd disorder and violence, commonly known as 'hooliganism', although considered prevalent in the 1980s, has now largely disappeared from German football stadia. However, incidents still occur regularly outside the confines of the football stadium.[1] Currently, the Ultra movement receives significant attention and has become one of the main foci of the police. Ultras are passionate and engaged fans, who claim to unconditionally support their club. As well as visual support, through a coordinated choreography, banners, large flags and the use of pyrotechnical devices, Ultras also support their team by singing, chanting and with the use of drums. Ultras have intense rivalries with other Ultra groups.

There is a large diversity in the groups that make up the Ultra movement, and within the various Ultra groups themselves. Ultra groups are often associated with football hooliganism and violence, but this is due to the fact that there is a general lack of research into the Ultras, as well as prejudices that exist about the movement.[2] However, recently there have been a number of social scientific studies on Ultra culture[3] that have started to illuminate the reality of the motivations and behaviour of Ultra groups.

4.1.2 The Stadia

Stadium attendance in Germany has grown substantially since the turn of the century. This is as a result of the number of new stadia that were built for the hosting of the 2006 FIFA World Cup. A further reason for the increased popularity of

[1]M. Gabriel, Problemgruppe Ultras? www.dvjj.de/sites/default/files/medien/imce/documente/veranstaltungen/dokumentationen/Gabriel_Pr%C3%A4sentation.pdf. Accessed 14 January 2015.

[2]S. Langner, Solidarität, Zusammenhalt und Engagement. Die Ultrabewegung in Deutschland: Eine explorative Interviewstudie zu einer neuen Fankultur. http://www.faszination-fankurve.de/sites/diplomarbeiten/downloads/download.php?name=arbeit?.pdf. Accessed 15 January 2015 (link no longer active).

[3]See Gabler 2011 and Ruf 2014.

football was the restructuring of the professional football leagues in 2008. In the 2010/2011 season, 17.4 million fans visited football matches in the two highest professional football leagues (Bundesliga: 13 million, and 2nd Bundesliga: 4.4 million).[4] This was an increase in attendance of 6 million fans (more than 50 %) since the start of the century.[5] If one compares the attendance of the Bundesliga (average attendance for the 2011/12 season: 44,293) with attendances in other international leagues (for example, the average attendance in the Premier League for the same period in 2011/12 was 34,601), the Bundesliga has the highest average attendance of any football league in the world.[6]

Most German stadia are newly built or substantially modernised with the latest and highest quality security and safety measures. All stadia contain high-resolution closed circuit television (CCTV) cameras, covering the entire stadium. There are sophisticated control rooms, in which the police can supervise the fans on CCTV screens. In most stadia there is a police station with a cell block. It is claimed that the safety and security measures in German stadia are amongst the most sophisticated in the world.[7]

4.1.3 Fan Disorder

Fan disorder and criminality in connection with sports events other than football is relatively rare. However, incidents are by no means limited to football. To a lesser extent, there have been problems at ice hockey matches, and in the last couple of years there have also been incidents where fans have lit pyrotechnics at ski jumping events. A crucial difference with the situation at football is that such incidents at these events are viewed as expressions of the fans' enthusiasm ('Gänsehaut-Atmosphäre', 'Hexenkessel') and not as violations of the criminal law.

Football still carries a certain stigma with it. Despite the significant variance in the nature and seriousness of instances of football-related criminality, disorder and violence, all incidents, major and minor, at and around football matches tend to be characterised by police statistics or in the stadium ban procedure as football-related violence. At the time of writing, the main concern inside stadia is the illegal use of pyrotechnics (mostly flares). The use of fireworks can be an offence under the Law on Explosives.[8] Violent offences such as assaults against rival fans

[4]See http://www.dfb.de/bundesliga/statistik/zuschauerzahlen/. Accessed 29 January 2016.

[5]Ibid.

[6]For an analysis of average attendances, see www.weltfussball.de/zuschauer/eng-premier-league-2011-2012/1/.

[7]DFL 12 December 2012, DFL Security Paper. www.cdn.static.bundesliga.de/media/native/autosync/antragspaket_1_sicheres_stadion_-_antraege_001_-_016_-_final.pdf. Accessed 13 January 2015 (link no longer active).

[8]Sprengstoffgesetz, 10 September 2002 (BGBl. I S. 3518).

are rare occurrences inside stadia. Situations where fans invade the pitch have also become very rare. The number of injuries at football matches is actually below average compared to major crowd events like ‘Oktoberfest’.[9]

Outside stadia, during the transit to games and in city centres, violent offences and incidences of public disorder do occur. Sometimes this takes the form of organised fights between rival groups of fans. Also ‘scarf-pulling’, whereby fans ‘steal’ the scarves with club emblems of rival supporters to gain credibility among their own group is increasingly common. The public prosecutor in these cases often prosecutes on the basis of robbery (‘Raub’, § 249 StGB), even though in most cases there is no intention to keep the scarves in possession. Younger fans in particular may engage in spraying graffiti and ‘stickering’ (‘Sachbeschädigung, § 303 StGB). Fans sometimes chant the abbreviation ‘ACAB’ (‘all cops are bastards’) or wear this abbreviation on a t-shirt as a reaction to the police; these fans can be prosecuted for insulting the police (‘Beleidigung, § 185). Finally, fans attempting to escape arrest by the police can be prosecuted for resisting a law enforcement officer (‘Widerstand’, § 113 StGB).

The lack of differentiation between offences outside and inside the football stadium is one of the key issues in the debate on fan disorder. The media, a number of important policy—makers, the police and the German football association tend not to differentiate between various forms of disorder, but label all incidents ‘football hooliganism’. There is a tendency to oversimplify and group various problems of supporter behaviour together as the same phenomenon. This grouping of various forms of football-related disorder can also be seen in the fact that the police and the football association in various published statistics and regulations use the overly broad concept ‘(in) relation to a football match’. This concept is used in the ‘Guidelines to Impose a Stadium Ban’,[10] as well as in the police’s situation reports and statistics on football.[11]

The result of the failure to differentiate between various forms of fan behaviour is that the discussion on fan disorder has a tendency to miss the important points. Furthermore, the police statistics that are used often lack a solid foundation and therefore have only limited utility. For the purposes of informed discussion on football-related disorder, proper definitions need to be applied and the concept of football-related disorder should not be used in an overly broad fashion.

[9]See for example the data collected by the campaign ‘ich fuehl mich sicher’ on www.ich-fuehl-mich-sicher.de/hintergrund.html and de-de.facebook.com/ichfuehlmichsicher.

[10]DFB, 1 January 2014, Stadionverbotsrichtlinien des DFB. http://www.dfb.de/fileadmin/_dfbdam/24339-Richtlinien_zur_einheitlichen_Behandlung_von_Stadionverboten.pdf. Accessed 29 January 2016.

[11]LZPD (2011/12) ZIS-Bericht 2011/2012. www.polizei-nrw.de/media/Dokumente/Behoerden/LZPD/130912_ZIS_Jahresbericht_11_12.pdf. Accessed 15 January 2015.

4.1.4 Police Statistics

All preliminary investigations into football-related disorder are registered by the Central Information-Point Sports Operations 'ZIS'. ZIS collates data from the whole of Germany and publishes an annual report.[12] ZIS statistics do not contain any information regarding convictions, but consist merely of data pertaining to police investigations and other measures such as detentions ('Freiheitsentziehungen'). The data contains statistics on injuries in relation to football but does not specify the cause of those injuries.[13] This means, for example, that individuals who are injured by accidentally falling down stairs in the stadium or injuries sustained as a result of the use of pepper spray by the police, are included in these statistics. The police vehemently refuse to make the grounds for injuries sustained inside the stadium public and justify this refusal by stating that to do so would pose a risk to public order and public security and would complicate the work of the police.

German police place football fans into three different categories; this categorisation is based on a report on Sports and Security from 23 July 1991 and has not been updated since.[14] However, the criteria for this categorisation are secret and are not made public by the police.

Category A: peaceful fans
Category B: fans who under certain circumstances have violent tendencies
Category C: fans who actively look for violence

In the 2010/2011 statistics, the police estimated that the 18 clubs in the Bundesliga had a total of 4,090 fans in Category B and 1,583 fans in Category C. For the clubs in the 2nd Bundesliga, there were 3,150 Category B fans and 862 Category C supporters.[15] However, because the criteria and the basis for the categorisation of fans are not made public by the police, it is impossible to assess the meaning and/or the accuracy of these statistics.

The general statistics of the police regarding offences and the statistics of the Justice Department regarding criminal convictions make no record of a relationship between convictions and football matches or events. In the experience of lawyers familiar with the problem of football-related violence, it is contended that football-related offences are investigated more stringently than comparable offences outside of a football context and that they are punished on average much more severely than comparable offences with no such relation to football.

---

[12]The data can be found on www.polizei-nrw.de/artikel__68.html.

[13]LZPD (2012/13) ZIS-Bericht 2012/13. www.polizei-nrw.de/media/Dokumente/12-13_Jahresbericht_ZIS.pdf. Accessed 15 January 2015.

[14]This categorisation can be found on http://dip21.bundestag.de/dip21/btd/17/080/1708051.pdf. This overly simplistic categorisation of fans was abandoned by police in the UK in the early 2000s.

[15]Above n. 11.

4.2 The Gap Between the Real Situation in the Stadia and the Media Coverage

DFL and German Professional Football League officials acknowledge that there is a difference between the media perception of stadium security and the reality.[16] A number of media outlets and politicians have suggested that there has been a strong increase in violence in the stadiums. However, evidence suggests otherwise; the report by the ZIS (2010/2011) does not provide any evidence for a substantial rise in violence in football stadiums. On the contrary, recent reports issued by the ZIS show a marked decline in all statistical categories regarding football-related disorder. The number of criminal investigations into football-related disorder declined from 6,030 (2008/09) and 6,043 (2009/10) to 5,818 (2010/11). The number of football-related arrests declined from 9,174 (2008/09) to 6,784 (2009/10) and 6,061 (2010/11). The number of police hours spent on football matches declined from 1.5 million (2008/09) to 1.2 million (2009/10) and 1.1 million (2010/11).[17]

The only increase in that period is in relation to the number of persons injured in relation to football matches. This number rose from 579 (2008/09) to 784 (2009/10) and 846 (2010/11).[18] In this regard, it should be noted that the police statistics do not take into account the number of persons injured by the police[19] and that a substantial part of the increase in related injuries can be attributed to more widespread use of more modern and larger chemical anti-riot agents by the police.[20] A further contributing factor to this rise in injuries is that league attendance in the past 10 years has risen to 6 million supporters.

The decline in the number of arrests suggests that criminality, violence and disorder in and around stadia are decreasing. This decline has occurred despite both an increased police presence and video surveillance inside stadia, leading to the increased likelihood of offences inside stadia being detected. The image these statistics presents becomes even clearer when football is compared to other mass

[16]DFL (27 September 2012) Information und Diskussion über weitere Schritte zur Umsetzung der Ergebnisse der Sicherheitskonferenz in Berlin und der Innenministerkonferenz (Sicheres Stadionerlebnis), S. 5. www.faz.net/Dynamic/download/Kommission_Sicherheit_Mitgliederversammlung_27_09_2012.pdf. Accessed 14 January 2015.

[17]LZPD (2010/11) ZIS-Bericht 2010/11. www.polizei-nrw.de/media/Dokumente/10-11Jahresbericht-oeffentlich.pdf. Accessed 15 January 2015.

[18]Ibid.

[19]Piraten Fraktion (2 July 2013) Realistische Erfassung von Sicherheitsproblemen—Reform der Datenerfassung und—auswertung der Zentralen Informationsstelle Sporteinsätze (ZIS). www.piratenfraktion-nrw.de/wp-content/uploads/2014/01/16-3438.pdf. Accessed 15 January 2015.

[20]Zeit.de (22 August 2013) Schalke kritisiert Polizeieinsatz gegen seine Fans. www.zeit.de/sport/2013-08/schalke-saloniki-polizei-einsatz. Accessed 15 January 2015.

events: for example the famous 'Oktoberfest' in Munich. During the 17 days of the Oktoberfest in 2011, the police recorded over 11,000 injuries, and reported 2,175 incidents and 499 violent offences (of which 120 were serious offences).[21] Despite this, those attending Oktoberfest do not have the same stigma attached to them as football spectators.

A high-level security meeting on the security situation in football stadia took place in Berlin on 17 July 2012. At this meeting, the football associations, clubs and the Federal Ministers of the Interior discussed the theme of 'fan violence'. Crucially, representatives of the fan organisations were not invited to this meeting. Ignoring the aforementioned statistics, many politicians played up the security problems in stadia in the build-up to this meeting. The participants at the meeting reported a (perceived) significant increase in football-related violence and demanded more stringent measures against football fans, including measures that would significantly encroach on both the civil rights and human rights under the ECHR of football fans.[22]

The depiction of football fans in the media has generally been negative and has contributed significantly to the stigmatisation of supporters. An extreme example comes from a television talk show where Ultras were compared to the Taliban.[23] On another occasion, Federal Prosecutor General Range, whose field of competence is counter terrorism, publicly called for electronic tags to control football fans, ignoring the fact that such a measure would be unconstitutional.[24] In the discussion on football-related disorder, politicians often use warlike rhetoric. They urge 'the state not to capitulate in the fight against violence in the stadiums'.[25] Those making these bold statements pay little attention to the fact that the measures they propose often infringe upon the civil rights of football fans, and that their statements contribute little to a constructive discussion on the reality of football-related disorder in Germany. However, this sort of rhetoric does provide fertile ground for severe limitations on the civil and human rights of football fans. In most of these instances, measures are taken which violate rights protected by the ECHR, especially the right to private and family life (Article 8 ECHR) and the

---

[21]Arbeitsgemeinschaft Fananwaelte (23 August 2012) Stellungnahme der Arbeitsgemeinschaft Fananwälte zum deutschen 'Sicherheitsgipfel' im Juli 2012. www.fanseurope.org/de/news-2/news-2/604-statement-fanlawyers-security-summit-germany-ger.html. Accessed 15 January 2015.

[22]P. Linke, 18 Juli 2012, Strenges Durchgreifen bei Pyrotechnik. www.fr-online.de/sport/fussball-sicherheitsgipfel-strenges-durchgreifen-bei-pyrotechnik,1472784,16644638.html. Accessed 15 January 2015.

[23]A. Bock, 25 May 2012, Ultras: Die Taliban der Fussbalfans! http://www.11freunde.de/artikel/best-2012-ein-abend-mit-sandra-maischberger. Accessed 15 January 2015.

[24]Sueddeutsche.de (25 May 2012) Range fordert elektronische Fußfesseln für Fußballrowdys. www.sueddeutsche.de/sport/gewalt-im-fussball-elektronische-fussfesseln-fuer-fussball-rowdys-gefordert-1.1366479. Accessed 15 January 2015.

[25]For example right-wing CDU politician Danny Eichelbaum, Mitteldeutsche Zeitung, www.mz-web.de (27.05.2012).

right to freedom of movement (Article 2 of Prot. 4 ECHR). For example, the systemic collection of personal data, the constant video surveillance of football supporters, identity checks of football supporters without a reasonable suspicion of any wrongdoing and body searches to which football supporters are subjected are all potentially disproportionate and arbitrary breaches of Article 8 ECHR.

4.3 Security Concepts

4.3.1 Development of Security Concepts

In 1991 the permanent Conference of the Minister of the Interior of the Federal States ('IMK') determined that a common policy was needed to improve the security situation at sports events and founded a working group on 'National Concept Security and Sports'.[26] In response to violence associated with football matches the IMK, together with all the other parties involved, approved the National Concept Sports and Security ('NKSS') in 1993.[27] The NKSS contains recommendations regarding social work, stadium regulations, exclusion orders, security services, stadium security and rules for the cooperation of the parties involved. The NKSS is overseen by the National Committee Sports and Security ('NASS'), which comprises stakeholders including the authorities and sports organisations. Representatives of fan projects are also involved in these discussions. However, they have no official powers with respect to the NKSS. At the time of writing, the last time the NKSS was updated was in 2011.

As a result of the NKSS, high security standards have been implemented in all stadia, nationwide football banning orders have been implemented and for (currently) 51 cities all over Germany there are social and educational fan projects. Furthermore, as a result of the NKSS there are special police officers with specialised knowledge of the fan groups ('szenekundiger Beamter—SKB's'). SKB's are police officers specifically tasked with supervising football fans. They work in civilian clothes and are present at virtually all the matches, domestically as well as internationally. The task of these SKBs is to compile and evaluate intelligence regarding violent or potentially violent fans and compile and evaluate information regarding incidents at football matches. The SKBs are furthermore the contact points for both the fans and the persons within the clubs who are responsible for fan matters.

[26]Arbeitsgruppe Nationales Konzept Sport und Sicherheit (December 1992) Ergebnisbericht. http://www.kos-fanprojekte.info/pdf/nkss-1292.PDF. Accessed 15 January 2015.

[27]Nationaler Ausschuss Sport und Sicherheit, Nationales Konzept Sport und Sicherheit. www.kos-fanprojekte.de/fileadmin/user_upload/material/soziale-arbeit/Richtlinien-und-Regeln/nkss_konzept2012.pdf. Accessed 15 January 2015.

Fan projects have been established in most German cities and are an important element in giving fans a voice. They engage in social educational work and support fans in various everyday issues surrounding football and fandom. Although fan projects existed in a number of places prior to the establishment of the NKSS, the NKSS has strengthened and developed them. They were first developed in the 1982 report Sports and Violence, which was initiated in 1979 by the Ministry of the Interior,[28] and are designed to play a significant role in the prevention of violence. The goal of fan projects is to lead to the peaceful resolution of conflicts and to reduce delinquent behaviour. These goals are accomplished by actively engaging the fan projects in the everyday life of the fans, for example by accompanying them to away games, visiting the meeting places of the fans, streetwork initiatives, organising youth events, education, cultural events, organising leisure activities outside football, supporting fans in organisational matters and engaging in public relations.

4.3.2 The 2006 World Cup

The implementation and further development of the NKSS dovetailed with an increase in repressive measures against football fans, which reached new heights in 2006 when the FIFA World Cup took place in Germany. For the 2006 World Cup, security concepts with large personnel and organisational costs were implemented and stadia and surrounding infrastructure were equipped with new and modern security measures. The authorities intended to clamp down on football-related disorder and prevent any incidents from occurring. Reporting duties were extensively imposed and further measures limiting civil rights and Human Rights under the ECHR were implemented. Large numbers of police officers were deployed during the World Cup but after the tournament a de-escalation of the new security measures and resources did not take place. The measures implemented during the World Cup stayed in force and the number of police hours spent on football has only nominally decreased.

4.3.3 Practical Implementation

Football fans have increasingly come to the attention of politicians and the police. Although, as we have seen, official statistics suggest that violence in stadia has decreased, the subject of football violence continues to dominate the media landscape. This is even more notable given the steady increase of

[28] See for example www.kos-fanprojekte.de/index.php?id=fanarbeit-in-deutschland.

football coverage by the media. The media in their coverage of football fans use a number of extreme terms, like for example 'Chaoten' (idiots), 'Gewalttätern' (violent offenders) and 'Randalierern' (rioters), which enhance stereotypes about all football fans and not only the small violent minority. As a result of these stereotypes, football fans are confronted with increasingly sophisticated security concepts and a comprehensive media strategy of demonisation.

In short, football fans (and especially Ultras) are viewed as a security risk and a societal problem, and this in turn leads to more elaborate security innovations by the police and the football clubs to counter the perceived risks posed by them. Every week hundreds of police officers from police departments all over Germany are deployed at and around football stadia, including the special football officers (SKBs), and for international football matches the police cooperate with other European police forces.

The police have established a special database for sports fans; 'Violent Offenders Sports' contains the personal data of 15,000 persons (per 2012).[29] Minor incidents (following which the police merely note a person's details) can lead to a fan's personal data being registered on the database. Even if an investigation for a football-related offence leads to a dismissal of the case (§ 153 StPO or § 153 a StPO), the personal data of the fan remains on the database. The dismissal of a case on the basis of § 170 Abs. 2 StPO, where the public prosecutor sees no reason to pursue a public complaint, also does not mean that the individual's data is removed from the Violent Offenders Sports database. Such systemic collection of personal data encroaches upon the rights protected by Article 8 ECHR.

On match days, fans are under constant police observation. Fan trains and buses rented by spectators are accompanied by the police. Even before the fans board the train or bus they may be stopped and searched. Once at the place of destination, visiting fans are often escorted to the stadium by the police in a narrow column under constant video surveillance. At the stadium entrance fans are again confronted with meticulous body searches to prevent them from bringing prohibited items (such as fireworks or banners) into the stadium. During the match, fan sections are under constant video observation by police. If the police anticipate disorder, visiting fans are held back in their section for an undefined period of time to ensure that home fans have left the stadium. Only once the home fans have dispersed are the visiting supporters allowed to embark on their return journey. This 'holding back' of away fans in their section is a form of police custody which is regularly used in the context of football fans. However, for police custody on the basis of the Police Law a concrete danger has to exist emanating from each person in custody. The indiscriminate application of police custody to groups of football supporters is therefore contrary to the law.

[29]See www.polizei-nrw.de/artikel__4596.html.

4.3.4 Current Developments

At the beginning of the 2011/2012 season a meeting between fan representatives and the DFB took place. The goal of this meeting was to develop a concept under which the use of fireworks inside the stadium, under certain strict regulations, would be allowed. The fans issued a legal opinion which set out a framework under which the use of fireworks could be regulated.[30] This campaign of the fans to legalise fireworks ('Pyrotechnik legalisieren') led to an official response from the DFB.[31] The fans, until that time had obeyed the ban on fireworks inside the stadiums. However, in response to the fan campaign, the DFB refused to discuss the issue of fireworks inside the stadium further and stated that it had never seriously considered legalising the use of fireworks inside stadia.[32] The stand-off between fans and DFB led to a marked increase of the use of fireworks inside stadia in the period immediately following the DFB's decision.

In the aftermath of the discussions in the media regarding the issue of fireworks inside the stadium, a number of politicians (including the Federal Minister of the Interior), police representatives, representatives of the police unions ('Polizeigewerkschaften') and representatives of the clubs and the DFB remarked that there had been a substantial increase in violence in connection with football matches. This led to a high-level security meeting on 17 July 2012, organised with the participation of the Ministers of Interior of the Federal States and representatives of the 36 clubs which comprise the two highest professional leagues. During this meeting, a catalogue of more severe measures to curtail fan disorder was agreed. Furthermore, on 23 July 2012, a meeting was held between representatives of the DFB and the DFL and the Conference of Ministers of the Interior, the Ministers of Interior of the Federal States. As a result of this meeting on 27 September 2012 the 'Security Commission' of the DFL presented the concept 'Secure Stadium Experience'.

4.4 Individual Measures Against Football Supporters

4.4.1 Stadium Bans

The most important and far-reaching measure that the clubs can impose on football fans is the stadium ban. Stadium bans are generally nationwide, which means that they are valid for all matches in the highest four leagues in Germany.

[30]This opinion and other relevant information regarding this campaign can be found on the website: www.pyrotechnik-legalisieren.de/blog/start.html.

[31]R. Ulrich, 8 December 2011, Bewusst Getauescht. www.11freunde.de/artikel/streit-um-dfb-gutachten-zur-pyrotechnik. Accessed 15 January 2015.

[32]J. Uthoff, 15 September 2011, Bengalos auf Eis. www.taz.de/!78182/. Accessed 15 January 2015.

A stadium ban is a private law ban restricting access to certain premises. The legal basis for the stadium ban is found in the rights of the owner of the premises to ban potential troublemakers in order to guarantee security at the event in question.

The stadium ban is regulated in the Stadium Ban Guidelines from the DFB. According to these Guidelines, the initiation of an investigation by the police (for example for breach of the peace) suffices for the imposition of a stadium ban. A conviction by a court is not necessary for the imposition of a stadium ban; the mere suspicion of having committed an offense is sufficient. In 2009, the Federal Court of Justice (BGH) held that a nationwide stadium ban could also be imposed on the basis of a mere suspicion at the start of preliminary proceedings against the suspect.[33] This is the case even when the proceedings are later dismissed. A constitutional complaint has been filed against this decision of the Federal Court of Justice, but the Federal Constitutional Court has not to date ruled on this case.

Normally, stadium bans are imposed by the clubs upon a request from the police. The police in these cases hands the personal data of the person concerned to the club. A further, independent assessment of the facts, in most cases, is not carried out by the clubs. Because a stadium ban is a private law measure, civil rights protection only indirectly extends to the individual concerned. The legal nature of a stadium ban is considered preventive. The unique character of the stadium ban is found in the fact that the Stadium Ban Guidelines are closely related to the criminal law, since the underlying acts for which the stadium ban is imposed are suspected criminal offences. The length of the stadium ban is related to the severity of the alleged offence, giving the ban (a technically private law preventive measure) a punitive character and effect. Fans also experience stadium bans as a punishment, notwithstanding the private law preventive character. Therefore, a stadium ban should be viewed as an 'alternative criminal law' measure. The nation-wide effect of stadium bans is possible because the clubs have authorised each other to accept stadium bans from other clubs. This is one of the conditions the DFB imposes on the clubs if they wish to be granted a license for the professional leagues.

The imposition of stadium bans in practice raises a number of important legal questions. Stadium bans are imposed on the basis of a request of the police, whereby the personal data of the person concerned is forwarded to a private party (the football club concerned). This practice gives the police powers which under normal circumstances they would not possess or would only be able to exercise under extremely limited circumstances. The imposition of stadium bans in this manner does not have an express legal basis in the Police Laws and violates the wording of the Law on Criminal Procedure, which only allows a transfer of data by the public prosecutor. Stadium bans are private law bans and therefore the presumption of innocence might not apply. However, the transfer of data by the police in the procedure leading to the imposition of a stadium ban is an act by a public body and can therefore be seen as a penalty. This means that Article 6

[33] BGH, 30.10.2009—V ZR 253/08.

ECHR (the right to a fair trial) can become applicable to the imposition of stadium bans. The Federal Constitutional Court has held that the presumption of innocence applies to public acts which in its effects are equal to penalties. This is also in line with the jurisprudence of the ECtHR.[34] For Article 6 (2) ECHR to become applicable, the sanction must have both a preventive and a repressive character. The presumption of innocence is therefore applicable to procedures in which penalties or measures with a punitive character are imposed. For this reason, Article 6 ECHR is also applicable to the imposition of stadium bans. In requesting a stadium ban, the police forwards information regarding ongoing investigations to the clubs without a legal basis. This should be classed as an unauthorised transfer of data from criminal files, which is prohibited in accordance with § 203 Abs. 2 StGB i.V.m. § 353b StGB.

The transfer of data from the police to the clubs is executed by the State Information—Point Sports (LIS), of the Federal State of the relevant football clubs. The LIS in practice sends a request to the club to issue a nationwide stadium ban. The police requesting the stadium ban compile a file containing the personal data of the person concerned, the criminal charge and a short description of the incident under investigation. This file is forwarded by the investigating police department to the LIS concerned. The LIS then forwards this file to the club in whose area the alleged offence took place or to the DFB (if the alleged offence took place during a journey to or from the match). It has to be kept in mind during this whole process, that the majority of incidents do not take place within stadia. The police departments justify this elaborate transfer of personal data by pointing to the DFB's Stadium Ban Guidelines. The DFB Guidelines are however an internal guideline from a private association and for this reason can never provide a legal basis for a police measure.

The transfer of personal data by the police to private parties for preventive goals is regulated in the respective State Police Tasks Law (for example for the State of Bavaria in Article 41 BayPAG) which states that the transfer of personal data is only lawful in exceptional circumstances, and requires the police to demonstrate that such a transfer is strictly necessary. This necessity required by the Police Law, however, is in most cases not present, because the police themselves could investigate football fans for offences they commit. This means that a delegation of the power to impose measures on football fans to a private third party is not strictly necessary. In order to use measures, in accordance with the Police Law (e.g. exclusion orders), a concrete danger-assessment is required. The mere initiation of a police investigation should not be sufficient to impose such measures. The practice, in which personal data is transferred to clubs who are then tasked with imposing stadium bans, is used to circumvent the strict requirements of the Police Law. What makes this practice even more problematic is that the transfer of personal data is a substantial encroachment

[34] ECHR, *Engel and Others v. the Netherlands*, App. Nos. 5100/71; 5101/71; 5102/71; 5354/72; 5370/72, Judgment of 8 June 1976.

on the personality rights and the right to informational self-determination of the individual concerned, which follows from the constitutional right to self-determination (Article 2 GG) and Article 8 ECHR.

The Law on Criminal Procedure is applicable to criminal investigations. The access to official records is exclusively regulated in the Law on Criminal Procedure, § 475 StPO. The constitutional principle on self-determination, with regard to information, would be violated if personal data is transferred to a third party. The transfer of this data to the LIS is only allowed in connection with a possible criminal investigation into the suspect. During ongoing criminal investigations, the transfer of data is governed by § 474 ff. StPO. A transfer of information by the police can only be done upon a valid application to the public prosecutor demonstrating sufficient grounds for such a transfer (§ 475 StPO). It is not the police, but the public prosecutor who decides upon such a request (§ 478 StPO). A violation of these articles is a violation of the Constitutional principle of informational self-determination.

It is not uncommon for large groups of fans to be made the subject of a criminal investigation, even though it is clear that only a small minority of the individuals within that group actually committed the offences. In such cases it is often difficult for the police to identify the perpetrators, hence police investigations target all the individuals identified as being part of the group. This situation can for example arise when the window of a bus is broken or where one individual within a group of supporters steals something at a service station. In these cases there is often a problematic reversal of the presumption of innocence. A criminal investigation requires the presence of a reasonable suspicion against the person concerned. This reasonable suspicion is in many instances established by the mere fact that an individual was travelling on the same bus as other football fans or was a member of a certain group of supporters, without any further substantive evidence identifying the individual concerned as the suspect. Since a criminal investigation has been started against all individuals making up the group, a stadium ban can then be imposed on all of them. In these cases, the threat of a stadium ban is often used to force members of the group to disclose information regarding the identity of the individual who committed the offence, even though the members of the group have a right to refuse to cooperate with the police.[35] This is a further erosion of the basic civil rights of football supporters. This practice is reminiscent of 'Sippenhaft': a policy whereby a whole group was punished for the deeds of individuals and is a clear violation of the rule of law, especially the guilt principle (*nulla poena sine culpa*) and Articles 6 and 11 ECHR (freedom of association).

In cases where a criminal investigation is opened into a group of football supporters, the investigations can last for months during which the stadium bans remain valid. The police in these cases justify the long duration of the investigation by pointing at the large number of suspects. By investigating large groups in this way, the police can potentially fabricate a justification for an

[35] Auskunftsverweigerungsrecht des Beschuldigten, §§ 136, 163a StPO.

investigation to ensure stadium bans are in place against groups considered to pose a risk of violence or disorder. This contradicts the constitutionally guaranteed principle of expediency and the presumption of innocence.[36] In many instances and after a period of many months, the case is dismissed by the prosecutor and the stadium ban is repealed. In these cases, the fans have been penalised without having been found guilty of committing an offence. Even after a dismissal of the case, it usually takes a couple of weeks before the clubs revoke the stadium ban, even though the clubs are legally obliged to revoke the ban immediately.[37]

For many fans the visit to the stadium in a community and the association within a social group are the most important elements of fandom. A stadium ban is therefore a very severe penalty for football fans and infringes the civil rights of the fans under German law and potentially human rights under and Articles 8 and 11 ECHR, and Article 2 Prot. 4 ECHR. A stadium ban for all stadiums in Germany, imposed merely on the basis of a suspicion of certain acts is therefore disproportionate and infringes the civil rights of the fans under German law. For these reasons, there is a pressing need to change the DFB Stadium Ban Guidelines and the practice of the police and the clubs of the professional football leagues with regard to their implementation.

4.4.2 Transferring League Punishments onto the Fans

Under certain circumstances football fans can be held accountable by a club for fines levied against them. This can have a significant financial impact on individual supporters, especially given the fact that the DFB can impose substantial fines. The international football associations and the DFB have the jurisdiction to sanction clubs for supporter misbehaviour, such as setting off fireworks, throwing objects on the playing field, or letting 'streakers' enter the field of play. Such sanctions can include monetary fines, points deductions, and the obligation to play matches behind closed doors. Sanctions imposed by the associations are not criminal or civil law penalties. The associations (for example UEFA and the DFB) base these sanctions on their statutes and disciplinary regulations. The members of these associations, most notably in this regard the clubs, have agreed to these statutes and are bound by them. The regulations regarding these sanctions can be found in the Legal and Procedural Regulation for the DFB[38] and the UEFA Disciplinary Regulations.[39] It is not necessary that the club is at fault for the imposition of such sanctions. The clubs are penalised based

---

[36]Which follows from the rule of law principle Article 20 (3) Basic Law ('Grundgesetz') and the right to a fair trial on the basis of Article 6 ECHR.

[37]n. 10, § 7.

[38]Rechts- und Verfahrensordnung (RuVO) des DFB.

[39]UEFA-Rechtspflegeordnung (RPO).

on the rule of strict liability which contradicts the fault principle and elementary principles of German law.[40] The strict liability rule has been accepted by the Court of Arbitration for Sports[41] despite being validly criticised in legal circles because such punishment without guilt is illegitimate.[42]

Since 2006, a legal jurisprudence has developed, almost under the radar, which gives the clubs the possibility to recover monetary damages from fans incurred as a result of penalties imposed by the football associations for fan disorder. The State High Court ("OLG") Rostock on 28 April 2006 ruled that a club could recover penalties from fans, paid by the club for fan disorder. In such a case, when there are more wrongdoers, the damages have to be divided proportionally amongst them. If for example a fine of 15,000 Euros is imposed for the lighting of 30 fireworks, any individual fan can only be fined 500 Euro (1/30 of the total fine).[43] This has been confirmed by the State Court ('LG') in Karlsruhe.[44] The clubs, however, in some cases ignore this ruling and bring an action for damages against individual supporters for the whole amount of the fine, even though the fine was imposed for imposed for different incidents in which more persons were involved. This is especially problematic, because the levels of fines involved are often disproportionate and more than most fans can afford.

In contrast, in Austria (see Chap. 8) the Vienna District Court denied a claim for damages brought by a club against supporters.[45] In its judgment, the Vienna District Court reviewed the decision of the Rostock State High Court and decided not to follow this judgment. The Vienna District Court held that sports associations impose penalties to prevent future outbreaks of disorder, rather than to compensate for actual damages suffered. For this reason these fines could not be transferred to the fans. In comparison with many other European countries, the case law in Germany on this issue is very harsh on football fans. Transferring association fines to supporters is legally a highly questionable practice; the goal of a penalty imposed by the association is to penalise the club and not the supporters. Such a penalty is often imposed for damages, which are illusory in reality. For example, high fines are imposed by the football associations for setting off fireworks, despite the fact that these offences do not lead to actual damage.

A further problem is posed by the fact that these sanctions against the clubs are based on the disciplinary procedures of the associations. The individual stadium visitor is not party to these disciplinary proceedings and has absolutely no access to information or the right to be heard in these proceedings. Furthermore, clubs are not motivated to appeal any penalty, because they can recover the fine from the fans. The disciplinary procedures of the associations are therefore unique, because

---

[40]Orth 2009.

[41]CAS 2007/A/1217—*Feyenoord Rotterdam v. UEFA*.

[42]Supra n. 40.

[43]OLG Rostock (Urteil v. 28.04.2006, Az. 3 U 106/05).

[44]LG Karlsruhe (Urteil v. 29.05.2012, Az.: 8 O 78/12).

[45]Judgment of the Vienna District Court of 25.01.2011, Az.:34 R 163/10p.

the criminal law fair trial guarantees are not applicable. Appeals have little or no prospect of success. Usually clubs will accept the penalties imposed on them rather than appealing the decision. However, the club's refusal to appeal could later come back to haunt them, because by doing so, theoretically the clubs violate their legal duty to minimise damages[46] which they later seek to recover from the fans. A lower fine would mean that the fans have less to pay back to the club.

At the time of writing this case law is accepted—at least before most courts of first instance. This means that each supporter runs the risk that, in addition to sanctions such as the stadium ban and the collation of their data on the Violent Offender Sports database, they could be held liable for substantial fines imposed on the clubs by the associations. However, the legal validity of this measure has not yet been definitively addressed by the Federal Court.

4.4.3 Police Measures

Because Germany is a federal state, for each of the 16 federal states there is a Law on the Duties of the Police. Police Law is a matter for the federal states. This leads to different legal standards and a difference in the practical application of police powers. Furthermore, there are differences locally between the various cities and municipalities. Such local differences can be quite substantial but generally the police have the same powers and responsibilities throughout the whole country. A variety of measures are available for the police and all such measures are governed by public law. This means that in the application of these measures civil rights and human rights under the ECHR are directly applicable.

4.4.3.1 Exclusion Orders (Stadium, Train Station, City Centre)

When there is sufficient evidence that an individual poses a danger, an exclusion order can be imposed upon them. An exclusion order is a public law measure. An exclusion order requires a concrete and motivated prognosis of the threat posed by the individual. The prerequisites for a public law exclusion order are thus higher and the mere initiation of a criminal investigation is not sufficient. Compared to private law stadium bans, there are fewer public law exclusion orders. However, there is a tendency to impose more public law exclusions.

The public law exclusion order can pertain to the stadium, the area around the stadium and even for the whole city centre, for certain train connections, or in individual cases even for the whole federal state. Most of the time, such orders are imposed before high risk matches. In these cases, the police determine whether a match qualifies as high risk. Exclusion orders are imposed on the basis of the

[46]This duty exists in accordance with § 254 BGB.

Police Laws of the federal states and are categorised as preventive measures. An exclusion order requires a determination that the individual will commit offences or will be involved in offences in a certain area in the future. As evidence for this prognosis of the future behaviour of the individual concerned, the authorities consider their past behaviour and previous convictions. Football supporters are regularly confronted with measures for incidents that occurred around football matches, for which no criminal convictions were obtained. The presumed or expected threat posed by football supporters is based on entries into the police database of supposed incidents, in which a broad range of police actions are entered, such as the mere personal identification of football supporters.

In this regard it must be kept in mind that football supporters, in the course of visiting a football stadium, are in a situation where they are under constant police supervision. Football supporters' identities are checked much more regularly by the police than citizens attending other events. Every further identity check by the police or by fan officers raises more of a suspicion regarding the behaviour of football supporters. This in turn leads to an increasing number of checks and further preventive measures even when no specific offence is reasonably suspected.

4.4.3.2 Reporting Duty

Based on the same preconditions as exist for exclusion orders, a reporting duty can be imposed. The supporter concerned in this case has to report to the local police station of their place of residence at set times to prevent them from travelling to away matches, for example during certain high risk matches. Should a supporter violate this reporting duty, they will be liable for a fine of several hundred Euros.

4.4.3.3 Detention

Fans can also be detained for the duration of a football match on the basis of stringent preconditions. However, for such a measure to be imposed, there needs to be an individual risk assessment. The ECtHR in its decision in *Ostendorf v. Germany* has held that preventive detention can be justified, if the detention complies with Article 5 (1)(b) ECHR.[47] Therefore, such detention can be justified when the person concerned has violated an explicit order by the police, or where there is sufficient evidence that the person concerned will commit an offence.

---

[47]ECHR, *Ostendorf v. Germany,* Application No. 15598/08, Judgment of 7 March 2013.

4.4.3.4 Travel Bans

Travel bans also require an individual risk prognosis. The authorities in these cases consider existing rivalries with foreign fan groups. However, travel bans are very serious measures and have to meet more stringent preconditions.

4.4.3.5 Police Visits ('Gefährderansprache')

A police visit means that the police will visit the supporter at his or her home or workplace or send a letter to the fan to inform them that they are under surveillance and that any possible offences will have legal consequences. However, the legal basis for this practice is questionable and is not regulated by the Police Law. This measure is especially problematic because of its impact on the private sphere of the person concerned.

4.5 The 'Violent Offenders Sports Database'

At the time of writing, the personal data of almost 13,000 individuals is registered in the Federal 'Violent Offenders Sports Database'. The majority of this data was compiled in relation to football. The collection and registration of this data is justified on the grounds that it improves security at sports events. Being registered on the Violent Offenders Sports Database can have severe consequences for the individual concerned. Their car could be searched extensively in a normal traffic check, a travel ban could be imposed on them around the time of away matches, and they could receive a personal visit from the police at their workplace to instruct them that they will be under intense police surveillance during upcoming football matches.

Often merely being 'in the wrong place at the wrong time' can be sufficient to result in a supporter being registered on the Violent Offenders Sports Database. The registration of an individual supporter can follow the detention of a large group of football supporters by the police at or around a football match, without a criminal offence having taken place. Even when the public prosecutor does not see sufficient grounds for initiating a criminal investigation against a supporter, their data is still registered on the Violent Offenders Sports Database. Especially problematic is the fact that the supporters concerned are not informed that they have been registered on the database. This means that they cannot appeal their registration, even though the collection of the data potentially violates the right to private life protected by Article 8 ECHR.

The police deal very diversely with the registration of individuals on the Violent Offenders Sports Database. Some police departments take great care when registering individuals on this database but other departments have much lower standards for registering individuals. Often it is only sufficient to have been stopped and searched by the police in the vicinity of the stadium to be registered on the database.

For these reasons, supporters allege that the Violent Offenders Sports Database gives the police an arbitrary instrument to repress them. Furthermore, supporters state that the database has little value in actually determining whether a particular individual is a violent offender because of the large quantity of data collected and because of the differing police practices with regard to the collection of data and the registration of persons on the database. Being registered on the Violent Offenders Sports Database leads to the stigmatisation of the individual concerned. However, the database in practice does not lead to more security at football matches, does not prevent violence and does not improve the prosecution of offenders. There are serious questions regarding the constitutionality of the data regulation. At the very least, the data regulation should be changed so that in the future only the data of persons who have been found guilty of an offence in connection to a sports event are registered. Otherwise there is an illegal encroachment into the privacy rights of the person concerned which may violate Article 8 ECHR. A registration on the basis of a case that was dropped by the prosecutor should no longer be possible. Registrations should further be reviewed after a period of 3 years and every registration should be communicated to the person concerned, affording them the opportunity to appeal the registration.

4.6 Conclusions

As seen before, football-related disorder or 'hooliganism' is an issue that receives considerable attention from the authorities. A large number of often far-reaching measures can be imposed upon supporters. However, the supporters themselves are also aware that the police measures they experience each week are a problem which affects all fans and the football community as a whole. To gain a common voice and protest against the excesses of the security measures, football supporters have for a long time been organising themselves. Organisations like Pro Fans, BAFF and Unsere Kurve can be mentioned in this respect. In terms of the legal protection of football fans the Fanrechtefonds (Supporters Legal Aid) also deserves recognition. Finally, at club level, legal aid organisations for fans exist, like the Rot-Schwarze Hilfe (Red Black Support) in Nuremberg. Such initiatives currently exist at many professional football clubs. Among many fan groups, there is a willingness to look past rivalries and club colours to raise a common voice against repressive, disproportionate and often ineffective measures.

References

Gabler J (2011) Die Ultras: Fußballfans und Fußballkulturen in Deutschland. Papyrossa, Köln
Orth JF (2009) Gefährdungshaftung für Anhänger? SpuRt 2009:10–13
Ruf C (2014) Kurven-Rebellen: Die Ultras—Einblicke in eine widersprüchliche Szene. Die Werkstatt, Göttingen

Chapter 5
Regulating Football-Related Violence in France

Anastassia Tsoukala

Abstract Due to the low profile of football crowd disorder until the mid-2000s, counter-hooliganism measures remained event-linked rather than embedded in a global strategy. Present legal provisions and police tactics are heavily influenced by risk-management policies, thereby producing multifold confusion. This confusion is visible in terms of value ranking: protection of human life, property, and public order tends to be guaranteed at the expense of the rule of law. In terms of objectives to be reached: 'law and order' tends to be established at the expense of the democratic legal order. Finally in terms of the means to achieve these objectives, counter-hooliganism tends to rest upon institutionalisation of control and direct punishment of deviance.

Keywords France · Counter-hooliganism · Risk · Deviance · Civil rights

Contents

Anastassia Tsoukala is Associate Professor, University Paris 11, Faculty of Sport Sciences; Senior researcher, GEPECS, University Paris 5-Sorbonne.

A. Tsoukala (✉)
University Paris 5, Sorbonne, France
e-mail: tsoukala.anastassia@gmail.com

A. Tsoukala et al. (eds.), *Legal Responses to Football "Hooliganism" in Europe*,
ASSER International Sports Law Series, DOI 10.1007/978-94-6265-108-1_5

5.1 Introduction

Following the gradual expansion of organised football crowd disorder in continental Europe from the early 1970s, the phenomenon became established in France in the early 1980s. In a country where sports fans were traditionally more enthusiastic for bicycling and rugby, and prevalent centralised state-orientated policies were subduing regionalist politics and traditions,[1] football was not inflaming sport crowds enough to anchor and stir up powerful fandom and fandom-related rituals. Quite unsurprisingly then, throughout the 1980s serious incidents remained scarce. Accordingly, until the early 1990s control of what was seen as an essentially foreign problem[2] rested upon generic law and policing practices.

The perceived low levels in significance of domestic football crowd disorder also explains to some extent a certain lack of interest in the subject in French academia. Although in the mid-1980s Alain Ehrenberg and Christian Bromberger framed two influential explanatory theories of the phenomenon,[3] the subject matter remained marginal in social sciences until the late 1990s and, with the exception of the author's work[4] and a few reviews,[5] remains underexplored when it comes to analysing relevant legal and policing issues.

In the lawmaking realm, the first shift occurred in 1993 when, in the aftermath of widely reported aggression against riot police, Parliament introduced a counter-hooliganism law[6] that sought to control football fans by criminalising an array of acts inside football stadia. In full compliance with the key principles of the rehabilitative, danger-oriented crime control model,[7] the first reaction of the lawmaker was to punish individual offenders for the social harm produced by their offences. From then on, and despite the fact that, compared with other European countries, football stadia remained relatively free of violence until the late 1990s, control of football crowd disorder was regularly an issue in many different legal texts. While the proliferation of legal and policing measures does suggest rising concern on the part of the authorities, the absence of constant crowd disorder led to an essentially reactive regulatory model. More often than not, innovative lawmaking and policing were event-linked rather than embedded in a global counter-hooliganism strategy.

This is not unrelated to the way authorities were prioritising internal security threats. From the 1980s onwards, social unrest in France has been mostly identified with youth living in socially and economically disadvantaged suburban

[1] Dietschy 2010.

[2] Tsoukala 2009a, p. 31.

[3] Ehrenberg 1984; Bromberger 1984.

[4] Tsoukala 1995, 2001, 2003, 2007, 2009a, b, 2011a, b, 2013.

[5] Simon 2008; Hourcade 2010; Lestrelin 2012; Otero 2012.

[6] Law 93-1282 of 6 December 1993 in relation to the safety of sporting events.

[7] Garland 1985.

areas.[8] The suburban areas where the riots seemed to predominantly occur came to be seen as emblematic of petty crime, antisocial behaviour and young people's conflict with the police. Their specific importance in terms of policing social unrest was further reinforced by the overall weak engagement of youth in violent politics. Though France has been occasionally hit by political violence, in recent decades domestic politics have been characterised by the absence of urban guerrilla groups and, broadly speaking, low levels of regular involvement in violent protests by youth other than those originating from the aforementioned suburbs. In this context, scarce youth-originating football-related incidents were certainly worrisome but were not believed to be a source of major concern among government and police officials.

This somewhat target-loose counter-hooliganism policy was, by definition, particularly receptive to external influences. Hence, while importing police practices applied in other fields of domestic police action, it was to a great extent shaped by supranational sports and security-related lawmaking and policing principles. As it will be shown below, the evolving regulation of football-related violence was also reflecting the rising influence of the risk-focused mindset in crime control policies. The turning point came in 2006 with the formal introduction of suspicion-grounded forms of punishment under the form of administrative football banning orders (AFBOs), which drew a dividing line between previous, danger-oriented controlling policies and present trends to privilege risk management-oriented ones.

5.2 Controlling Danger

Due to the low levels of football crowd disorder throughout the 1980s, both public and sport authorities did not see the need to rank it among security threats, and adopted a casual approach to the issue. In line with the then prevailing rehabilitative crime control model, the consensus was that society should tackle the origins of this violent behaviour by addressing its structural causes and changing the 'crime-generating' aspects of the violent fans' environment. Hence, until the early 1990s, football crowd disorder was attributed to many different social causes, ranging from the commercialisation of football to declining ethics and overall social lax attitude.[9] In admitting its deep social and psychological roots, senior sport officials further believed that the phenomenon could not be efficiently dealt with by ordinary policing. Police control was certainly seen as a necessary step to maintain law and order but only if it could be supported with long-term social preventive measures.[10]

---

[8]Dubet and Lapeyronnie 1992; Mucchielli 2001; Bonelli 2007, 2008.

[9]Bambuck 1990, pp. 9–10.

[10]Paillou 1990, pp. 31–40.

A similar attitude was found among law enforcers who were seeking to control football crowds by both informal and formal preventive measures rather than coercive ones. In the former case, policing football stadia relied heavily on negotiations with both ordinary and violent football fans. Informal discussions between fans and police officers, with the latter pointing out the disastrous impact of probable future convictions on teenager's lives,[11] are believed to have substantially limited football-related violence for many years.[12] Informal police work was further expected to be enhanced by the implementation of a wide-scale preventive policy likely to encompass a broad array of actors, ranging from sport officials and teachers to referees and journalists.[13]

The overwhelming impression that domestic football-related violence was not serious enough to justify specific reactions on the part of the lawmaker was shaken in 1993. The incident that took place on the terraces of the Parisian Parc des Princes stadium led to the introduction of the aforementioned first counter-hooliganism law. However, because it was not believed to be representative of the overall phenomenon, it did not lead to the formal transposition in football stadia of risk-based police practices, such as undercover policing and profiling, which were already targeting youth living in disadvantaged suburban areas.[14] Control of football crowd disorder was limited to criminalising a series of acts deemed to endanger public order if they were committed inside stadia.[15] This control was further enhanced following the introduction of Law 95-73 of 21 January 1995 on orientation and planning in relation to security, and of the correlated ministerial decree 96-926 of 17 October 1996, that were respectively providing for the installation and operation of CCTV cameras inside stadia.

The rise in surveillance practices and the ensuing reinforcement of deviancy control[16] was not accompanied by any significant shift in sentencing policies, the rationale of which remained attached to offence-based, rather than suspicion-based, judicial reactions. The 1993 law provided up to five-year-long football banning orders but only as a judicial sentence handed down for people convicted for football-related violent offences committed inside stadia. Throughout the 1990s, judges were being frequently criticised by law enforcers for not handing down enough banning orders for them to act as a deterrent. While these criticisms stemmed from the usual tension between zealous, pragmatic law enforcers and social interest-balancing judges unwilling to punish severely what was still seen as unremarkable disorderly behaviour, the low volume of judicial football banning orders (JFBOs) was also related to the fact that the 1993 law could only be

---

[11] In its early phase, football crowd disorder was an issue for young fans: Mignon 1998, p. 220.

[12] Chatard 1990, pp. 42–43.

[13] Idem, pp. 43–45.

[14] Bonelli 2001, 2008, p. 383 f.

[15] For example: consuming alcohol, introducing dangerous objects into a stadium, invading the pitch, inciting hate and violence, racist behaviour.

[16] Armstrong and Giulianotti 1998.

implemented inside stadia. Football-related offences committed elsewhere were punished according to the provisions of the general Penal Code. In the perspective of the 1998 Football World Cup, the introduction of Law 98-146 of 6 March 1998 relating to the safety and promotion of sporting activities reinforced judicial power in that it expanded the field of application of the law to encompass offences committed outside stadia.

5.3 Managing Risk

5.3.1 Conceptual Background

The public perception of football crowd disorder changed significantly in the aftermath of the 1998 Football World Cup which was marked by large-scale clashes between English fans, local youth and police in Marseille and, above all, the violent assault on a police officer that left him in a coma and permanently disabled. As I have argued elsewhere,[17] events can play a significant role in shaping public discourses and triggering legal and policing reforms only and to the extent that they are also catalysts for ongoing social and political processes. In other words, harsher counter-hooliganism policies may frequently be introduced in the aftermath of serious incidents, and justified by the seriousness of the latter, but in fact their successful introduction is possible only if they encapsulate relevant ongoing trends and satisfy an array of interests at stake, be it social, political or other. From this standpoint, the impact of the aforementioned events on future French counter-hooliganism policies should be understood in combination with many other domestic and international factors, unrelated to football crowd disorder. The rationale of twenty-first century counter-hooliganism was integrated in a rapidly changing security landscape where control of rising domestic social unrest and Islamist radicalism was heavily influenced by risk-focused policies, growing politicisation of security, and the legitimised erosion of civil rights and liberties in the name of the 'war on terror'.

One of the key common denominators of this security context was the redefinition of security threats following a global approach[18] that emancipated itself from ordinary law-based objective definitional criteria. In full compliance with the risk-based mindset, security threats were no longer prioritised according to their seriousness and deviant or criminal nature, to be dealt with by increasingly standardised measures likely to ease the subjective and politically-related sense of insecurity, which could be troubled by minor or major deviant or criminal behaviour. In an era of growing social, economic and ultimately existential

[17] Tsoukala 2011a, p. 602.

[18] Bigo 1996.

uncertainty[19] and the weakening of the political elites' legitimacy, government capacity to keep law and order and reduce feelings of insecurity, ranked at the top of the political agenda, thereby reinforcing the aforementioned fusion. The henceforth prevailing global perception of security threats relied upon merging definitional processes and law enforcement policies where football crowd disorder was turned into a subgroup of urban security-threatening behaviours, along with urban riots, demonstrations and cultural events. The conceptual ground of this definitional shift is to be found in a preliminary note for an experts' meeting convened by the JHA Council in 1998,[20] where the term 'offence' was replaced by 'conflict'. Conflict was defined broadly enough to include both crime and disorder as any act contrary to the public's perception of normality or which adversely affects their quality of life.[21] As I have noted elsewhere,[22] the ensuing blurring of the boundaries between delinquency, deviance and ordinary behaviour is not founded on any kind of legal concept but on an essentially political one, since the note specifies that conflict has the potential to have an adverse effect on the status quo.[23]

When it comes to sporting issues, at the EU level this merging process was formalised for the first time when, under the generic term 'meeting', the Joint Action of 26 May 1997 with regard to cooperation on law and order and security brought together football-related violence with a whole array of potentially urban security-threatening events.[24] In the early 2000s, at the French lawmaking-and-police level there was certainly a rise in surveillance practices inside and outside stadia but legal reforms still had an EU rather than domestic origin. The 2003 creation of a police database on football fans served with JFBOs stems from a 2002 Council Decision[25] on the EU-wide establishment of national football information points for coordinating and facilitating the exchange of relevant information between law enforcement agencies in connection with football matches with an international dimension.[26] Once created, however, the national football information point boosted undercover policing and intelligence gathering, thereby contributing to the normalisation both of surveillance practices inside the territory and exchange of intelligence with foreign security agencies.

[19]Castel 2003; Bauman 2007; Young 2007.

[20]The note 7386/98 ENFOPOL 45 was sent from the Presidency of the Council to a Cooperation Group of experts on public order to prepare an expert's meeting on public order and conflict management to be held in Brussels on 15 April 1998.

[21]Council of the EU 1998, 3.1.

[22]Tsoukala 2009a, p. 108.

[23]Council of the EU 1998, 3.2.

[24]Council of the EU, 1997.

[25]Council of the EU 2002b.

[26]For a thorough analysis of relevant EU legislation: Tsoukala 2009a, p. 105 f., 2011b.

5.3.2 Control and Direct Punishment of Deviant Behaviour

Risk-oriented policies became prevalent in the mid-2000s. Law 2006-64 of 23 January 2006 on the fight against terrorism, internal security issues and border controls included one provision that enabled administrative authorities to serve football banning orders for a maximum of three months, upon anyone whose behaviour was deemed to threaten public order during a sporting event.[27] This shift had a multifold political origin. On the one hand, the introduction of this legislation cannot be dissociated from the rise in violent clashes between football fan groups during the 2005/06 season; on the other, it should be seen as a government reaction to the unprecedented wave of urban riots that shook the country in 2005[28] and had only been controlled when the government declared a state of emergency. In this respect, it is not coincidental that in introducing formal control and direct punishment of deviant behaviour under the form of AFBOs, the 2006 law mirrored security practices already at work in the suburbs. In the same period, law enforcers overtly adhered to the EU broad-sweeping definition of security threats. It is telling that from then on, the training programme of the Academy of National Gendarmerie Officers included a seminar on 'Crowd regulation at the occasion of sporting and cultural meetings'.

During the 2006/07 season, 401 football fans were served with AFBOs[29] and their personal data was entered onto a new specific national police database. However, as the AFBOs' scope was still complying with the rehabilitative crime control model in that they were targeting individuals accused of committing criminal offences,[30] they were not thought to be efficient enough. This last vestige of prior crime control policies was rejected in 2007 when the lawmaker specified that the conduct being penalised by such orders did not have to constitute a criminal offence. It was sufficient for it to amount to 'behaviour that is generally threatening to public order'.[31] Specific danger stemming from concrete individual offences was thus being replaced by vague risk stemming from membership of deviant groups likely to breach public order. From then on, AFBOs have been on a constant rise, outnumbering JFBOs. For example, at the end of March 2011, there were 258 fans served with AFBOs and 168 with JFBOs.[32] It is noteworthy that this extra-judicial punishment of deviance went together with criminalisation of deviant behaviour as any person who breached such an order was liable to a fine.[33] 'Potentially threatening' fans became even more vulnerable from 2009 on, following the creation of a counter-hooliganism police division that enhanced

[27]Law 2006-64, Artcle 31.

[28]Mucchielli and Le Goaziou 2006.

[29]Assemblée Nationale, Report No 396.

[30]Circular INT/D/06/00077/C.

[31]Circular INT/D/07/00089/C.

[32]Ligue de Football Professionnel (LFP) 2012, p. 9.

[33]Law 2006-64, Article 31.

surveillance and undercover policing. The prevalence of deviancy control is clearly shown by the ratio of people brought to trial among those served AFBOs. For example, of the 249 Paris Saint Germain and Saint Etienne fans arrested and given AFBOs on 7 August 2010 only four were brought to trial.[34]

Prioritisation of deviancy control is also clear when one considers that long before any possible assessment of their efficiency was possible, AFBOs were being criticised as inefficient due to their short duration. A 2007 Parliamentary Report thus recommended their length be increased to 6 months,[35] whilst the authors of a 2007 Senate Report wanted it increased to a whole year.[36] Those emphasising the comparatively greater number of fans subjected to similar banning orders in the UK did not attribute this discrepancy to the relatively low crowd disorder in France. Instead they saw it as evidence of a lax government stance. Quite unsurprisingly then, Law 2010-201 of 2 March 2010 on the fight against violent groups increased the length of AFBOs to 6 months, or 12 months in case of recidivism.[37] Accordingly, any person who breached such an order was liable to a 12 month prison sentence and a fine.[38] 1 year later, Law 2011-267 of 14 March 2011 on internal security allowed the length of these banning orders to be increased to 1 year and extended to 2 years in case of recidivism. Henceforth, this measure, targeting behaviour 'likely to cause serious public disorder' could be applied to an exceedingly broad and vaguely defined array of people as it encompasses 'people who claim to be or behave as if they were football supporters'[39] as well as any member of a suspended or dissolved football fans' group. The deviancy-oriented nature of this new piece of legislation becomes flagrant if one takes into consideration statistics on football-related violence. During the season 2010/11, for example, the vast majority of the 282 reported incidents that took place both inside and outside of First Division stadia were not violence-related: 50.1 % were related to the use or transport of fireworks, 13.1 % to alcohol consumption, and 3.9 % to ticket touting. Among the rest, only 10.6 % were related to use or threat of physical violence, 6.7 % to missile throwing, and 1.7 % to verbal abuse.[40]

The introduction of AFBOs was only one facet of a more elaborate counter-hooliganism policy that focused on increased control of fans' behaviour and movement. Law 2006-784 of 5 July 2006 on the prevention of violence at sporting events provided for football supporters' clubs or groups to be dissolved or have their activity suspended for one year if their members had been collectively and regularly engaged in violent acts. This provision was implemented for the first

[34]Le Monde 2010a.

[35]Assemblée Nationale, Report No. 396.

[36]Sénat, Report n° 467, p. 36.

[37]Law 2010-201, Article 10.

[38]Ibid., Article 10 1c.

[39]Law 2011-267, Article 61.

[40]Ligue de Footbal Professionnel 2011, p. 49.

time in 2008, leading to the dissolution of 'Faction Metz' and 'Association Nouvelle des Boulogne Boys'.[41] The latter referred the case to the Council of State, which ruled that, in light of previous regular and serious events involving members of the club,[42] dissolution was not a disproportionate security measure.[43] In 2011 this ruling was supported by the European Court of Human Rights that declared the supporters' club application inadmissible.[44] Following the introduction of the aforementioned 2010 law, executive power to order the dissolution of football supporters' clubs or groups was extended to encompass particularly serious offences, be they individual or collective. When, in the same year, two more Parisian football supporters' clubs were disbanded,[45] their members referred the case to the Council of State. In applying the 2010 law, the Court backed the government decree because members of these clubs had been involved in a particularly serious offence that caused the death of a supporter.[46]

Disruption of football fans' activities as a form of police control was further extended to monitoring their freedom of movement. The aforementioned 2011 law provided for organised away match trips to be prohibited if they were believed to be likely to cause a serious breach of public order.[47] This measure was applied for the first time in November 2011 to Paris Saint Germain and Olympique de Marseille supporters who were respectively wishing to attend the match in Marseille and the return match in Paris. The 2011 law further provided for individual fans' freedom of movement to be restricted if it was believed that their presence at a designated away match could threaten public order.[48] In all cases, breach of these orders is punishable with a 6-month prison sentence and a fine.

---

[41]ANBB was punished for unfurling an offensive banner in the stands during a match at the Stade de France stadium on 29 March 2008.

[42]Namely several violent clashes between members of the club and the police or rival teams' supporters that had taken place between 2006 and 2008.

[43]CE, 25 July 2008, Appl. n° 315723.

[44]Ruling 5th Section 22 February 2011, *Association Nouvelle des Boulogne Boys v. France*, App. n° 6468/09. The applicant association complained that, under Article 6 1 and 3 (right to a fair hearing) of the European Convention on Human Rights, it had not had the time or the wherewithal to prepare its defence. It also alleged that insufficient reasoning had been given for the dissolution, and complained, under Article 11, of interference with its freedom of association. Regarding the right to a fair hearing, the Court ruled that the criminal aspect of Article 6 was not applicable in this case because the proceedings did not concern a 'criminal charge'. Regarding freedom of association, the Court ruled that the dissolution measure constituted an interference with the applicant's right to freedom of association which was prescribed by the French Sporting Code and which pursued the legitimate aim of preventing disorder or crime.

[45]Les Authentiks and Supras Auteuil 91. Dissolution of Parisian football supporters' clubs went along with disbanding of two fans' clubs in the South of France: Brigade Sud de Nice (2010) and Butte Paillade 91 (2011).

[46]CE, 13 July 2010, App. n° 339257 and 339293.

[47]Article L. 332-16-1 of Sports Code.

[48]Article L. 332-16-2 of Sports Code.

5.4 Jeopardising Civil Rights and Liberties

5.4.1 Suspicion-Grounded Policies

Most of the key components of the risk-oriented legal provisions and police measures discussed above share one key point: they seek to circumvent judicial control in order to impose liberty-restricting measures that rest upon suspicion rather than proof. In so doing, police measures reinforce pre-existing patterns of deviant behaviour control, until then limited to surveillance practices, while legal provisions innovate by introducing direct punishment of deviant fans. Needless to say, both trends are jeopardising civil rights and liberties of fans in distinct complementary ways that suggest significant shifts in social values ranking. Protection of human life, property, and public order has entailed jeopardising, if not negating, privacy,[49] presumption of innocence,[50] principles of legality[51], proportionality of penalties,[52] and freedom of movement.[53] As will be argued below, these value conflicts are not conjectural. They are structural parts of risk-management policies and they emerge whenever football fans are turned into key targets of the social control apparatus because they belong to an alleged risk group.

In one respect, enhanced control of deviance through increases in surveillance mechanisms, intelligence gathering, and restrictions on fans' freedom of movement, falls within the much criticised grey zone of policing, where the line between order and disorder becomes blurred as the social control apparatus veers off course in order to maintain 'law and order'. It has frequently been stated that police strategies and practices can fuel, if not create, disorder, either because their conception is erroneous in terms of respecting rule of law, in that they rest upon liberticidal control of deviance, or because their implementation is flawed and they produce perverse effects.[54] Erosion of the legislative and judicial powers to the benefit of the executive, as one of the direct consequences of the use of

---

[49]Guaranteed under: Article 2 of the 1789 Declaration of the Rights of Man and the Citizen [DRMC] (confirmed as autonomous freedom by the Constitutional Council: Appl. 99-416 and 99-419 of 9 November 1999); Article 8 of the European Convention on Human Rights [ECHR]; Article 7 of the Charter of Fundamental Rights of the EU [CFREU].

[50]Guaranteed under: Article 9 of the DRMC; Article 6§2 of the ECHR; Article 48§1 of the CFREU.

[51]Guaranteed under: Article 8 of the DRMC (repeated in Article L 111-3 of the Penal Code); Article 7§1 of the ECHR; Article 49 of the CFREU.

[52]Introduced by: Constitutional Council, Appl. 86-215 of 3 September 1986; also guaranteed under: Article 49 of the CFREU.

[53]Guaranteed under: Articles 2 and 3 of the Protocol n° 4 to the ECHR; Article 45§1 of the CFREU.

[54]Cohen 1971; Anderson et al. 1996; Della Porta and Reiter 1998; Armstrong and Giulianotti 1998; Palidda 1999; Stott 2003; Balzacq and Carrera 2006; Fillieule and Della Porta 2006; Stott et al. 2006; Bonelli 2007; Bigo and Tsoukala 2008; Tsoukala 2009a.

discretionary police power, surveillance devices and proactive control measures in football stadia in particular, has been criticised in academia since the early 1980s.[55]

Yet, in another respect, these measures mark a turning point in criminal justice because, from the moment they are introduced by the lawmaker, they imply institutionalisation of both control and direct punishment of deviance. One of the key differences between danger and risk-based crime control models is that in the latter, control of deviance is no longer a form of social control that has veered off course. It is no longer a question of policing practices situated in an implicitly tolerated grey zone, but of a key component of the legal system which is intrinsically linked to the way in which crime control policies actually operate.[56] Marginalisation of proof and the subsequent growth of suspicion as a justificatory basis for the setting in motion of the social control apparatus are core elements of the risk-based mindset. The ensuing institutionalisation of the control of deviance should be analysed therefore along with other aspects of the risk-based crime control model, ranging from proactive risk management policies to impersonal group-based profiling criteria, which have been widely discussed by many different scholars from both sides of the Atlantic.[57] When it comes to assessing its intrusive capacity, it is clear that the institutionalised control of deviance tends to become so inclusive that it can no longer be attributed to sporadic deviations by a criminal justice system that otherwise complies with the rule of law. It is indicative of the formal insertion into the criminal justice system of previously illegal practices that imply a genuine legal upgrading of this type of control of deviance.

These legally upgraded forms of control and direct punishment of deviant behaviour become all the more concerning from a human rights perspective when we take into account the rising interoperability of police databases.[58] From the early 2000s, football crowd disorder was at the heart of an EU-wide exchange of intelligence, with the Council considering that national football information points could, should the need arise, exchange information regarding other matters besides sporting events.[59] In line with the guiding principles of the Hague Programme and the Stockholm Programme that stress the importance of developing exchanges of information and criminal intelligence in the EU, this position is presented in a 2010 Note that places interoperability of police databases at the core of the future European Information Exchange Model.

In light of these remarks, it is interesting to see how this tension between the rule of law and risk-management policies is formally denied by officials involved both in the decision-making process and the implementation of counter-hooliganism.

---

[55]Trivizas 1980, 1984; Williams 1980; Armstrong and Hobbs 1994; Armstrong and Giulianotti 1998.

[56]Tsoukala 2009a, b.

[57]Feeley and Simon 1992; Beck 1999; Broadhurst 2000; O'Malley 2000; Lyon 2001; Silver and Miller 2002; Johnston and Shearing 2003; Ericson 2007; Carlen 2008.

[58]Geyer 2008; Türk 2009.

[59]Council of the EU 2002a, annexe: Chapter 1, Section 2.

The embarrassment among law enforcers and sport officials is clearly illustrated in the case of AFBOs. While relevant administrative decisions rely on police or intelligence reports or other allegedly informative facts[60] that seek to frame 'potential threatening behaviours', both public and sport authorities deny the existence of any possible discretionary power of law enforcers. It is telling that in a 2012 document of the Football League, AFBOs were presented as being mostly handed down to fans who have regularly been involved in violent or racist acts.[61] In other words, official presentation of usually threat-related AFBOs seeks to identify them with strictly offence-related JFBOs. In practice, however, the designation of who is 'potentially threatening' rests upon vague criteria when gathering relevant intelligence. Personal data may be entered in police files for many different loosely defined reasons that are structured around the subjective assessment of the dangerousness of a given behaviour in a given context. Hence, more often than not, the decision-making process blurs the borders between the executive and the legislative powers or between the executive and the judiciary ones.

5.4.2 Blurring Borders

As I have shown elsewhere,[62] both public and private security agents take over the sphere occupied by lawmakers in determining what behaviour will be included in the field of action of the social control apparatus. Situated beyond the border dividing legality and illegality, their discretionary power draws new lines between social disturbance and potential threat, and social disapproval and punishment, in an attempt to reshape a certain social order as a response to seemingly growing disorder. To the extent that their wish to contain disorder is shared by lawmakers, their power is law-framed; but as this very way of proceeding counters many principles of the rule of law, the content of this power cannot be possibly defined in legal terms. Verbal abuse or excitement may therefore be tolerated on a permanent or temporary basis as a worrying sign to justify future clampdown if repeated, or immediately seen as threatening enough to justify an AFBO. Regular implementation of such vaguely-defined police powers inevitably produces arbitrariness and it was telling that around 250 Paris Saint Germain fans who participated in December 2010 in an incident-free protest against the introduction of new security measures in the Parc-des-Princes stadium have been served with

[60]For example: going regularly to notoriously disorderly sections of the stadium; being member of a violent fans' group; having been already arrested or convicted for violent acts or alcohol consumption.

[61]Ligue de Footbal Professionnel 2012, pp. 7–8.

[62]Tsoukala 2013.

AFBOs,[63] thereby becoming the subject of an indirect restriction on their freedom of assembly.

The use of this discretionary power may further allow public security agents to take over the position held by judges in deciding who is socially dangerous enough to be punished. AFBOs may then be served upon arrested fans if police officers believe they should be put under control until their case is brought before the Court. AFBOs may also be imposed upon convicted fans if intelligence officers consider that they remain dangerous even when their sentence comes to an end. Being grounded on a henceforth limitless suspicion, punishment thus becomes endless. It may start from the moment of arrest, or in anticipation of a probable conviction that may be imposed or not. It may be repeated if the person is not convicted and, in case of conviction, as soon as the JFBO expires it may be handed down again, as many times as necessary, until the person is 'disgusted' and stops going to stadia forever.[64]

Subsequent confusion between the roles of the different powers is not new as such. What is new is that, until recently, similar confusion was usually related to the way the police operate and was analysed as a perverse effect of policies which otherwise complied with democratic standards. However, now the separation of powers is being deliberately flouted by the legislator who, in institutionalising the confusion, is fully accepting its consequences.

5.4.3 Risk-Based Policies and the Judicial

The role of suspicion in counter-hooliganism has never been at the heart of public debate. With the exception of the Communist Party,[65] which regularly denounces securitisation in football stadia,[66] mainstream political parties have expressed concern only during parliamentary debate on the aforementioned 2011 law. Human rights groups and journalists have paid little, if any, attention to liberticidal counter-hooliganism measures, and the vast majority of scholars have focused on other fan-related issues, such as the way fans are perceiving fandom and are being organised in (in)formal groups, and their relation to politics. Moreover, the absence of a nationwide representative body of football supporters, along with traditional distrust of authorities, has initially prevented many fans from bringing their case before the Court, thereby creating an impression of passivity which has in turn been presented by both police and sport officials as indirect evidence of their well-grounded policy.

---

[63] Communist Party 2011.

[64] View expressed to the author by an intelligence officer (Interview: March 2011).

[65] From 2008, the Communist Party is part of the Left Front.

[66] Its Sport Commission has been active in organising public debates on the issue.

In fact, the only resistance to AFBOs stemmed from judges, who frequently opposed the introduction of the risk-based mindset in the judicial sphere. Administrative Courts did not support AFBOs that were not grounded on sound evidence. In the last 4 years, around 80 % of AFBOs have thus been annulled.[67] Particularly striking is the example of the Administrative Court of Montpellier which, in May 2010, annulled 24 of 36 AFBOs imposed in February 2010 against fans of the local football team.[68] In the following months, the Administrative Courts of Paris, Versailles and Dijon annulled many AFBOs imposed against Paris-Saint-Germain fans during the 2006/07 season and ordered the police to pay 10,200 Euro compensation.[69]

However, this broadly shared rule-of-law-abiding judicial stance cannot fully protect football supporters' rights because it is limited to a mere evaluation of the way AFBOs are being implemented. Judges assess AFBOs' compliance with the rule of law but they are not calling into question their legal nature. Despite the jurisprudence of the European Court of Human Rights that punitive measures should be defined in law according to their effect rather than their label,[70] the question of whether football banning orders may constitute penalties and, hence whether people served with such penalties might be provided with ordinary procedural guarantees has not been raised before the Courts. In official documents, it is stated that AFBOs are not a penalty but a preventive administrative measure. When certain left-wing MPs referred the constitutionality of AFBOs provided by the aforementioned 2011 law to the Constitutional Council, the Court ruled that such orders complied with the Constitution so long as restrictions on freedom of movement were proportionate to the aim of protecting public order and their imposition could be controlled by the Administrative Courts.[71] Yet, in practice, fans who have been served with 'football bans on suspicion' have their freedom of movement inside the country or abroad severely restricted for long periods of time—a penalty which is imposed with none of the procedural guarantees provided by the criminal justice system.[72] This is all the more important as AFBOs produce legal effects at the EU level for much longer periods of time than their formal duration. As personal data is stored for a minimum of 5 years, and given the obligation to transmit information on football bans to countries staging international football matches or tournaments,[73] people served with AFBOs may be prevented from attending an international fixture well after the period of the initial penalty has come to an end.

---

[67]Otero 2012, p. 101.

[68]Midi libre 2010.

[69]Le Monde 2010b.

[70]Delmas-Marty 2002, p. 448 f.

[71]Constitutional Council, Decision n° 2011-625 DC of 10 March 2011.

[72]For an analysis of similar questions regarding UK fans: Pearson 2005; Blackshaw 2005; Stott and Pearson 2006; James and Pearson 2006.

[73]Council of the EU 2003, Article 5.

5.5 Conclusions

In spite of its apparent coherence, an analysis of French regulation of football-related violence uncovers a multifold confusion. In terms of value ranking, protection of human life, property, and public order tends to be guaranteed at the expense of the rule of law. In terms of objectives to be reached, 'law and order' tends to be established at the expense of the democratic legal order. In terms of the means to achieve these objectives, counter-hooliganism tends to rest upon the institutionalisation of control and direct punishment of deviance.

Far from being exceptional, the confusion that stems from the many different structural shifts within the (inter)national political and security fields from the 1970s on[74] lies beneath all current Western crime control policies and has been increasingly criticised in academia. From this standpoint, what happens in and around French football stadia should be seen as a mere illustration of expanding rule-of-law-disregarding governance in twenty-first century liberal democracies. French counter-hooliganism strategies offer insights into many key features of this ongoing struggle between past and present regulatory modes of the state-citizen relationship, ranging from the introduction of liberticidal security devices and the consensual acceptance of the shrinking of civil rights and liberties in the name of the protection of security, to the subtle denial of any questioning of the juridical-political foundations of the regime.

For what matters here, efficient resistance to these trends has to go well beyond the judicial sphere to encompass both human rights and fans' groups. French human rights defenders have never included football fans among targeted social groups to be protected. Conversely, even if government and sport officials are still unwilling to engage in negotiations with fans,[75] effective protection of the latter's civil rights and liberties will never be guaranteed unless they become aware of what is at stake and they actively seek collaboration with human rights groups while, of course, elaborating their own alternative proposals.

References

Anderson M, Boer M den, Cullen P et al (1996) Policing the European Union. Clarendon Press, Oxford

Armstrong G, Hobbs D (1994) Tackled from behind. In: Giulianotti R, Bonney N, Hepworth M (eds) Football, violence and social identity. Routledge, London, pp 196–228

Armstrong G, Giulianotti R (1998) From another angle: police surveillance and football supporters. In: Norris C, Moran J, Armstrong G (eds) Surveillance, Closed Circuit Television and Social Control. Ashgate, Aldershot, pp 113–135

Balzacq T, Carrera S (eds) (2006) Security versus Freedom. Ashgate, Aldershot

---

[74] Tsoukala 2010.

[75] Hourcade 2012.

Bambuck R (1990) Le message du ministre. In: Association Française pour un sport sans violence et pour le fair play. La violence et le vandalisme dans le sport. AFSVFP, Paris, pp 9–10
Bauman Z (2007) Liquid Times. Polity, Cambridge
Beck U (1999) World Risk Society. Polity, Cambridge
Bigo D (1996) Polices en réseaux. Presses de Sciences-Po, Paris
Bigo D, Tsoukala A (eds) (2008) Terror, Insecurity and Liberty. Routledge, London
Blackshaw I (2005) The "English Disease" – Tackling Football Hooliganism in England. International Sports Law Journal 2:90–91
Bonelli L (2001) Renseignements généraux et les violences urbaines. Actes de la recherche en sciences sociales 136–137:95–103
Bonelli L (2007) Policing the youth: towards a redefinition of discipline and social control in French working-class neighbourhoods. In: Venkatesh S, Kassimir R (eds) Youth, Globalization and the Law. Stanford University Press, Chicago, pp 90–123
Bonelli L (2008) La France a peur. La Découverte, Paris
Broadhurst R (2000) Criminal careers, sex offending and dangerousness. In: Brown M, Pratt J (eds) Dangerous Offenders. Routledge, London, pp 109–126
Bromberger C (1984) L'Olympique de Marseille, la Juve et le Torino. Esprit 4:174–195
Carlen P (ed) (2008) Imaginary Penalities. Willan Publishing, Cullompton
Castel R (2003) L'insécurité sociale. Seuil, Paris
Chatard R (1990) La mission du Service d'Ordre. In: Association Française pour un sport sans violence et pour le fair play. La violence et le vandalisme dans le sport. AFSVFP, Paris, pp 41–45
Cohen S (ed) (1971) Images of Deviance. Penguin, Harmondsworth
Communist Party (2011). Press release: Plutôt que cibler les hooligans, le gouvernement criminalise tous les supporters
Council of the EU (1997), Joint Action of 26 May 1997 with regard to cooperation on law and order and security, OJEC L 147
Council of the EU (1998) Note from the Presidency of the Council to the Cooperation Group, 7386/98 ENFOPOL 45
Council of the EU (2002a) Resolution of 6 December 2001 concerning a handbook with recommendations for international police cooperation and measures to prevent and control violence and disturbances in connection with football matches with an international dimension, in which at least one Member State is involved, OJEC C 22
Council of the EU (2002b) Decision 2002/348/JHA of 25 April 2002 concerning security in connection with football matches with an international dimension, OJEC L 121
Council of the EU (2003) Resolution of 17 November 2003 on the use by Member States of bans on access to venues of football matches with an international dimension, OJEC C 281
Della Porta D, Reiter H (eds) (1998) Policing protest. The Control of Mass Demonstrations in Western Democracies. University of Minnesota Press, Minneapolis
Delmas-Marty M (2002) Le paradoxe pénal. In: Delmas-Marty M, Lucas de Leyssac C (eds) Libertés et droits fondamentaux. Seuil, Paris, pp 437–461
Dietschy P (2010) Histoire du football. Perrin, Paris
Dubet F, Lapeyronnie D (1992) Les quartiers de l'exil, Seuil, Paris
Ehrenberg A (1984) Le football et ses imaginaires. Les Temps Modernes 460:841–845
Ericson R (2007) Crime in an insecure world. Polity, Cambridge
Feeley M, Simon J (1992) The new penology: notes on the emerging strategy of corrections and its implications. Criminology 4:449–474
Fillieule O, Della Porta D (eds) (2006) Police et manifestants. Presses de Sciences Po, Paris
Garland D (1985) Punishment and Welfare. Gower, Aldershot
Geyer F (2008) Taking Stock: Databases and Systems of Information Exchange in the Area of Freedom, Security, and Justice. CEPS Working Paper 9
Hourcade N (2010) Principes et problèmes de la politique de lutte contre le hooliganisme en France. Archives de Politique Criminelle 32:123–139

Hourcade N (2012) Tolérance zéro dans les stades ? Répression ou prévention pour les supporters extrêmes. Le Sociographe 38:59–69

James M, Pearson G (2006) Football Banning Orders: Analysing their use in court. Journal of Criminal Law 6:509–525

Johnston L, Shearing C (2003) Governing Security. Routledge, London

Le Monde (2010a) PSG: les 249 supporters interpellés interdits de stade. 10 August 2010

Le Monde (2010b) Des interdictions de stade cassées par les tribunaux. 11 August 2010

Lestrelin L (2012) Droit et radicalisation de la lutte contre le hooliganisme en France. In: Guillaumé J, Dermit-Richard N (eds) Football et Droit. LGDJ, Paris, pp 109–125

Ligue de Football Professionnel (2011) Observatoire de la sécurité, des affluences et recettes du football professionnel. Bilan de la saison 2010/11. LFP, Paris

Ligue de Football Professionnel (2012) Mesures en matière de sécurité. Interdictions de stade, de déplacement, restriction d'aller et venir des supporters et dissolution d'associations. LFP, Paris

Lyon D (2001) Surveillance Society. Open University Press, Buckingham

Midi libre (2010) Annulation de 24 interdictions de stade. 7 May

Mignon P (1998) La passion du football, Odile Jacob, Paris

Mucchielli L (2001) Violences et insécurité. La Découverte, Paris

Mucchielli L, Le Goaziou V (eds) (2006) Quand les banlieues brûlent… Retour sur les émeutes de novembre 2005. La Découverte, Paris

O'Malley P (2000) Risk societies and the government of crime. In: Brown M, Pratt J (eds) Dangerous Offenders, Routledge, London, pp 17–33

Otero C (2012) Prévention et sanction des agissements des supporters: entre ordre (public) et désordre (juridique). In: Guillaumé J, Dermit-Richard N (eds) Football et Droit. LGDJ, Paris, pp 95–108

Paillou N (1990) Débat de la matinée. In: Association Française pour un sport sans violence et pour le fair play. La violence et le vandalisme dans le sport. AFSVFP, Paris, pp 31–40

Palidda S (1999) Polizia e immigrati: un'analisi etnografica. Rassegna Italiana di Sociologia 1:77–114

Pearson G (2005) Qualifying for Europe? The Legitimacy of Football Banning Orders 'On Complaint' under the Principle of Proportionality. Entertainment & Sports Law Journal 1

Silver E, Miller L (2002) A Cautionary Note on the Use of Actuarial Risk Assessment Tools for Social Control. Crime & Delinquency 1:138–61

Simon G (2008) Police des stades et libertés publiques: le dispositif préventif et répressif de lutte contre la violence en France et en Europe. In: Simon G (ed) Le stade et le droit. Dalloz, Paris, pp 179–190

Stott C (2003) Police expectations and the control of English soccer fans at Euro 2000. Policing: An International Journal of Police Strategies and Management 4:640–655

Stott C, Pearson G (2006) Football Banning Orders, Proportionality, and Public Order Policing. Howard Journal of Criminal Justice 3:241–254

Stott C, Adang O, Livingstone A, Schreiber M (2006) Policing, Crowd Dynamics and Public Order at Euro 2004. Home Office, London

Trivizas E (1980) Offences and Offenders in Football Crowd Disorders. The British Journal of Criminology 3:276–288

Trivizas E (1984) Disturbances Associated with Football Matches. British Journal of Criminology 4:361–383

Tsoukala A (1995) Sport et violence. Sakkoulas/Bruylant, Athens/Brussels

Tsoukala A (2001) La gestion policière du hooliganisme: Angleterre, Italie, Pays-Bas. In: Basson J.-C. (ed) Sport et ordre public, IHESI/La Documentation française, Paris, pp 159–174

Tsoukala A (2003) Les nouvelles politiques de contrôle du hooliganisme en Europe: de la fusion sécuritaire au multipositionnement de la menace. Cultures & Conflits 51:83–96

Tsoukala A (2007) Security Policies and Human Rights in European Football Stadia. CEPS, Challenge Research Papers 5

Tsoukala A (2009a) Football Hooliganism in Europe. Security and Civil Liberties in the Balance. Palgrave Macmillan, Basingstoke

Tsoukala A (2009b) Combating football crowd disorder at the European level: an ongoing institutionalisation of the control of deviance. Entertainment and Sports Law Journal 2

Tsoukala A (2010) Risk-focused security policies and human rights: the impossible symbiosis. In: Salter M (ed) Mapping Transatlantic Security Relations. Routledge, London, pp 41–59

Tsoukala A (2011a) Timing 'dangerousness': football crowd disorder in the Italian and Greek press. Sport in Society 5:598–611

Tsoukala A (2011b) Combating football-related violence in the EU: A law-abiding process? In: Robin G (ed) Football, Europe et régulations. Presses Universitaires du Septentrion, Villeneuve d'Ascq, pp 123–132

Tsoukala A (2013) Controlling football-related violence in France: law and order versus rule of law. Sport in Society 16(2):140–150

Türk A (2009) La difficile quête d'un équilibre entre impératifs de sécurité publique et protection de la vie privée. Cultures & Conflits 76:115–133

Williams J (1980) Football Hooliganism: Offences, Arrests and Violence—A Critical Note. British Journal of Law and Society 1:104–111

Young J (2007) The Vertigo of Late Modernity. Sage, London

Chapter 6
Punishing and Monitoring the Greek Football Fans: Civil Liberties at Stake?

Diamantis Mastrogiannakis

Abstract The aim of this chapter is to trace the development of Greece's counter-hooliganism legislation. Specifically, it analyses the legal regulation and measures adopted over the past 35 years to punish, tackle, and control football supporters' violent behaviour in and around stadia. Contrary to other countries and contexts, where the issue of the violation of human rights of supporters has captured scholars' attention, in Greece this field of study remains largely unexplored. This study shows the way in which Greek football crowds progressively became the target of draconian legislation and how, during the 1980s and 1990s, legal responses aimed to punish violent behaviour in a limited spatial and temporal context; before, during, and after football matches, both in and around stadia. From the beginning of the twenty-first century, this reasoning changed radically to a point where football fans became the subject of increased punishments and surveillance measures. Following a proactive reasoning, and dominated by a risk rationality, legal network provisions expanded in time and space to the extent that they identified supporters' clubs' composition; controlled fan travel; and introduced electronic surveillance within stadia.

Keywords Football · Hooligan · Greece · Law · Policing · Human rights

---

Diamantis Mastrogiannakis is Lecturer of Sociology of Sport, Mediterranean College, Thessaloniki.

D. Mastrogiannakis (✉)
Mediterranean College, 9 Valaoritou Street, Thessaloniki, Greece
e-mail: diamantis.mastrogiannakis@univ-lille2.fr

A. Tsoukala et al. (eds.), *Legal Responses to Football "Hooliganism" in Europe*,
ASSER International Sports Law Series, DOI 10.1007/978-94-6265-108-1_6

Contents

6.1 Introduction

Although scholars have investigated the violation of supporters' human rights with reference to other countries,[1] in Greece this matter remains an unexplored field of study. According to the institutional point of view, the violent behaviour of Greek football supporters is a recent phenomenon. But historical facts prove the opposite. From the beginning of the Greek football championship in 1910 until the start of the Second World War, numerous incidents were reported, both in national and local newspapers.[2] This violent conduct re-emerged during the 1950s and the 1960s, only to decrease from 1967 to 1974 during the seven-year dictatorship. The fact that these incidents were spontaneous and unorganised up to this period relates to the game's evolution. In addition, they took place primarily within stadia, but by the end of the 1970s a radical transformation had taken place. Henceforth supporters' movements were organised on an institutional basis. Incidents were not related anymore to the game's evolution but took place more frequently outside stadia, before and after the match, between rival fans, supporters, and the police.

However, although supporters' violent behaviour was becoming more organised, and violent incidents were spreading all over the country, it was not until 1986 that the first counter-hooligan law was promulgated to tackle this phenomenon. In fact, up to this point, due to the lack of an explicit legal context, sentences against offenders were pronounced according to the provisions of the penal code or civil law, and they followed ordinary juridical procedure. From the mid-1980s on, a specific legal framework started to be introduced which sought to control supporters' conduct; identify and map the members of supporters' clubs; and punish supporters' violent behaviour. Far from being continuous, this framework can be divided into two periods, going, respectively, from 1986 to 2000 and from 2000 onwards.

---

[1] Armstrong and Hobbs 1994; Armstrong and Guilianotti 1997; Falacho 2001; Pearson 2005; Spaaij 2012, 2013; Testa 2012, 2013; Tsoukala 1995, 1999, 2002, 2003, 2008, 2009.

[2] Koulouri 2000, p.111; Gogos 2006, p. 42.

This division rests on three correlated points. The first one concerns the frequency of law production. During the first period, anti-hooligan laws and amendments were promulgated at a relatively slow pace, while throughout the second period legal regulations were being produced at much more regular intervals. The second point relates to the two dominant perceptions underlying the legal background of the aforementioned periods. That is to say, during the 1980s and the 1990s legal provisions were dominated by a situational reasoning limiting anti-hooligan actions to the spatial and temporal frame of the football game. Hence, offenders were punished in a less severe way because their violent behaviour was believed to have social roots.[3]

However, during the second period the situational logic was replaced progressively, but not definitively, by proactive practices and risk-oriented rationalities and responses extending 'counter-hooligan mechanism'[4] action in time and space. Henceforth, specific police units, Sports Ministry Commissions and professional football clubs were charged with controlling and surveying supporters' clubs. At the same time, offenders were punished more severely as their violent action was gradually seen as disconnected from its social roots; hooliganism was merely a result of 'organised and planned' initiatives.[5] As a consequence, all possible effective means were legitimised in order to tackle violent conduct.

The last point concerns the internal structure of the 'counter-hooligan mechanism'.[6] Comparing the two aforementioned periods, we can see a clear evolution of the anti-hooligan mechanism's configuration from a vertical, state-centred vision to a more horizontal and fluid instrument as counter-hooligan responses linked together public and private rationalities and knowledge, overlapping the distinction between the public and private sphere. As a result, a variety of local and national 'experts', security professionals and think-tanks coming from State institutions and bureaucracies, and others belonging to heterogeneous private corporate interests looked to construct the social image of 'hooligans' and legitimise and impose the appropriate responses to tackle violent behaviours.

---

[3]Tsoukala 1995, p. 401.

[4]According to Foucault's definition of "mechanism: as a web of power relations, as a set of procedures different from others, as a strategic configurations, as a set of heterogeneous institutions, instruments of prohibition and prescription, heterogeneous material elements and discourses of a certain kind; as an assemblage of multiform combinations of rationalities and technologies of government", Foucault 2004.

[5]The Greek anti-hooligan legal framework did not originate exclusively from Greek parliamentary activities, or decisions of the executive power. It also originated from processes that were taking place in the transnational European space; processes that involved public and private authorities, especially sport organisations, which had an impact on the Greek counter-hooligan legal framework.

[6]For an overview of Security Mechanisms developed in the context of Sport Events see Mastrogiannakis and Dorville 2012, 15–44.

6.2 The Lenient Period

The first counter-hooliganism law came into effect in September 1986,[7] and was reinforced by the ratification of the Council of Europe's Convention On Spectator Violence.[8] It focused primarily on two main objectives: on the one hand, legislation sought to define the spatial and temporal context in which violent actions took place; on the other hand, it defined the actions which, when committed in the precise spatial and temporal context, could be punished, as well as the penalties to be given to the offenders.

6.2.1 Punishing the Offenders

The Legislators' first priority was to define and punish the actions that essentially characterised spectators' violent behaviour, both in and around sports venues.[9] In this sense, as a sanction the law prescribed imprisonment ranging from 10 days up to 2 years for those offenders who: (a) threw projectiles, (b) invaded the football field, and (c) carried objects likely to cause injury.[10] Furthermore, since it was believed that the use of alcohol or drugs might cause supporters to be violent, those under the influence of the aforementioned substances were prohibited entry into sports venues. An imprisonment sentence relating to these offences could be transformed into a fine of 3,000 drachmas[11] per day of imprisonment. In this case, offenders were now hit by a banning order from football venues, ranging from 3 months to 2 years; and they were legally obliged to attend the nearest police station before, during, and after each football match. In case of violation, an offender was sanctioned with 2 months imprisonment; a sanction that could not be transformed to a pecuniary one.

Greek legislators were more severe towards other actions and here the transformation of a custodial sentence to a fine was forbidden. In order to legitimise this decision, they introduced the notion of 'dangerousness'. The criteria that determined the characterisation of an offender as 'dangerous' were the circumstances in which the act was committed, and the complicity. Thus, if an

[7]Law 1686/1986, 'Metra prolipsis kai katastolis tis bias stous athlitikous xorous kai alles diatakseis' (Preventive and repressive measures against violence in the sport grounds and other amendments), Greek Government's Official Journal, No. A 138, September 16, 1986.

[8]Law 1787/1988, "Kurosi tis Europaikis Sumbasis gia tin bia ton theaton kai tin anarmosti sumperifora stis athlitikes ekdiloseis kai idiaitera stous agonistikous xorous" (Ratification of the European Convention On Spectator Violence), Greek Government's Official Journal No. A 130, June 15 1988.

[9]See also Tsoukala 1995, pp. 399–417.

[10]Law 1686/1986, n. 7 above. For more details see Tsoukala 1995.

[11]Approximately 9 euros.

offender was judged as 'dangerous' for the course of a football game or was found guilty of: (a) threat, (b) defamation, (c) actions against property, (d) obstructing traffic, (e) brawling, or, (f) injury, then a 1-year custodial sentence was imposed.[12]

A Ministerial Decree published in 1989[13] slightly modified the sanctions against offenders. Considering that the existing provisions were efficient to tackle and prevent supporters' violent behaviour, the legislator introduced a minor change. Henceforth, a convicted supporter should be banned for a minimum of 3 months, and a 'dangerous' one should be excluded from all football grounds for at least 1 year.

6.2.2 The Spatial and Temporal Context

Legislative priority in defining which actions should be punished depended on their spatial and temporal context. In order to deal with these two issues the law maker focused on the main characteristics of supporters' violent behaviour. Therefore, where behaviour occurred during the match, legal provisions defined the 'temporal' context as the period of the football match itself, and the 'spatial' context as the terraces and auxiliary facilities. However, as the aforementioned conditions did not cover the range of the phenomenon (i.e. hooliganism was occurring outside football stadia both before and after each game), legal provisions were extended to include both the period in which football spectators gathered in the stadia, and the period in which they began to leave. Regarding spatial conditions, the legal provisions were extended to encompass those places far from football stadia where violent incidents might occur.

6.3 The Harshest Period

Situational counter-hooligan measures were considered efficient to tackle football crowds' violent behaviour until the beginning of 2000 because they were based on the premise that the roots of supporters' disorder were fundamentally social. From the beginning of the new millennium, this conceptual background of the counter-hooliganism legal framework would be influenced and progressively replaced by a new one. Football supporters' disorder was considered to be an archaic, non-civilised conduct adopted by persons who did not belong to Greek civil society and did not share its ethos. Thus, they had to be eradicated from sport venues by

---

[12]Law 1686/1986, n. 7 above.

[13]Ministerial Decree 2403/1989, 'Metra prolipsis kai katastolis tis bias stous agonistikous xorous' (Preventive and repressive measures against violence in the sports grounds), Greek Government's Official Journal, No. B 719, September 26 1989.

any means on the grounds that 'hooliganism is a phenomenon strange to Greek society and culture', so that 'football stadia will be accessible to families and citizens…as appropriate to modern and civilised societies'.[14]

6.3.1 Punishing the Offenders

The hardening of legal responses against offenders was progressively put into effect from 2002. Initially, the length of the correctional punishment to the offenders considered as 'dangerous' was extended to a fixed sentence of 2 years, in addition to a promulgated ban order from 6 months to 2 years. The ban order was thereafter executed after the correctional sentence had finished.[15]

In September 2004, just before the beginning of the professional championship, these measures were still seen as inadequate to maintain order. As a consequence, the conservative government, supported by the opposition, voted for a new law, which enforced existing amendments.[16] The law annulled the transformation of an imprisonment sanction to a pecuniary one, and imposed a two-year sentence. In addition, it prescribed that those offenders should be judged within 30 days of the alleged offence. However, the effect of this amendment was relatively weak in that it included a 3 to 5-year suspension of the sentence.[17]

A new counter-hooliganism law issued in 2006 ordered the banning of the temporal suspension of the sentence and the direct incarceration of offenders.[18] As a result, for the next 3 years various and multiple violent incidents in and outside football grounds were recorded, resulting from organised supporters' reactions to the increased incarcerations.[19] Only in 2009, just before the national elections, was a new legal provision issued by the conservative government.[20] In the wording, the

[14]'The Minister of Public Order declared himself satisfied and optimistic regarding professional football's progress', Eleftherotupia, 1 December 2004; Mastrogiannakis 2010, p. 315.

[15]Law 3057/2002, 'Tropopoiisi tou nomou 2725/1999, rithmisi thematon Ypourgeiou Politismou kai alles diatakseis' (Modification of the Law 2725/1999, regulation of the affairs of the Ministry of Culture and other amendments), Greek Government's Official Journal, No. A 239, October 10 2002.

[16]Law 3262/2004, 'Tropopoiisi tou nomou 2725/1999 kai alles diatakseis' (Modification of the Sports Act 2725/99 and other amendements) Greek Government's Official Journal, No. A 173, 15 September 2004.

[17]According to Article 99 of the Greek Penal Code.

[18]Law 3472/2006, 'Themata tou Ypourgeiou Dikaiosunis kai alles diatakseis' (Issues related to the Ministry of Justice and other amendements) Greek Government's Official Journal, No. A 135 4 July 2006.

[19]Mastrogiannakis 2010.

[20]Law 3773/2009, 'Organotiki Epitropi ton Mesogeiakon Agonon 2013 kai alles diatakseis' (Organising Committee of the 2013 Mediterranean Games and other amendments) Greek Government's Official Journal, No. A 120, 21 July 2009.

direct imprisonment of offenders was banned, and the alternative of a three-year suspension was restored, along with a stadium-banning order. However, in the case of a subsequent offence, the sanction of incarceration would not be suspended. The issue of immediate incarceration became prominent in 2012. If violent incidents became uncontrollable, it was suggested that in the case of serious criminal behaviour before, during, or after football matches, offenders should be imprisoned at once.[21] Thus, if the offender had used a weapon, or any other object that could threaten human life, and if the seriousness of this act, its circumstances and the offender's motives proved that the individual would engage into further antisocial and criminal behaviour—they would not qualify to have their imprisonment sanction transformed into a pecuniary one.

6.3.2 From State Control to Private Power Discretion

The first amendment regarding supporters' associations was put into effect by the late 1980s.[22] Lawmakers intended to make supporters' groups aware of their responsibilities in preventing violent incidents, and promoting their collaboration with local police forces. The only penalty that was prescribed was the prohibition on obtaining tickets for football matches. The control of supporters' associations was subjected to major change by the end of the 1990s.[23] This was evidenced by the introduction of the Law 2725/1999, and its developments in 2002, in addition to the 2003 Ministerial Decree's legal regulations that provided for financial, legal, and identity controls.

As regards financial control, it was stipulated that each sports association should keep a record of expenses and incomes to be certified by the public authorities. There were three main conditions prescribed: first, in order to be officially recognised by the State authorities, a supporters' association had to obtain a professional football club's written approval. Secondly, an association's internal rules had to provide for disciplinary sanctions to any of its members that provoked, or engaged in violent incidents. The final condition obliged all association board members to divulge any criminal records of theirs to the State authorities. Each sports association had to provide to the Professional Sports Committee (a State bureaucratic unit) the following elements on an annual basis: (a) an official copy of their members' list, (b) any board member's criminal record, (c) the associated professional football club's written approval, and (d) members' written statements certifying that they have not previously incurred any sanctions according to counter-hooligan legislation. Furthermore, to penalise any association

---

[21]Law 4049/2012, 'Antimetopisi tis bias sta gipeda, tou ntoping, ton prosinenoimenon agonon kai alles diatakseis' (Controlling football related violence, doping, match fixing, and other amendments). Greek Government's Official Journal, No A 35, 23 February 2012.

[22]Ministerial Decree 2403/1989, n. 13 above.

[23]Mastrogiannakis and Dorville 2012, p. 125.

that did not comply with the conditions, legislators could order the closure of their offices, and sanction whoever had participated in the activities of an illegal supporter's association to two years' imprisonment.

The issue of supporters' association control became crucial in Greece's counter-hooligan policy in 2008 and 2012. Legislators suppressed the term 'supporters' associations' in favour of the term 'supporters' clubs'. These were henceforth deemed to support and sustain their associated professional football team. Furthermore, they should be assigned and constrained to promote 'fair play'. Counter-hooliganism was no longer only a matter for the State; professional clubs now had to be involved in relevant policies to the extent that from this time on they were assigned responsibility for any violent behaviour, and punished accordingly. Thus, the issue of supporters' clubs was allocated to the professional football clubs, which were required to control them, but the overall supervision remained at the hands of the Ministry's bureaucracy, as the clubs' data had to be submitted annually. Besides, in order to obtain its legal recognition each 'club' had to acquire a professional team's written consent and include the same data as was submitted earlier to the Professional's Sport Committee.[24] It was also decreed that each supporter who wished to be a member of a 'club' had to be provided with an identity card supplied by the professional team. Furthermore, football clubs were required to organise and supervise supporters' collective travel to away matches.

Finally, football clubs had the discretionary power to ask for the dissolution of a supporters' club which had not adhered to the provisions of the Law. But while professional football clubs were held accountable for their supporters' behaviour, the law gave them the option to filter football fans at the stadia entrance. The 2012 Act authorised sport authorities to ban supporters' entrance into grounds if this decision was justified according to objective criteria, and the local police authority was notified. However, these objective criteria were not defined; there were no particular principles justifying the filtering of fans. The possibility of banning football supporters was established following a more or less arbitrary estimation based on the circumstances and their behaviour, which could be considered suspicious or likely to lead to violent action during the match.

6.3.3 *The Politics of Risk Assessment, and Its Exceptional Responses*

The will to extend counter-hooliganism actions to prevent violent incidents was clearly expressed through the establishment of the Permanent Committee Against Supporters' Violence in 1999. Considered as the central counter-hooliganism

[24](a) An official copy of their members list, (b) an official declaration providing information regarding the existence of annexe associations in the Greek territory, (c) board members' criminal records, (d) members' written statements certifying that they have not incurred any sanctions according to counter-hooligan legislation.

bureaucratic unit within the Ministry of Sports, the Permanent Committee was charged with various relevant functions. Far from being independent, the Permanent Committee is under the direct control of each Minister. It is the Minister who defines its composition; the Permanent Committee is comprised of bureaucrats, police officers and delegates from the Greek Football Federation, Greek Professional Football League and Professional Football Clubs. Excluding supporters' associations' representatives from the meetings, and following a short-term vision, one of the Committee's main tasks was to evaluate, every Monday, the risk that they considered forthcoming matches to represent. The evaluation of each game as risky or not was based on information obtained by the football clubs and provided by the police, as well the historical rivalries between opposing supporters. Founded upon this rationality, the Committee's proposals were never innovative. During the past 14 years, its resolutions regarding counter-hooliganism, and particularly high risk matches, have produced broadly two responses, which have always been adopted throughout Ministerial Decisions. Firstly, if a football match was considered high risk, the Committee's proposition was to prohibit all visiting supporters' collective and organised travel to the sporting venue. Secondly, supporters could not purchase tickets on the day of the match.

Some other more radical responses were promoted less frequently during a period when the phenomenon was considered uncontrollable in Greece by many commentators.[25] In order to avoid any possible meeting between rival fans from different districts or towns, an identity card control was established by local police forces outside stadia. In this sense, if a supporter did not originate from the district/town where the football game was taking place, he or she was not allowed access to the sporting venue. This practice was lawful to the extent that it was adopted according to the principal of exceptional measures as a means to guarantee order and security.

6.3.4 Police Bureaucratic Procedures and the Question of Supporters' Records

The need to create a special counter-hooliganism bureaucratic unit was first formulated in 1997. In the context of the pre-Olympic preparation, Greek Police Authorities signed a bilateral agreement with British Police. This initiative was aimed at learning from British expertise in counter-terrorism, which had been a major domestic political issue for the Greek society since the mid-1970s, and one considered to be the most serious threat to internal security and the image of a 'peaceful society' that the country wished to promote for the 2004 Olympics. The British authorities suggested the greater use of electronic surveillance for suspects,

[25] This measure was put into effect for one month in 2003.

and the identification and infiltration of groups considered to be involved in terrorist activities, or displaying a certain 'threatening' ideology for the dominant political, economic and social order.[26]

But the British support was not limited to the transfer of counter-terrorism knowhow. As Greek police authorities considered the British counter-hooliganism model to be a successful one, they took advantage of the bilateral collaboration and addressed the question of football hooliganism. In sharing the idea of establishing a central bureaucratic unit and creating a special record that should be provided by two main sources, the UK authorities made a twofold suggestion. Firstly, that professional clubs should communicate information about violent or potentially violent supporters (ironically this was not a useful or common tactic in the UK). Secondly, that Greek police should create a unit tasked with infiltrating supporters' associations, and assuring their surveillance during football matches in order to identify violent individuals.[27]

Before this collaboration, the Greek Police had already been using infiltration and intelligence techniques; the Greek Police Investigation Department had deployed this strategy during its operations to monitor and to identify violent supporters since the early 1980s, and during the same period the first hooligan records were progressively set up. While undercover police officers could collect data regarding supporters, or assist as witnesses providing evidence against accused supporters during legal proceedings, inscription onto the hooligan record was determined by the court's decision. This is to say that if a defendant was judged guilty, they would be automatically added onto a hooligan database for a three-year period.

This method of recording supporters' data was subjected to a major transformation in the early 2000s (although it is difficult to pinpoint the exact period). From now on, it was no longer a question of evidence, and of a final judicial decision proving the culpability of an individual; the simple fact of being seized by the police before, during, or after a football match, was enough for an individual to be put on the hooligan database for at least five years.[28] However, the police's hooligan record was not only enriched with seized supporters' data; the police also requested access to supporters' documents submitted to the Professionals' Sport Committee; a request that was not refused, and which enabled the Police to retrieve such data from criminal records.[29]

This qualitative change could be attributed to a certain extent to the internal restructuring of the Ministry of Public Order in order to respond to the ongoing homogenisation of Police exchange practices at the European level. In fact, at the beginning of 2000, the existing Greek police criminal records started to fuse into a

---

[26]Mastrogiannakis 2010.

[27]The information quoted come from interviews with an officer of the Greek Secret Services and the Vice President of the Greek Police Union.

[28]Interview with the Vice President of the Greek Police Union, 27 March 2007.

[29]Interview with a member of the Professionals' Sport Committee, 30 March 2007.

general digital one. In this new record, potential or actual 'dangerous individuals', were classified according to political or criminal identities, such as 'anarchists', 'terrorists', or 'hooligans', and the threat that they offered or seemed to offer, i.e. to internal security, public or political order.[30]

As far as the British police suggestion regarding the creation of a central bureaucratic unit is concerned, it was only 7 years later that the establishment of this unit took place.[31] Imposed by the constraints of the Council of the European Union,[32] it was in reality an 'imaginary unit' to the extent that, due to bureaucratic inertia, for 2 years the service was not equipped with police officers. The continuous violent incidents and the creation of an ad hoc Committee on the 7th of June 2005,[33] within the Ministry of Public Order (which included the Minister and the Deputy Minister of Public Order, the Deputy Minister in Charge of Sports, the President of the Permanent Committee Against Violence, Sport Judges and the Professional Football Clubs Union), accelerated the nomination of 32 Sport Liaison Officers, which took place in October 2006.[34] These officers, who were experienced Olympic and European campaigners working for the Greek Police, were assigned to two main decentralised police units, established in Athens and Thessaloniki, within the National Security Offices charged with the 'Prevention of Organised Football Violence'.[35] Their main task consisted of promoting the collaboration between Professional Football Clubs, Football Authorities and the Police. In this respect, these officers had to create contacts with the leaders of the supporters' associations and the Sport authorities in order to collect information about their activities during match days.

At a central bureaucratic level, the Greek National Information Football Unit was established on the 4th of December 2006.[36] Its international task was to collaborate and exchange information with the National Information Football Units of the other European Countries. Additionally, Unit officers were assigned to draft a common document to be distributed to all the peripheral Police Departments. The aim was to build up a central database in which information concerning incidents, the number of police forces, the details about football matches, and the number of arrests, was collated.

---

[30]The information quoted comes from interviews with an officer of the Greek Secret Services, and the Vice President of the Greek Police Union; see also Mastrogiannakis and Dorville 2012, p. 125.

[31]Decision of the Greek Police Headquarters No. 7001/2/1349-γ.

[32]Decision 2002/348/JAI, 'La sécurité lors de matchs de football revêtant une dimension internationale'. Journal Officiel des Communautés Européennes, 25 avril 2002.

[33]During the period 2005–2006 five meetings were organised.

[34]Presidential Decree 213/2006, 'Football Liaison Officers'. Greek Government's Official Journal, No. A 212 9th of October 2006.

[35]Ibid.

[36]Presidential Decree 252/2006, 'Ethiko Grafeio Pliroforion Agonon Podosfairou' (Greek National Information Football Unit). Greek Government's Official Journal, No. A 263, 4th of December 2006.

6.4 Conclusions

The aim of this chapter was to highlight the evolution of the Greek counter-hooliganism legal framework. It shows how, during the past three decades, Greek supporters have progressively been the subject of increased regulation—a target of a legal dynamic process that went hand in hand with the evolution of the dominant perception of the phenomenon and the offenders. In this regard, Greek jurisdiction initially revealed itself as tolerant, considering social conditions as the primary cause of football crowds' violent conduct. Consequently, sanctioning offenders following lenient, indulgent, and inclusive responses was deemed sufficient to tackle violent incidents.

However, since 2000 the aforementioned perception of the social roots of hooliganism progressively ceased. From that time onwards, a new moral rhetoric has been introduced and has transformed hooliganism's social image and the actions taken to deal with it. It has now been replaced by explanations and perceptions in which hooligan behaviour is perceived as irrational, antisocial, and contrary to dominant cultural values and moral principles. Hooligans now represent an extraneous hostile minority, a threat to Greek society—the dangerous ones. Therefore, sanctioning offenders is no longer appropriate in terms of tackling football supporters' conduct, and guaranteeing order and security in and around sports venues. As a result, new anticipatory techniques of identification, profiling, social categorisation and surveillance are legitimatised and put into effect in order to control and tackle supporters' behaviour. Rather than being efficient, given that football crowd disorder and violence remains a serious problem in Greece, the counter-hooliganism responses previously mentioned raise major questions concerning Greek football crowds' civil and human rights. This is particularly the case with regard to the establishment of hooligan records, the arbitrary criteria according to which these records are supplied, and the opaque use of them (or their potential use in the future). Officially the maintenance and use of hooligan records operate under the protection of the Hellenic Data Protection Authority. In practice, Police Authorities remain uncontrolled so far as the use of the data is concerned. In this sense, the legitimate use of the data is relative. Given that these practices are not transparent, we do not yet know if and where the legitimacy is violated.

Also of importance is the progressive reinforcement of the private sector's discretionary power. Greek football crowds are facing new arbitrary control techniques to the extent that their entry into football stadia now depends upon the will of professional football clubs. These control techniques are arbitrary because there are no objective criteria that can justify a potential refusal into a sports venue. Objectivity and certainty are therefore now alien concepts in the experience of Greek football supporters when it comes to their ability to attend matches.

References

Armstrong G, Hobbs D (1994) Tackled from behind. In: Guilianotti R, Bonney N, Hepworth M (eds) Football violence and social identity. London, Routledge, pp 196–228

Armstrong G, Guilianotti R (1997) Legislators and interpreters: the law and 'football hooligans'. In: Armstrong G, Guilianotti R (eds) Entering the field. Berg, pp 178–195

Falacho L (2001) Les mesures prises pour lutter contre le hooliganisme à l'épreuve des libertés publiques. Revue du droit public 2:419–445

Foucault M (2004) Sécurité, territoire, population. Cours au Collège de France (1977–78). Gallimard/Seuil, Paris

Gogos N (2006) Supporters' trust in Europe? Some sociological reflections on the organized football supporters in England and Greece. Master II dissertation, University of Leicester, unpublished

Koulouri C (2000) Sport et société bourgeoise. Les associations sportives en Grèce 1870–1992. L'Harmattan, Paris

Mastrogiannakis D (2010) La lutte contre le hooliganisme en Grèce: 'Jeux' et 'enjeux' des politiques anti-hooligan. Thèse de Doctorat, Université Lille 2, unpublished

Mastrogiannakis D, Dorville C (2012) Punishing in situ governing by distance: risk management and practices in the Greek counter-hooligan policies. In Mastrogiannakis D, Dorville C (eds) Risk management and sport events. Le Manuscrit, Paris, pp 111–133

Pearson G (2005) Qualifying for Europe? The legitimacy of football banning orders 'on complaint' under the principle of proportionality. Entertainment and Sports Law Journal 3:1–10

Spaaij R (2012) The football laboratory: policing football supporters in the Netherlands. In: Mastrogiannakis D, Dorville C (eds) Risk management and sport events. Le Manuscrit, Paris, pp 49–91

Spaaij R (2013) Risk, security and technology: governing football supporters in the twenty-first century. In: Mastrogiannakis D, Dorville C (eds) Special issue: Security and sport mega-events: a complex relation. Sport in Society: Cultures, Commerce, Media, Politics 16:91–110

Testa A (2012) Bare sovereignty: the football banning order and the Italian fun. In: Mastrogiannakis D, Dorville C (eds) Risk management and sport events. Le Manuscrit, Paris, pp 91–110

Testa A (2013) Normalisation of the exception: issues and controversies of the Italian counter-hooliganism legislation. In: Mastrogiannakis D, Dorville C (eds) Special issue: Security and sport mega-events: a complex relation. Sport in Society: Cultures, Commerce, Media, Politics 16:91–110

Tsoukala A (1995) 'I politiki ton Europaikon Organon enanti tou Xouligkanismou kai i epiptosi tis sto Elliniko Dikaio' (Counter-Hooligan European's Institutions responses to the Greek law). Iperaspisi 2:399–417

Tsoukala A (1999) I astinomefsi ton athlitikonekdiloseon. I antimetopisi tou houliganismou stinAglia, tin Italia kai tin Ollandia. Sakkoulas, Athens

Tsoukala A (2002) Le hooliganisme et la protection de la sécurité intérieure en Europe. Quels enjeux? Revue Internationale de Criminologie et de Police Scientifique 3:310–321

Tsoukala A (2003) Les nouvelles politiques de contrôle du hooliganisme en Europe: de la fusion sécuritaire au multipositionnement de la menace. Cultures et Conflits 51:83–93

Tsoukala A (2008) Dispositif de sécurité contre le hooliganisme et droits des supporters en Europe. In: Busset T, Jaccoud C, Dubey JP, Malatesta D (eds). Le football à l'épreuve de la violence et de l'extremisme. Lausanne, Antipodes, pp 189–208

Tsoukala A (2009) Football hooliganism in Europe: Security and civil liberties in the balance. Palgrave Macmillan, Basingstoke

Chapter 7
Football-Related Disorder in the Netherlands

Peter T.M. Coenen

Abstract In this chapter, we look at the historical background of football-related disorder in the Netherlands, and current legal developments regarding the policing of football matches. The situation regarding intelligence gathering on football-related disorder and the 'Hooligans in Beeld' project are discussed. The new Football Law and selected case-law on the Football Law are analysed. Finally, the author makes recommendations for the development of legal responses to football-related disorder in the Netherlands.

Keywords Football-related disorder · The Netherlands · Intelligence gathering · Hooligans · Hooligans in beeld · Football law · Human rights

Contents

At the time of writing this chapter, Peter Coenen (deceased) was Assistant Professor of Law at Maastricht University in the Netherlands. Any further correspondence related to this chapter could be addressed to G. Pearson at the address specified below.

P.T.M. Coenen (✉)
School of Law, University of Manchester, Manchester, UK
e-mail: geoff.pearson@manchester.ac.uk

A. Tsoukala et al. (eds.), *Legal Responses to Football "Hooliganism" in Europe*,
ASSER International Sports Law Series, DOI 10.1007/978-94-6265-108-1_7

7.1 Introduction

The Netherlands has a long history of football crowd disorder and violence. During a match between Feyenoord and Tottenham Hotspur in 1974, football-related disorder was broadcast for the first time to the whole country on television, and since that match, football-related disorder has become a recognisable part of professional (and amateur[1]) football in the Netherlands.[2] During the 1980s, crowd disorder became a regular phenomenon at football matches.[3] In that period, especially in The Hague, Utrecht, Amsterdam, and Rotterdam, opposing 'sides' established themselves and gained notoriety.[4] During the 1990s, the rivalry between Ajax and Feyenoord supporters largely dominated the headlines. This rivalry culminated in a large-scale fight in a field next to the highway in Beverwijk, where one Ajax supporter was killed.[5] Football-related incidents still occur relatively regularly at professional football matches in the Netherlands; however, there is a great variation in the degree and intensity of such incidents.[6]

An important instrument to curtail football-related disorder was supposed to be provided by the '*Voetbal Wet*', or Football Law, [7] which came into force on 1 September, 2010. The Football Law in its ultimate form has become incorporated into much broader legislation designed to deal with a myriad of different public order offences and deviant behaviour.[8] However, there are serious deficiencies regarding the effectiveness and necessity of the Football Law. Calls for more and tougher legislation on football hooliganism have continued after it came into force.

[1]There seems to be a significant degree of violence at and around amateur football matches in the Netherlands. The most notable recent incident was where a linesman was killed in a fight following a youth match. However, the scope of this chapter is limited to professional football matches.

[2]See for example Siekmann 1982 and Van der Brug 1994.

[3]Van der Brug 1994, p. 169.

[4]Ibid., p. 171.

[5]Spaaij 2007, p. 324.

[6]Ibid., p. 322. See also Spaaij 2006, 2011.

[7]The official name of the law is 'Wet Maatregelen Bestrijding Voetbalvandalisme en Ernstige Overlast', which translates as 'Act regarding Measures to Fight Football Hooliganism and Serious Nuisance'. However, the term Voetbal Wet or 'Football Law' is generally used to refer to this Act.

[8]The Dutch Football Law incorporates elements of the English legislation on football related disorder and anti-social behaviour orders. For a discussion on general problems associated with the legality of such orders and the regulation of risks, see among others Von Hirsch and Simester 2006; Garland 1996; Zedner 2007; Macdonald 2006. For the problems associated with football banning orders, see among others James and Pearson 2006; Pearson 2006; Stott and Pearson 2006, 2007.

7.2 Current Developments in the Netherlands

In recent years disorder inside the football stadium, although not completely absent, has become relatively rare.[9] Confrontations between groups of supporters intent on disorder have become displaced from the football stadium to other venues.[10] Typically, official travel arrangements are ignored and groups will show up in the city of an away match well before the game is played. Football supporters intent on disorder show an increased awareness of where they can strike, and they target specific matches or events with a small police presence or a small risk potential to escape detection and punishment. Pre-season or mid-season friendlies have increasingly become the context of serious disorder between rival groups of supporters intent on disorder. Such disorder can also have a transnational element. For example during a pre-season match between Roda JC and Club Brugge in Kerkrade on 23 July 2011, Brugge fans stormed the field to fight with Roda fans and the match had to be abandoned.[11]

There is evidence that football supporters have increasingly started to use new technologies. While most of this usage of technology is for innocent means, technological means are sometimes used to arrange confrontations between groups intent on disorder. Spaaij claims that in order to arrange confrontations, hooligans keep contact via cell phones or via the Internet with persons within rival groups. It is difficult for the police to monitor these communications and to prevent or respond to these prearranged meetings, thereby decreasing the risk of detection and punishment for the hooligans involved.

Another form of displacement has been the involvement of football hooligans in other forms of large-scale disorder or riots. In 2007, in the Ondiep neighbourhood in Utrecht, serious riots broke out after a man who had threatened police with a knife was killed by the police.[12] Hooligan followers of FC Utrecht were implicated in these riots.[13] Another illustration of this 'new hooliganism' could be seen at riots at the free dance festival Veronica Sunset Grooves on the beach at Hoek van Holland in 2009. During the festival there were a number of violent incidents[14] and later that night the police were confronted with major disorder by a large number of festival visitors. Officers fired numerous shots at the assailants,

[9]Spaaij 2007, p. 324.

[10]The majority of football supporters are peaceful and come to the stadium to enjoy a football experience. However, there is a small minority intent on disorder which also frequents football matches in the Netherlands. In this chapter, where the term hooligans is used, it is exclusively used to describe persons or groups with a specific intent to commit offences or cause disorder.

[11]D. de Hulster, 'Strafonderzoek naar rellen bij Roda', *Dagblad de Limburger* 26 July 2011.

[12]Nos.nl (13 March 2007) 'Weer onrustig in Utrechtse Ondiep'. http://nos.nl/artikel/61116-weer-onrustig-in-utrechtse-ondiep.html. Accessed 2 July 2014 (link no longer active).

[13]Ferwerda et al. 2010, p. 62. See also for example Rechtbank Rotterdam, 02-02-2010, BL1682.

[14]Ibid., p. 63.

killing one person and wounding a number of others.[15] The violence during these confrontations was intense, but such levels of aggression against the police are rare in the Netherlands.[16] It was claimed that a group of Feyenoord hooligans had specifically targeted this festival for disorder and had instigated the disorder, and some of the rioters had yelled 'Rotterdam Hooligans' during the riots.[17]

Such riots, far removed from football or the football stadium, raise the questions regarding the precise nature of the connection between the behaviour of such hooligans with football. Is there a nexus with football, or are these hooligans part of a larger societal problem targeting large-scale events for disorder? If the latter, it calls into question the necessity and the effectiveness of repressive and preventive measures specifically taken against all football supporters. For this same reason, the term Football Law used to describe the anti-hooliganism legislation in the Netherlands is problematic, because of this lack of connection to football.

7.3 Intelligence Gathering on Football 'Hooliganism'

Football 'hooliganism' has become part of a policing and intelligence infrastructure.[18] For a long time, the Dutch authorities, have been active in gathering intelligence on football supporters.[19] The CIV, the central information point on football hooliganism, has been gathering data on football hooliganism since it was established in 1986. The CIV was the first central intelligence gathering organisation on football supporters in Europe, established 2 years before the UK's 'Football Intelligence Unit' (see Chap. 3 in this volume).[20,21] The CIV is a part of the Dutch police, whose task it is to collect and exchange information regarding football events, security and football hooliganism.[22] The CIV further provides risk assessments regarding individual football matches and advises the police on the strength of the police presence needed at individual football matches.[23] The CIV has become the National Football Information Point for the Netherlands, and as such is active in exchanging information with other NFIP's in Europe.[24]

---

[15]Ibid.

[16]Ibid.

[17]Ibid.

[18]For a discussion of the football banning order industry in England and Wales, see Hopkins 2013.

[19]Van der Brug 1994, p. 185.

[20]C.J. van Netburg, 2005 Voetbalvandalisme. www.civ-voetbal.com/sites/default/files/voetbalvandalisme_tcm44-84975.pdf. Accessed 2 July 2014.

[21]For a discussion of the role of NFIP's in Europe, their impact on the rights of football supporters and their role in the risk- regulation infrastructure, see Tsoukala 2009a and Tsoukala 2009b.

[22]See http://www.civ-voetbal.com/.

[23]Ibid. n. 20

[24]See http://www.civ-voetbal.com/node/1.

Recently, the police have started to implement a new form of intelligence-based approach to football supporters. The project 'Hooligans in Beeld' (HiB) focuses on collecting information on specific groups of supporters deemed to pose a high risk of being involved in football-related disorder.[25] Regional police forces collect information regarding the behaviour of certain supporters, their identities and their roles within the relevant supporters' group as a whole, and their relations with other supporter groups, which operate in the police district.[26] The information collected focuses not only on problematic behaviour at football matches, but also charts information on other public order offences. The goal of HiB is to increase the visibility of high-risk supporter groups and the individuals that make up these groups.[27] This is supposed to lead to an increased knowledge about groups or individuals who are involved in football-related disorder. This method furthermore gives the authorities more insight into the group dynamics within these groups and the role played by the individuals that make them up. The authorities, on the basis of this information, should be enabled to respond to the deviant or offending behaviour of individuals in a much more targeted manner. Knowing the identity of individuals involved in football-related disorder theoretically offers the authorities the opportunity to respond at an early stage and prevent riots. Knowing the identity of these individuals further increases the chance of detection and punishment once disorder does occur. Targeting leading figures within a group is also designed to lead to a decrease in the problematic behaviour of other members within the group.

HiB is an example of the shift from post-fact punishment to a pre-crime risk assessment and prevention framework.[28] However, HiB raises a number of questions regarding the way the targets are selected for inclusion in the database. Being included in the HiB database, and therefore being targeted with possible corresponding preventive and repressive measures, has a substantial effect upon the privacy of the person concerned.[29] Therefore, the selection for inclusion in the database has to be done carefully and correspond with the principles of necessity and proportionality. Furthermore, it is important that there is a clear procedure for ensuring that when the reasons for inclusion of a person in the database are no longer present, then the person's data is removed from the database. Additionally, there must be clear guidelines about the situations in which and with whom the data can be exchanged. If the information collected is exchanged with private organisations, for example this is problematic from the perspective of the privacy rights of the person concerned.[30] There is furthermore an issue regarding the

[25]Adang and Ferwerda 2007, p. 57.

[26]Ibid.

[27]Ibid.

[28]Zedner 2007, Maguire 2000.

[29]The right to privacy is guaranteed in the Netherlands in Article 10 of the Dutch Constitution and by Article 8 of the European Convention on Human Rights.

[30]See www.hetccv.nl/binaries/content/assets/ccv/dossiers/uitgaansgeweld/hooligans_in_beeld_procesbeschrijving.pdf, which states that the information collected under certain circumstances can be exchanged with private actors, like football clubs and the local catering branches.

presumption of innocence with respect to HiB. Especially when HiB is viewed as a whole concept, including intelligence gathering and possible repressive and preventive measures. The collection, use and exchange of data in the HiB database, therefore has to be carefully balanced against the presumption of innocence and the proportionality and necessity of the inclusion in the database.

7.4 The Football Law

The Dutch Football Law, although originally conceived to deal with the problem of football-related disorder exclusively, has been included in a much broader proposed law to counteract various forms of public order offences and deviant behaviour.[31] The term *Voetbal Wet*, commonly used to describe the law, is therefore misleading, since the Football Law in its ultimate form is intended to counteract all sorts of structural disorder and not exclusively football-related disorder. However, the term Football Law is used, because politically and in the media it is easier to gain acceptance for a law relating to 'hooliganism' and football in general. The negative stigma attached to football supporters unfortunately seems to be abused, because it prevents an objective and unbiased public discussion about the necessity and proportionality of the measures introduced by the Football Law.

The Football Law is specifically designed to target violations of public order and deviant behaviour by groups (for example youths or football supporters), who through their (usually, but not necessarily criminal) behaviour, create an unsafe environment in the areas or neighbourhoods where they congregate.[32] One of the main goals of the Football Law was to enable the police to proactively deal with a variety of groups perceived as problematic within society. A further problem which the law was supposed to solve is that the police were often unable to pinpoint offences to a specific, individual perpetrator, and therefore were unable to obtain criminal convictions. Even if the police were able to pinpoint the offence to an individual and punish them for that act, this often did not reduce the safety of the environment in the perception of the authorities. Therefore, the Football Law enables the authorities to implement measures against persons merely suspected of involvement in such offences, or penalise deviant behaviour that is not an offence. This is problematic from a rule of law perspective.

The Football Law is designed to present the authorities with proactive powers to confront groups and individuals that cause structural violations of public order, through short-term administrative measures. 'Structural' on the basis of the Football Law, means that there has to be a structural element to the violations of

---

[31]As mentioned above (n. 8), the Football Law combines a lot of the elements of Anti-Social Behaviour Orders and Football Banning Orders. The Football Law as such has become a catch-all for deviant behaviour in the Netherlands.

[32]Tweede Kamer 2008, Memorie van Toelichting, 31467 nr. 3, KST118583, SDU.

public order that can be addressed on the basis of the Football Law. This means concretely that there has to be evidence of at least more than one violation of public order.[33] The Football Law is further designed to provide the authorities with tools to target the internal dynamic of such groups. The behaviour specifically targeted by the Football Law is structural (though not necessarily criminal) disorder, through which public order is violated.[34] Specific examples of such behaviour are intimidation, threatening behaviour and vandalism.[35] The person targeted by the Football Law engages in such behaviour individually or within the group he or she forms a part of.[36] However, as mentioned above, for the powers under the Football Law to become available, there has to be a pattern of (criminal) behaviour that structurally violates public order.

The Football Law intends to target the small core group of supporters who engage in violence or disorder in the context of live football matches. Groups of hooligans in the Netherlands are generally analysed as loosely structured groups with a dynamic membership.[37] At the core of these groups is a small number of people, who have been members of the group for a while and who hierarchically are more important within the group.[38] Accordingly, although the evidence suggests that such groups are not strict hierarchical groups with a static membership, the Football Law targets a relatively small core of supporters, believed to be responsible for the majority of the violent incidents at and around professional football matches and other events in the Netherlands.[39]

The Football Law has expanded the powers of mayors of municipalities under the Municipalities Law and for prosecutors under the Criminal Code and the Code of Criminal Procedure. The Football Law strengthens the competences of the mayor under the Municipalities Law to deal with structural violations of public order. On the basis of the Football Law mayors can impose the following measures: an area ban, a group ban (which means that not more than three people are allowed to group together at certain designated public spaces within a municipality) and/or a reporting duty.[40] The precondition for imposing any of these measures is that the person concerned has repeatedly violated public order individually or in a group; or that the person concerned has played a leading role in such a group that repeatedly

---

[33]A proposed change of the Football Law was presented to the Second Chamber of Parliament in March 2014, which would soften this structure element to also enable measures to be introduced to first- time offenders and which would extend the periods for which measures could be imposed.

[34]Wet Maatregelen Bestrijding Voetbalvandalisme en Ernstige Overlast 2010, n. 7 above.

[35]Tweede Kamer 2008, Memorie van Toelichting, 31467 nr. 3, KST118583, SDU.

[36]Ibid.

[37]Ibid. See also Spaaij 2006, 2007. For a description of a Dutch group of football supporters, see Kievits 2012.

[38]Tweede Kamer 2008, Memorie van Toelichting, 31467 nr. 3, KST118583, SDU.

[39]Audit-Team Voetbal Vandalisme 2008.

[40]Wet Maatregelen Bestrijding Voetbalvandalisme en Ernstige Overlast 2010, n. 7 above.

violated public order.[41] Measures can be imposed for a maximum of 3 months at a time and can be extended three times with further 3 month periods, to a maximum of 12 months.[42]

The Football Law further introduces new competences for the prosecutor under the Criminal Code and the Code of Criminal Procedure to deal with structural violations of public order in anticipation of a verdict for a criminal offence. The powers for the prosecutor under the Football Law are linked to the prosecution for a criminal offence of the person concerned. The prosecutor can impose a measure against a person suspected of committing an offense that resulted in a serious violation of public order and where there is a serious risk of further violations of public order; or where there is a serious risk of harmful behaviour by the suspect regarding other persons; or where there is a serious risk of harmful behaviour by the suspect regarding goods.[43] If this precondition is fulfilled, the prosecutor can impose an area ban, a contact ban (which means that the suspect is not allowed to have contact with a person or certain persons), a reporting duty and/or a counselling duty (this means that the suspect has to receive counselling that could help him or her refrain from criminal behaviour). The prosecutor can impose a measure for a maximum period of 90 days. This period can be extended three times with further 90-day periods, but cannot exceed 360 days. A measure imposed by a prosecutor will end when there is an irrevocable verdict in the case against the person concerned. The measures possible on the basis of the Football Law, which are most relevant in a football context are the reporting duty, group ban and area ban. Such measures can be imposed individually or cumulatively.

After an amendment of the Second Chamber of Parliament, a new Article 141a was added to the Criminal Code. This article stipulates that a person, who intentionally provides opportunity, means or information resulting in violence against goods or persons will be criminally liable.[44] Under this article, the person who for example puts a message on a message-board calling for a fight between rival supporters at a certain time and place, can be prosecuted. It is questionable, however, whether this is a measure that is really effective in preventing hooligan confrontations. With this article, the new-media, or virtual, behaviour of persons who, typically, have nothing to do with actual violence or disorder is criminalised. As we have seen, supporters intent on disorder have become increasingly sophisticated in preventing detection and thus probably will not announce their intention to commit offences on the Internet or via social media.[45] This article furthermore opens

---

[41]Ibid. This is an administrative procedure by the mayor, without judicial involvement. So the mayor has to comply with the principles of proper administration, for example the principle of careful information gathering of Article 3:2 General Administrative Law Act. However, the criminal standard of proof (beyond a reasonable doubt) does not apply when imposing such a measure.

[42]Bestrijding Voetbalvandalisme en Ernstige Overlast 2010, n. 7 above.

[43]Tweede Kamer 2008, Memorie van Toelichting, 31467 nr. 3, KST118583, SDU.

[44]Ibid.

[45]In contrast to Spaaij's claims above, n. 10 above.

the door for invasive investigative techniques potentially violating (online) privacy. This broad criminalising provision has to be balanced against the necessity and proportionality of such breaches of privacy.

A further important novelty of the Football Law approach is that because a measure can only be imposed for structural disorder, it is crucial that a dossier is compiled.[46] This dossier should provide detailed information regarding the specific behaviour of the person concerned, the behaviour of the group he or she is a part of, the group structure and dynamics, previous measures taken against this person and/or group and whether there is a reasonable fear of further violations of public order.[47] This dossier includes contributions from a variety of sources, such as the police, the prosecutor's office, the CIV and other instances.

7.5 Problems Related to the Football Law

In a Report published in 2008 the Audit-Team Football Vandalism (the 2008 Report) looked at the process of arrest, prosecution and punishment of football hooligans.[48] The fan groups of six Dutch clubs were the subject of this report: Feyenoord Rotterdam, Ajax Amsterdam, FC Groningen, NEC Nijmegen, Cambuur Leeuwarden and MVV Maastricht. The report concluded that, on the basis of the estimated number of hooligans and the number of football-related incidents, the number of arrests for football-related offences is relatively low.[49] On paper, according to the 2008 Report, there seemed to be an adequate and elaborate framework to deal with hooliganism: the legal framework to deal with hooliganism was judged to be sufficient, the Prosecutors Office had issued clear guidelines regarding the prosecution of hooligans, and the Policy Framework for Combating Football Hooliganism established a clear tolerance level with regard to hooliganism.[50] However, few hooligans were arrested and even when they were arrested, the instances in which they were convicted were relatively low. The legal framework in place was therefore not sufficiently used. Further, the Dutch Football Law follows the English example by introducing civil/administrative banning orders for behaviour that is either not criminal or which is difficult to prove in order to secure a conviction. This raises the same legitimacy concerns that have been identified with respect to the English banning order on complaint.[51]

[46]Tweede Kamer 2008, Memorie van Toelichting, 31467 nr. 3, KST118583, SDU.

[47]Ibid.

[48]Audit-team Voetbal Vandalisme 2008.

[49]Ibid.

[50]Ibid.

[51]See Pearson 2006, James and Pearson 2006 and Stott and Pearson 2007. See also Maguire 2000.

Incidents at and around football matches have persisted despite the introduction of the Football Law in 2010. The 2008 report concluded that in practice the legislative framework to deal with hooligans was under-used or even ignored,[52] and that for the most part, hooligans could act with a certain level of impunity. There were a number of reasons for this. One reason mentioned in the 2008 Report was that the maintenance of security within the stadiums was a task left to the clubs and therefore there is no significant police presence within stadia; another reason was that the focus of the police was primarily aimed at preventing disturbances and not in detecting and prosecuting offences; and finally in many cases the police were unable to obtain enough evidence to pursue a criminal conviction (an assessment that in most cases led the police not to arrest).[53]

The result of this approach was that the prospect of a criminal conviction had little deterrent effect for hooligans because the chance that they would be successfully prosecuted and convicted for their acts was remote. The 2008 Report therefore proposed that the legal framework and the house rules of the individual clubs should be more actively monitored and maintained.[54] Football supporters who did not follow these rules should, it argued, be held accountable for this not only by the clubs and the KNVB but also by the police and the prosecutors.[55]

Another problem raised in the 2008 Report was that where acts of hooliganism were prosecuted, there was no uniformity in the process of prosecution and punishment throughout the various cities and districts in the Netherlands.[56] This led to legal uncertainty among all the stakeholders. The Audit-Team therefore proposed that there should be clarity on a national level regarding which offences should be prosecuted, and how these prosecutions should be executed.[57]

A final overall conclusion drawn in the 2008 Report was that there was a lack of an effective approach in focusing on the small core group of hooligans that are at the centre of the activities of their particular groups.[58] The 2008 Report proposed that an effective policy should aim to deal with this small core group of hooligans: a theory that is mirrored in the Explanatory Memorandum to the Football Law and that was high on the agenda in the legislative history leading up to the Football Law.[59]

Accordingly, even with an elaborate legislative framework already in place, the authorities do not effectively support the approach of the clubs and the KNVB in their efforts to deal with hooligans. In too many cases, the clubs are left on their own to deal with those engaging in acts of violence or disorder. Most professional

[52]Audit-Team Voetbal Vandalisme 2008.

[53]Ibid.

[54]Ibid.

[55]Ibid.

[56]Ibid.

[57]Ibid.

[58]Ibid.

[59]Ibid.

football clubs in the Netherlands are relatively small organisations with a budget to match. For the maintenance of the safety and security in the stadium, in a lot of cases these clubs depend on a relatively small organisation and on the work of volunteers. This puts a huge strain on the clubs in terms of finance and personnel. Therefore, an effective approach to football crowd disorder requires that the measures possible for the clubs and the KNVB (the stadium ban) are complemented and supported by effective legal measures.

Thus far, the Dutch Football Law has not proven to be an effective tool against hooliganism; a large number of Dutch municipalities have chosen not to use the new powers against those engaging in football-related violence or disorder.[60] These municipalities feel that the conditions for imposing the new measures are too demanding and require too much administrative effort and they choose to deal with public order violations under the legal framework in existence prior to the Football Law.[61] Many municipalities and districts feel they do not need to apply the additional powers conferred by the Football Law.[62] Some of the municipalities have argued that the new law does not add anything to the existing powers to deal with public order problems and therefore they choose to use those instruments with which they are already familiar. These municipalities add that to deal with immediate threats to public order posed by groups of football supporters, the emergency powers already in force remain the more effective instrument.[63]

Furthermore, there remain serious doubts about the effectiveness of the Football Law because of the relatively short duration of the measures and the amount of work needed to impose them.[64] When the duration of the measures possible under the Football Law are compared with the lengthy Football Banning Orders possible in England (between 3 and 10 years), the Dutch measures are of a relatively short duration. Measures imposed under the football law have a limited duration of 3 months and can be prolonged for a maximum period of about 1 year. However, it must be kept in mind that the Dutch measures, like Football Banning Orders on Complaint, do not follow upon a conviction for a football-related offence. Accordingly, extending the period of the measures, as has now been proposed in an amendment to the Football Law, would lead to serious questions regarding the legitimacy of these measures.[65] The Football Law should not be used to gradually introduce more draconian and long-lasting measures on football supporters, a fear that seems to materialise with the amendments introduced to the Football Law in March 2014.

[60] See also Pro Facto 2012.

[61] Inspectie Openbare Orde en Veiligheid 2012.

[62] Ibid.

[63] Ibid.

[64] See also Pro Facto 2012, p. 84.

[65] It would be virtually impossible to maintain that measures on the basis of the Football Law have a preventive character, if these measures have a much longer duration. Penalties for football related disorder are imposed by the Courts after a trial, whereas the mayor and the prosecutor have certain additional powers to maintain public order or in anticipation of a criminal trial.

Another problem is that it has been difficult for the authorities to compile a quality dossier on the persons concerned, which complies with the demands of the Football Law and the guarantees of Dutch law in general.[66] Particularly in the context of hooliganism, it has proven difficult to compose a dossier that meets the demands of the Football Law.[67] The first evaluation of the Football Law with regard to compiling a quality dossier on those suspected of being engaged in football-related violence or disorder reached a number of conclusions: 'hooligans' have a low number of criminal antecedents compared to some other groups that violate public order; the quality of the police observations in many cases has proven of insufficient quality to withstand judicial scrutiny; hooligans commit acts of violence or disorder in a large group and therefore it is often impossible to pinpoint who did what exactly within this group; and the exchange of information on hooligans between the various stakeholders is not at such a level that it enables the authorities to compile a comprehensive file.[68] After 4 years of operation of the Football Law there are still serious problems regarding the compilation of dossiers. The Football Law groups a variety of violations of public order of different character and nature under one law.[69] However, for building a dossier, a number of terms in this law (i.e. the terms 'violation of public order', 'repeatedly' and 'fear for further violations'), have to be interpreted differently for each form of disorder.[70] Public order violations committed by hooligans differ in their temporal scope from other public order violations. Public order violations committed by hooligans in relation to football have to be tied to football matches and the football season and even then only to certain matches–disorder does not occur at every match. So it generally takes a longer time to build a dossier against those suspected of engagement in football-related violence or disorder.[71]

Furthermore, most individuals arrested in connection with football are first-time offenders.[72] In this case, a measure on the basis of the Football Law is impossible, since the law requires involvement in more than one incident for the imposition of a measure.[73] According to the evaluation of the Football Law in 2012, the 'hooligans' that were arrested were predominantly the 'hangers-on' and not the 'hardcore' hooligans, which made it impossible to compile a dossier on

[66]Such a dossier for example has to comply with the general principles of administrative law. Examples of such principles are the principle of careful information gathering (Article 3:2 General Administrative Law Act) and the principle of a reasoned decision (Article 3:46 General Administrative Law Act).

[67]Inspectie Openbare Orde en Veiligheid 2012.

[68]Inspectie Openbare Orde en Veiligheid 2011.

[69]Inspectie Openbare Orde en Veiligheid 2012.

[70]Ibid.

[71]Ibid.

[72]Ibid.

[73]For a discussion on best policing practices regarding football supporters and the prevention of offences by such first- time offenders, see Stott and Pearson 2007.

this alleged 'hardcore'.[74] With regard to these individuals, much is expected from the 'Hooligans in Beeld II' (HIB II) project.[75] This project stipulates that a database is compiled containing a 'top ten' of football hooligans for all the professional clubs in the highest Dutch football league, the *Eredivisie*, who are to be targeted for measures by the authorities.[76] The police and the prosecutor can compile information on these 'top-hooligans' in the HIB II database, therefore compiling a dossier on these individuals that can be used to impose measures.[77] However, the HIB II has some problems. One issue is that the police in many cases lack the experience necessary to build a dossier.[78] Police officers are experienced in building criminal cases, but the Football Law requires the police to collect information to build a dossier for an administrative measure.[79] Secondly, the level and quality of information entered into the database differs significantly between the various police forces.[80] Reasons for this difference are a lack of capacity within police forces, problems coordinating different information systems and the fact that certain forces do not see the necessity of the database.[81] For a discussion regarding the legal problems associated with the HIB database, see the previous paragraph in this chapter. In the proposed amendment to the Football Law, it would also become possible to impose measures against such first-time offenders. Again, it can be seen that the original Football Law is used as a gateway to gradually introduce more draconian measures and to substantially broaden the scope of the Football Law.

Once a dossier is composed and deemed sufficient for the imposition of a measure, a letter will be sent to the person concerned informing him or her of the intention to impose a measure.[82] This letter includes the motivation for the measure, the legal grounds for the measure, the facts giving rise to the measure, the exact conditions of the measure and an explanation regarding the procedure.[83] Once this letter is sent, the target will have the opportunity to respond to the intention to impose a measure. If the mayor, after taking note of the response of the person concerned, decides that a measure is still warranted, the measure can be imposed. Once the measure is communicated to the person concerned, the measure enters into force although the person concerned can then appeal to the courts to have the measure revoked. This procedure in practice has been quite cumbersome and time consuming. Especially in the

[74] Tweede Kamer 2008, Memorie van Toelichting, 31467 nr. 3, KST118583, SDU.

[75] Inspectie Openbare Orde en Veiligheid 2012.

[76] Ibid.

[77] Ibid.

[78] Ibid.

[79] Ibid.

[80] Ibid.

[81] Ibid.

[82] Ibid.

[83] Ibid.

context of football hooliganism, when a measure is sometimes urgent, this procedure has been experienced in practice as taking too much time and effort by the authorities.[84]

7.6 Early Case Law Regarding the Football Law

7.6.1 LJN BP5057, Amsterdam District Court[85]

This case concerned a request for an interim order regarding a measure imposed on the applicant by the mayor of Amsterdam. On January 22, 2011, a group ban on the basis of the Football Law was imposed on the applicant. This group ban was for the Amsterdam city centre and the area directly surrounding the Amsterdam Arena, the stadium of Ajax. The group ban was valid on the days before matches of Ajax and the Dutch national team and was imposed for a period of 3 months. Concurrently, the applicant received a reporting duty for the match days of Ajax and the Dutch national team. On these days, the applicant would have to report to a specified police station between 15 and 30 min after the start of the match.

The mayor of Amsterdam imposed this measure on the applicant and a number of other persons believed to belong to a larger group of Ajax hooligans. The mayor on the basis of the Football Law, imposed the measure on the applicant, because he had reasons to believe that the applicant was a member of a group that had repeatedly and structurally violated public order in Amsterdam. The mayor further had reasons to believe that the applicant would continue to be involved in violations of public order. The applicant in response to the measure, asserted that although he was a member of a group of Ajax supporters who regularly visit Ajax home matches, he has not been involved in any violations of public order. The applicant further asserted before the court that the mayor could not base his decision on events that happened before the entry into force of the Football Law.

The judge in his decision stated that the fact that an individual in the past has been involved in serious violations of public order can be a factor in determining whether there is a serious danger that that person will violate public order in the future. The judge continued to state that according to Article 3:2 of the General Administrative Law Act, in preparation of a decision the authorities must gather knowledge regarding the relevant facts and the interests which are at stake in each particular instance.

In this case, the relevant information regarding the applicant pertained to the areas where the applicant was normally present on or before match days and on five incidents noted as violations of public order. A number of these violations took place before the entry into force of the Football Law. The judge ruled that the

---

[84]Ibid.

[85]Rechtbank Amsterdam, 18-02-2011, LJN BP5057.

principle of legal certainty requires that only incidents which happened after the entry into force of the Football Law can be taken into account to determine whether a measure can be imposed on the basis of it.[86] The dossier regarding the applicant also mentioned two incidents which happened after the entry into force of the Football Law. One of these incidents happened at the Netherlands versus Sweden match on October 12, 2010, the other in Hamburg, Germany, where Ajax played HSV on January 8, 2011. With regard to this second incident, the judge found that incidents which happen in other municipalities in the Netherlands, or incidents which happen abroad can be considered relevant for the dossier.[87]

According to the decision, the determining factor when imposing a measure is whether there is a dossier which contains enough relevant information. This dossier needs to document the behaviour and incidents giving rise to the measure, the risk of future violations of public order, the group and the central figures within this group responsible for these violations of public order and especially the role of the individual concerned herein, and finally the urgency for imposing a measure.[88] The judge found that the dossier in this case was not detailed enough to justify a measure imposed under the Football Law. The five incidents mentioned before (of which only two were relevant for the decision) were only summarily described by the police commissioner. From the information contained in the dossier, it could not be established who had made the concrete observations, nor what the precise nature of the applicants' involvement in these incidents was.[89] The judge added that the mayor in a later stage of the proceedings could add enough information to justify the imposition of a measure against the applicant.[90] Further, it is not necessary to establish that the applicant himself has violated public order, or has committed any offences himself. The mayor merely needs to prove that the applicant was a member of a group that repeatedly violated public order or committed offences.[91]

Then the judge looked at whether the measure was motivated properly in the light of the proportionality principle.[92] According to the judge, one of the most severe measures possible under the Football Law had been imposed on the applicant. The judge found that for such a stringent measure to be handed out, the mayor should have made clear whether the measure is proportionate to the intended aim and whether a less stringent measure could have been taken to achieve this aim.[93] For all these reasons, the measure was suspended.

---

[86]LJN BP5057, at para 4.4.

[87]LJN BP5057, at para 4.5.

[88]LJN BP5057, at para 4.6.

[89]LJN BP5057, at para 4.7.

[90]LJN BP5057, at para 4.7.

[91]LJN BP5057, at para 4.7.

[92]The principle of proportionality is contained in Article 3:4(2) of the General Administrative Law Act.

[93]LJN BP5057, at para 4.8.

7.6.2 LJN BW1140, Amsterdam District Court[94]

This case deals with an appeal before the Amsterdam District Court of a decision whereby the mayor of Amsterdam had imposed a group ban and a reporting duty on the applicant. The applicant was alleged to be a member of a group of Ajax hooligans and was alleged to have been involved in a number of incidents of serious disorder. He received a group ban for the period from 26 January 2011 until 25 April 2011. During this period, ten football matches of Ajax and the Dutch national team were being played. The group ban applied to the ten match days and the evenings of the days preceding these matches and the reporting duty meant that the applicant had to report at a police station during these matches.

The applicant stated that the measures imposed on him violated the principle of legal certainty, since incidents that had occurred before the entry into force of the Football Law had been taken into account. The court held that the measures imposed on the basis of the Football Law were of a purely preventive character and could not be seen as punitive. Therefore, such measures do not fall within the notion of a criminal charge in accordance with Article 6 of the ECHR. The court further held that the measures implemented by the Football Law were not completely novel, rather that they expanded the already existing instruments to deal with public disorder. The court further found that one of the incidents the applicant had been involved in occurred after the entry into force of the Football Law. The court held that at that moment the applicant could have known that incidents that had happened prior to the entry into force of the Football Law could be taken into account when imposing a measure on him and that this was not a violation of the principle of legal certainty.

The applicant further argued that one of the incidents in which he had allegedly been involved occurred in Germany and could not be taken into account. The court held that for a measure to be imposed the only relevant question is whether the applicant had been involved in violations of public order by a group; where such violations occurred was irrelevant according to the court. The applicant's claims that it had not been proved that he had violated public order, but merely that he had been part of a group that had violated public order were also dismissed. The court found that the evidence established that the applicant was part of a group that violated public order in two instances, thereby fulfilling the requirements of the Football Law which requires at least two incidents in which public order was violated.

The court then looked at whether the final precondition for the imposition of a measure, whether there is a risk of further violations of public order, was fulfilled. It held that there had to be concrete evidence for such a risk. The court found that the incidents in which the applicant was found to be involved, the nature of the group of which the applicant was found to be a member, the behaviour of that

---

[94] Rechtbank Amsterdam, 03-04-2012, LJN BW1140.

group and the fact that the intervention of the police had not prevented the applicant from engaging in further activities with such groups was sufficient evidence that there was a serious risk of further violations of public order.

Finally, the court looked at whether the imposition of the measures on the applicant complied with the principles of subsidiarity and proportionality.[95] The court considered whether less stringent measures were available against the applicant and whether the measures imposed were necessary for the goal of the measures, the prevention of disorder. The mayor had indicated that a group ban and reporting duty were imposed to extract the applicant from the group he was a part of, which was responsible for structural violations of public order. The court found that a group ban was a less invasive measure than an area ban. The court further found that measures imposed on the applicant contained a temporal limitation for the ten match days and the evenings before these matches. For these reasons, it was held that the measure imposed conformed with the principles of proportionality and subsidiarity.

7.7 Conclusions

In the fourth year after its implementation, a number of conclusions can be made about the Dutch Football Law. The Football Law has not delivered the expected effective instrument to address hooliganism. There are valid reasons to question the effectiveness of the Law in its current form and there are serious concerns regarding the future and the direction it appears to be headed in. The Football Law provides an addition to the existing police powers and has proven more efficient for countering structural public disorder and structural violating disorder in the neighbourhood. The Football Law gives powers to the mayor and to the public prosecutor to impose measures with a relatively short duration. The major problem with the Football Law signalled by the stakeholders is that the period measures can be imposed for are too short to realistically make an impact on football hooliganism. A number of possible solutions have been mentioned to improve the Football Law and an amendment has now been introduced. The measures imposed on the basis of the Football Law are to be lengthened or the application of the 3 month period could be restricted to football matches or weekends, so extending the duration of the measures that way. However, before making such drastic changes to the Football Law, it is necessary to consider some possible problems with such solutions from a human rights perspective.

At the moment, the Football Law is specifically designed to *prevent* immediate and structural violations of public order. The measures imposed on the basis of the

[95]The principle of subsidiarity is contained in Article 3:3 of the General Administrative Law Act and the principle of proportionality is contained in Article 3:4(2) of the General Administrative Law Act.

Football Law are civil or administrative measures not designed for a long duration. Significantly extending the duration of the measures imposed on the basis of the Football Law would fundamentally alter its character, and would give such measures a definitively punitive character.[96] Under the current Football Law, the persons against whom such measures are imposed cannot benefit from the fair trial guarantees that should accompany punitive measures imposed as a result of a criminal trial.

The power to impose measures on the basis of the Football Law resides with the mayor and the public prosecutor. The mayor and the public prosecutor are both unfit to impose punitive measures of a long duration in the Dutch legal system; this is a role reserved for the judiciary. Although the measures imposed on the basis of the Football Law have punitive elements in them, at the moment the measures possible under the Football Law can be categorised under the public order powers of mayors and prosecutors. However, these public order powers can only be activated to prevent immediate violations of public order. If one therefore were to significantly extend the duration of the measures imposed on the basis of the Football Law, this preventive character and much of the legal justification of such measures would disappear. This would raise fundamental questions about the roles of the mayor and the prosecutor in imposing such measures and regarding a number of fundamental protections available under the criminal law, which are not available under the Football Law.

One of the problems of the Dutch approach to football-related violence and disorder and the Football Law in particular is that there seems to be insufficient attention to the specific characteristics of the phenomenon of hooliganism in the legislative process. In the discussion on the Football Law and hooliganism in general, it seems that a desire for publicity reigns and outdated rhetoric about hooliganism resurfaces. Political gain is placed above realistic and viable solutions. During the legislative process, the hooliganism aspect of the law was sidetracked and the Football Law became a catch-all for various types of antisocial behaviour. Where the Football Law has proven quite effective to address such other types of nuisance, for hooliganism the picture is quite different. The Football Law is lacking attention to a number of characteristics specific to the problem of hooliganism; it lacks a definitional approach to the problem and lacks the tools to address the specifics of the phenomenon.

The problem in the Netherlands is that the focus has shifted away (and is continuing to do so) from punishing hooligans for the offences they commit to a 'guilt by association' strategy. As was noted by the Report published in 2008 by the Audit-Team Football Vandalism, acts of football-related crime in too many cases go unpunished for a variety of reasons. Hooligans are not sufficiently

[96] See *Engel and Others v. the Netherlands*, App. No. 5100/71; 5101/71; 5102/71; 5354/72; 5370/72, 8 June 1976. For a discussion of the definition of punitive measures under the ECHR, see Trechsel and Summers 2006. For a discussion of this issue with regard to English football banning orders, see Pearson 2006.

arrested, prosecuted and convicted for the offences they commit, whether or not such offences have a nexus to football. Instead of remedying this situation, there is a push towards long-term preventive measures outside of the criminal law and a widening of the net. Significant money and time has been invested in attempting to obtain preventive measures against hooligans, and opportunities for prosecution and conviction are ignored.

The Netherlands should refocus its attention to a criminal law approach to hooligan offences, rather than follow the English preventive approach of the FBO on complaint. The primary goal should always be to arrest, prosecute and convict hooligans for the offences they commit. Acts of hooliganism (vandalism, assault, etc.) are criminal offences and should be dealt with according to the criminal law, whether they are committed at a football match or at some other (large-scale) event. The active and actual punishment for criminal behaviour sends a much stronger signal to society as a whole and hooligans in particular than 'preventive' measures. Only by really getting tough on that small core of hooligans can the problem of hooliganism really be addressed in a manner that is both effective and legal and in line with human rights standards.

References

Adang O, Ferwerda H (2007) Hooligans in beeld. Reed Business, Amsterdam

Audit-Team Voetbal Vandalisme (2008) Aanhouding, vervolging en bestraffing van hooligans. Rijksoverheid, The Hague

Ferwerda H, Van Leiden I, Van Ham T (2010) Het nieuwe hooliganisme; geweld ook buiten het voetbalveld. Justitiële verkenningen 36:54–68

Garland D (1996) The limits of the sovereign state strategies of crime control in contemporary society. British journal of criminology 36:445–471

Hopkins M (2013) Ten seasons of the football banning order: Police Officer narratives on the operation of banning orders and the impact on the behaviour of 'risk supporters'. Policing and Society 24:285–301

Inspectie Openbare Orde en Veiligheid (2011) Wet Maatregelen Bestrijding Voetbalvandalisme en Ernstige Overlast. Toepassing in de Praktijk. Inspectie Openbare Orde en Veiligheid, The Hague

Inspectie Openbare Orde en Veiligheid (2012) Wet Maatregelen Bestrijding Voetbalvandalisme en Ernstige Overlast. Toepassing in de Praktijk 2012. Inspectie Openbare Orde en Veiligheid, The Hague

James M, Pearson G (2006) Football banning orders: Analysing their use in Court. Journal of Criminal Law 70:509–525

Kievits Y (2012) Rotterdam hooligan. Just Publishers, Meppel

Macdonald S (2006) A suicidal woman, roaming pigs and a noisy trampolinist: Refining the ASBO's definition of 'Anti-Social Behaviour. The Modern Law Review 69:183–213

Maguire M (2000) Policing by risks and targets: Some dimensions and implications of intelligence-led crime control. Policing and Society: An International Journal 9:315–336

Pearson G (2006) Hybrid law and human rights–banning and behaviour orders in the appeal courts. Liverpool Law Review 27:125–145

Pro Facto (2012) Op doel? Evaluatie van de Wet Maatregelen Bestrijding Voetbalvandalisme en Ernstige Overlast. Rijksuniversiteit Groningen, Groningen

Siekmann R (1982) Voetbalvandalisme. De Vrieseborch, Haarlem

Spaaij R (2006) Understanding Football Hooliganism. Amsterdam University Press, Amsterdam
Spaaij R (2007) Football Hooliganism in the Netherlands: Patterns of Continuity and Change. Soccer and Society 8:316–334
Spaaij R (2011) Understanding Football Hooliganism: A comparison of six Western European football clubs. Vossiuspers, Amsterdam
Stott C, Pearson G (2006) Football banning orders, Proportionality and public order. Howard Journal of Criminal Justice 45:241–254
Stott C, Pearson G (2007) Football hooliganism: Policing and the war on the English Disease. Pennant Books, London
Trechsel S, Summers SJ (2006) Human rights in criminal proceedings. Oxford University Press, Oxford
Tsoukala A (2009a) Football Hooliganism in Europe. Security and Civil Liberties in the Balance. Basingstoke, Palgrave Macmillan
Tsoukala A (2009b) Combating football crowd disorder at the European level: an ongoing institutionalisation of the control of deviance. The Entertainment and Sports Law Journal 7(2)
Van der Brug HH (1994) Football hooliganism in the Netherlands. In: Giulianotti R et al (eds) Football, violence and social identity. London, Routledge, pp 169–189
Von Hirsch A, Simester A (eds) (2006) Incivilities: Regulating offensive behaviour. Hart, Oxford
Zedner L (2007) Pre-crime and post-criminology? Theoretical Criminology 11:261–281

Chapter 8
Legal and Policing Responses to Football Crowd Disorder in Austria

Ireen Christine Winter

Abstract Football crowd disorder and violence is perceived to be a significant problem in Austrian domestic football. As a result, the legislature, the football authorities and the football clubs have taken action to regulate the behaviour of football spectators and restrict the ability of those believed to pose a risk to public order from attending live matches. This chapter draws upon a study of the Bundesliga in 2007/08 which investigated football crowd behaviour and the utility of measures designed to ensure order and safety in and immediately around football stadia. It concludes that fan training and education are key to reducing problems and improving safety, and warns against the dangers of unnecessary high-profile policing. It also suggests that exclusion of those who have previously engaged in misbehaviour is not always the best approach to improving fan behaviour in Austrian football stadia.

Keywords Austria · Football crowds · Football hooliganism · Regulation · Law · Policing · Pyrotechnics

Contents

Dr. Ireen Winter is Head of Operational and Strategic Crime at the Federal Ministry of the Interior, Criminal Intelligence Service Austria.

I.C. Winter (✉)
Federal Ministry of the Interior, Criminal Intelligence Service, Vienna, Austria
e-mail: ireen.winter@bmi.gv.at

A. Tsoukala et al. (eds.), *Legal Responses to Football "Hooliganism" in Europe*,
ASSER International Sports Law Series, DOI 10.1007/978-94-6265-108-1_8

8.1 Introduction

In 1924 Austria became the first country in continental Europe to introduce professional football.[1] The success of the clubs, which were mostly concentrated around Vienna,[2] also contributed to the success of the national side which in 1930, as the so-called 'wonder-team', finished second at the European Cup of national teams.[3] Two years after the first regional championships, and initiated by former ÖFB official Hugo Meisl, the so-called Mitropacup began. Many international clubs participated in this forerunner of today's Champions' League.[4] The 'Staatsliga' was introduced in 1949, the 'Nationalliga' in 1965, and finally in 1974 today's 'Bundesliga': an association of the organisers of the professional championships of the two highest divisions in Austria.[5] From a legal point of view, the Bundesliga is a non-profit association. The twenty clubs—ten of which are in tipp3-Bundesliga powered by T-Mobile, and ten of which are in the 'Heute für Morgen' first league—are the regular members of the federation. In season 2012/13 more than 1.5 million people attended 180 games; almost 7,000 spectators per game were registered in the first division.[6]

Safety measures taken by the police have become a central part of safety management around football stadia in Austria. In this regard, the amendment of the 'Sicherheitspolizeigesetz' (Austrian security law—SPG)[7] that came into force on 01.01.2007 and the introduction of the 'Pyrotechnikgesetz' (Austrian pyrotechnic law)[8] that was enacted on 01.01.2010, provided not only further measures in an attempt to prevent violence at big sports events but also extended the special powers of the security authorities. It is the duty of the police to ensure the necessary balance between the biggest possible freedom of the spectators and the best possible safety standards.

[1]Horak et al. 1985, p. 5.

[2]As the oldest Austrian football club, in 1894 the 'First Vienna Football' was founded by English employees of a company called Rothschild.

[3]Only five nations participated in it.

[4]Winter 2007, p. 12.

[5]Limberger 2003, p. 97.

[6]Bundesliga (05 April 2013) http://www.bundesliga.at/index.php?id=144. Accessed 12 January 2015.

[7]BGBl I 113/2007.

[8]BGBl I 131/2009.

In order to meet safety considerations, the author, together with Bernhard Klob, carried out an empirical investigation of the Austrian T-Mobile Bundesliga in season 2007/2008 entitled 'Football and Security in Austria'.[9] In the main part this explorative study evaluated the current state of relevant factors and strategic measures to curtail violence amongst spectators. The study, which was published in 2011, also contains a detailed report on the personal opinions of football fans and of experts regarding safety measures in relation to football matches and the factors leading to violence. The evaluation was limited, however, to the stadium and its immediate surroundings. A discussion of the results of the investigation includes detailed recommendations for an optimal interaction of preventive and repressive measures that may contribute to guaranteeing safety at football matches. Based on the findings and recommendations of the evaluation of Winter and Klob, in the course of another study, a uniform training programme for spotters (training and professionalising for Spotters—Best European Practice Manual)[10] was developed for the first time and was incorporated in the regular training programme of the Austrian police starting in April 2013.[11]

In both studies, particular attention was drawn to legal aspects and powers as well as to measures restricting the freedom of the fans by the police and by the clubs. The present article focuses on these topics. Sections 8.2 and 8.3 deal with terminology and safety regulations as well as with legal principles. Section 8.4 provides an overview of the measures to be taken by the police and under house rules in relation to safety management at major sports events in Austria.

8.2 Football Games as Sports Events

Guaranteeing safety in and around the venues is one of the highest priorities for organisers of major football events. Safety measures range from preventive to repressive instruments. This also applies to club football in the highest divisions of the Austrian league. The respective organisers together with security authorities are confronted with the task of taking all the essential measures to guarantee the orderly conduct of football matches.

[9]Winter and Klob 2011, p. 231.

[10]Publication of the research study in six countries expected in 2015.

[11]Winter, Jaeger and Geissler 2012, p. 47 ff. Starting in April 2013, four weeks of standardised training per year was offered on a national level to train active spotters all over Austria. In Austria as well as in five other European countries, a current-state-analysis was carried out and based on this, basic and advanced training standards in particular for spotters in Austria but also flexibly applicable for the rest of Europe were developed in a so-called European Best Practice Manual that was published in English in autumn 2013 by Verlag fuer Polizeiwissenschaft.

8.2.1 Terminology

According to the prevailing opinion, football matches are sports or major sports events[12] that are according to Article 15, Section 3 B-VG subject to the respective regional event law as they are publicly accessible, organised competitions in front of an audience.[13] A concrete definition of the term can neither be found in the law nor in corresponding ministerial ordinances.[14] Indicators for the existence of such an event include a supra-regional structure, e.g. an event with several venues[15] (with an international dimension), a tournament cycle lasting for several days, the capacity of the venues, the duration of the organisational process[16] or the number of spectators[17] and any of these can be decisive.[18] With regard to the Bundesliga, matches of the highest as well as of the lowest division can be considered major sports events. Here, the football stadia offer space for a minimum of 3,000 spectators; they are within the jurisdiction of the 'Bezirksverwaltungsbehörden' (district administrative authorities)[19] and are therefore sports events with a supra-regional character.[20]

8.2.2 Legal Basis

Bundesliga matches are public sports events that require registration and for which the visitors are obliged to produce a paid ticket.[21] For the sake of danger defence and danger prevention, all games must be registered according to Article 15 Section 1 B-VG in due form and time with the competent authority. In this regard, all regional states take account of the European Convention on Spectator Violence and Misbehaviour at Sports Events and in particular at Football Matches.[22] On April 1, 1988, Austria became a formal party to this convention. In addition, since 1988, the Austrian Ministry of Interior (BMI) has been a member

[12]There is no definition as to when an event is considered "major", hence there is no minimum number of participants or spectators as a prerequisite.

[13]VwGH 24.05.2005, 2005/05/0014; further Wess 2008, p. 179; Mayer 2009, p. 164.

[14]Ordinance BMI 29.05.2009, GZ.: BMI-EE1920/0008-ZSA/2009. For the comparison with projects of international or Austrian meaning see § 1 Bundes-Sportförderungsgesetz 2005 i.d.F. BGBl I 143/2005.

[15]According to the prevailing opinion, a stadium is a venue as defined by the regional event laws; see Mayer 2009, p. 164.

[16]VwGH 06.09.2005, 2005/03/0076.

[17]Dissenting see Unabhängiger Verwaltungssenat (UVS) Styria 07.03.1995, 30.4-98/94.

[18]Mayer 2009, p. 164.

[19]In detail Feßl 1993, pp. 44–48.

[20]Mayer 2009, p. 142.

[21]Mayer 2009, p. 61.

[22]SEV-No.: 120, dated 01.11.1985.

of the 'standing committee' to prevent riots at football matches of the Council of Europe.[23] Pursuant to this, sports organisations also have responsibilities in safety matters and are required to more generally ensure the orderly conduct of the events they organise.

8.3 Maintenance of Public Safety and Order

In the area of conflict between large football crowds and the risk of disorder, guaranteeing the safety of spectators at football matches poses a great challenge for those responsible. What degree of safety is necessary for football? What measures are vital and proportionate? Does more police automatically mean more safety? Football matches have become large scale and costly safety events. As a result of the EURO 2008[24] and some safety-related incidents and fan riots in the Bundesliga, intense discussions on a private and official basis amongst those responsible occurred in Austria with regard to the possibilities of maintaining public safety and order. The European Convention on Spectator Violence and Misbehaviour at Sports Events and in particular at Football Matches, by which Austria is bound under international law, contains a number of obligations owed by the parties involved in safety matters. They focus in particular on the drawing up and implementation of measures to prevent and control violence and misbehaviour amongst spectators.

8.3.1 Tasks of the Organisers

Austrian law considers the organiser of Bundesliga football matches to be the hosting club.[25] As a natural person or legal entity, the hosting club is responsible for the observation of the rules, regulations and orders concerning the event. The hosting club is subject to the regulations of the ÖFB, in particular the 'Rechtspflegeordnung' (disciplinary regulations) including the rules regarding the 'Strafausschüsse' (penal committees) of the ÖFB, the safety regulations for competitions of the Bundesliga[26] which apply to the sports organisers as well as to the spectators, and the implementing rules of the Bundesliga. The ÖFB functions as a non-profit and umbrella association of the regional football federations in Vienna.

[23]For further details on the Ständigen Ausschuss Europarat (1994), see http://conventions.coe.int/Treaty/ger/Summaries/Html/120.htm.

[24]Sabitzer 2005, p. 6 f.

[25]Wess 2008, p. 180; following a decision of the Austrian Supreme Court dated 23.03.1993, 2 Ob 526/03, which in relation to sports events defines the organiser as the party that creates a dangerous situation by organising and carrying out the competition.

[26]Bundesliga 2007a, p. 1 ff; Bundesliga 2008b, p. 1 ff.

It is a member of the Fédération Internationale de Football Association (FIFA) and the Union des Associations Européennes de Football (UEFA).[27] The UEFA Disciplinary Regulations (edition 2008) and the FIFA disciplinary rules (edition 2009) form the basis for the Austrian regulations of the ÖFB and the Bundesliga.

8.3.1.1 ÖFB, Bundesliga

According to § 5 Sec 5 of the disciplinary regulations of the ÖFB, the competent boards, here the so-called penal committees[28] are responsible for all disciplinary issues, for penalising offences and infringements of the regulations and for ordering safety measures.[29] The stadium and security board, senat 3 of the Bundesliga is, according to §§ 23 Sec 8 of the Bundesliga safety regulations the decisive body with regard to internal investigations and penalties. This board is responsible for drawing up (and reviewing compliance with) safety guidelines in the licensing process by the clubs (§ 6 Sec 1). In addition, it is responsible for deciding whether to implement stadium bans throughout Austria in cases of spectator misbehaviour, and together with the security authorities for the assessment and the management of a so-called 'risk' match, normally categorised as such following previous incidents with fans of one or both teams, or due to other extraordinary reasons which suggest that dangerous situations can be anticipated.

8.3.1.2 Football Clubs

According to the regulations of the event law and of the Bundesliga safety guidelines, the hosting clubs are predominantly responsible for the protection of spectators in the stadium. As organisers, it is their responsibility to guarantee compliance with the respective house rules and official orders.[30] The main task of the organiser is the organisation and management of the matches. As a secondary obligation,[31] the hosting clubs are charged with securing order and safety within the stadium and its immediate vicinity.

§ 5 of the safety guidelines state that clubs are obliged to establish and maintain stable contact with the appropriate, officially recognised fan clubs. Under No. 8.4.3.4. of the licensing criteria, selected fan representatives should act as a link between the clubs, fan clubs and security authorities to facilitate the control of the spectators at (away) games. Fan representatives are also responsible for the registration and organisation of fan choreographies.

---

[27]Österreichischer Fußball-Bund 2007, p. 2.

[28]Österreichischer Fußball-Bund 2008, p. 5.

[29]Österreichischer Fußball-Bund 2009, p. 8.

[30]Jedelsky 2008, p. 196.

[31]Regarding the illustration of the German liability of organisers, see Wess 2008, p. 190.

This also includes in principle the clubs' preventive work with fans and the realisation of fan projects in an effort to handle any previous disorder. Fan work on the one hand includes the work of fan initiatives and socio-pedagogic fan concepts and on the other hand also the achievements of the fan clubs.[32] Apart from one initiative against racism supported by the EU commission (Fair Play), there is currently no official fan project dealing with the question of fan misbehaviour (or spectator violence) in Austria.

Fan coaching work of the clubs also only affects the organisation of journeys to away games, the sale of tickets and the taking care of the fan club. Fan choreographies are an inherent part of fan activity and in this regard, the fan representatives of the clubs regularly make contact with the individual clubs. According to the Bundesliga safety guidelines, fan choreographies are organised activities by fans that under the compliance with the subsequent regulations allow for living 'fan culture'. Planned fan choreography needs to be formally registered and recorded with those responsible for safety at the organisational meeting at the latest before the safety check, which usually takes place 2 h before the match, or in case of high risk games, several days before.

If legal prerequisites are met, and after input from the operational commander of the security authorities and the fan coaching, permission must be granted unanimously by the representatives of the authorities, the stadium administration and the representatives of the hosting club. Those responsible for safety then organise the admission, the registration of names and the sequence of the fan choreography. Here the fan representative of the security authority should provide assistance.

In 2001, fan clubs of almost all clubs of the Austrian 'Ober and Unterhaus' united for the movement 'The stand is ours!'. With the participation and support of Swiss fans, this movement aimed at demonstrating against modern football, progressing commercialisation, increasing restrictions of artistic freedom and repression by public authorities.[33]

8.3.2 *Tasks of the Police*

Major football matches usually attract a large number of spectators and therefore inherent safety risks need to be recognised by organisers and police. The primary role of the police in relation to football matches is to ensure the balance between the highest degree of freedom for the spectators and the best possible safety standards for them. As the police are mainly associated with repression and restrictions, however, the presence of police forces is often resented by the fans.

[32]Directorate General IV (2003, p. 8) regarding the social support in the EU manual on the prevention of violence in sports.

[33]See Verrückte Köpfe Innsbruck (01 April 2009) www.vk91.at/neu/presseaus/index.php?id=110. Accessed 12 January 2015 (link no longer active).

To ensure continuous communication between, and coordination of the police forces, a joint operation control should be appointed for each match. This should consist of representatives of the Bundesliga, of the hosting club, of private security firms and stewards, medical services, fire brigade and representatives of the security authorities (§§ 4 Sec 3 of the Bundesliga safety guidelines). In this context, the security authorities have the final decision-making power.

8.3.2.1 Organisation

On a regional level, the 'Landespolizeidirektionen' (National Police Directorates) have been the highest security authorities since 1 September 2012. The 'Landespolizeidirektor' (National Police Director) is the highest police authority in each federal state. In this context, the former 'Sicherheitsdirektionen' (Security Directorates), 'Bundespolizeidirektionen' (Federal Police Directorates) and 'Landespolizeikommanden' (National Police Commands) were dissolved and included in this new organisation.[34]

With currently more than 23,000 police officers, the Austrian security police is responsible for all matters relating to internal safety in the fight against crime, danger defence and prevention. The Austrian security police law, SPG, forms the legal basis of the security authorities and its organs. The key tasks of the security police are the maintenance of public safety and law and order and the general obligation to provide service (§ 3 SPG). In terms of maintaining law and order (§ 27 SPG), there is an inherent duty to respect the rights of the individual and the community. Finally, the special monitoring service (§ 27a SPG) is a task of the security police.

It is obvious from these regulations, that in the end, the police have to provide for safety if in a certain situation (e.g. an event) those responsible cannot or do not want to guarantee peace, order and the safety of the public. In the context of major sports events, this can become relevant if the organiser made no or insufficient arrangements.[35] In principle, any intrusion upon a person's rights has to be proportionate so that the person is affected as little as possible. The intrusion needs to be proportionate to the severity of the offence or misbehaviour. In addition, actions by the police need to meet the ultima ratio principle; hence, only the most moderate means sufficient to serve the purpose has to be applied.[36] By observing these principle conditions, the police have the possibility to exercise immediate commands.[37]

At football matches, the tasks of the police are carried out by uniformed law enforcement officers, operational units (EE and a special unit in Vienna, called

[34]Austrian Ministry of Interior, (02 February 2013) www.bmi.gv.at/cms/bmi/_news/bmi.aspx?id=7A5A70765696E6E6F4C6F3D&page=0&view=1. Accessed 12 January 2015 (link no longer active).

[35]Mayer 2009, p. 17 1 ff.

[36]Thanner and Vogl 2010, p. 76 ff.

[37]Thanner and Vogl 2010, p. 138.

'Wiener Einsatzgruppe Alarmabteilung, WEGA'). They primarily carry out the duties of the maintenance of public safety and order (Grosser Sicherheits und Ordnungsdienst, GSOD). GSOD refers to the use of units of officers who carry out their normal duties in different police stations. At matches with an international dimension and at matches of the two highest divisions, SKB/spotters are usually brought into action. Their duty is to draw up risk analysis assessments in order that preventive measures can be taken to reduce the risk of disorder or violence. The trained SKB/spotters are law enforcement officers who either work full-time, or besides their work as police officers at major sports events such as football or ice hockey matches.[38]

Contrary to many other countries, the SKB/spotters (at the time of writing numbering 175) are active within the fan environment and enter into dialogue with fans during and after major sports events. They operate in at least pairs,[39] and in plain clothes. Attached to only one club, and remaining in permanent contact with its supporters, they accompany fans at both home and away matches. The main focus of the SKB/spotters is male Ultras aged between 16 and 25. Intense evaluation, investigation and educational work through observation and contact with the fan scene is sought in order to provide information on the danger and disposition for violence. In each sports club, where due to the size and the potential for danger of the fan groups, it is necessary, an SKB/spotter must be appointed. In this context, the National Football Information Point exercises supervisory control over SKB/spotters and the gathering and international exchange of sports-related data and recommendations. Pursuant to a resolution of the Council of the EU, this National Football Information Point was included in unit II/11 as the central liaison and coordinating body of fan prevention.[40]

8.3.2.2 Powers

The powers of the security authorities at sports events fall under the Austrian security police law, SPG, and the 'Richtlinienverordnung' (§ 31 SPG). In this context, the police are obliged to observe the principle of proportionality[41] (§ 29 SPG) and the ultima-ratio principle (§ 28 Sec 3 SPG). According to these principles, an individual's rights may only be infringed upon if such a power is laid down in the Austrian security police law, SPG. Here a very strict standard needs to be applied. These civil rights exist in addition to human rights guaranteed to Austrian citizens under the European Convention on Human Rights.

[38]Winter, Jaeger, Geissler 2013, p. 31.

[39]See ordinance of the Austrian Ministry of Interior, BMI-SI1810/0050-ZSA/2005.

[40]See BMI (01 July 2009) www.bmi.gv.at/cms/bmi/_news/bmi.aspx. Accessed on 26 January 2016.

[41]For example Jedelsky 2008, p. 197.

Apart from a first general obligation to render assistance (§ 19 SPG) and the special monitoring service, the security police has certain key tasks[42] to fulfil under § 87 SPG. Officers should primarily use their command authority ('Stop!'). Only if the person shows no reaction is the officer entitled to threaten and in further course exercise coercion (moving persons away).[43] If an offence or an administrative offence was committed, a person can, as a last consequence, be arrested if s/he, despite having been warned, continues with or repeats the offence and less restrictive means in the sense of § 35 Z 3 VStG are not possible anymore. In practice, § 27 SPG in particular includes unwritten rules of behaviour of the individuals in public under the observation of the rules of an orderly communal life like selective norms of society. Social control is operative through the norms of society. In connection with football matches, this can include loud conflicts or the breach of the pyrotechnic law as administrative criminal offences.

8.3.2.3 Operational Procedures (3-D Philosophy)

During the European Championships of 2008, Austrian security authorities utilised the '3-D' philosophy (see Table 8.1).[44] This is a step-by-step operational procedure for police at sports events.[45] The first D stands for the intense dialogue between the fans and the patrol duty, i.e. primarily SKB/spotters, and should mirror the preventive work of the police using the means of communication and information. In this context, observance of the streets and the stadium is of particular importance.

If a conflict has already arisen, such as a minor dispute in the stadium, police should communicate the legal situation and attempt to settle the dispute according to § 26 SPG, identity verification (§ 35 SPG) by the SKB/spotter or uniformed police forces should contribute to deescalating the situation. Only if there are no milder means available to deescalate a situation that has already got out of control (e.g. an affray involving many people) may the officers take drastic action and use the necessary means to restore public safety and order.[46]

---

[42]In detail Hauer and Keplinger 2005, §§ 19 ff.

[43]Jedelsky 2008, p. 199.

[44]Austrian Ministry of Interior 2007, p. 1ff. Bundesministerium für Inneres (Hg.) (2007): Empfehlungen für die Durchführung von Public Viewing im Rahmen der EURO 2008 - Schweiz. In: Enquete EURO 2008. Public Viewing - Das ganze Land wird Stadion! Maßnahmen der Bundesregierung. Wien, 1–15.

[45]See also Adang and Schreiber 2008, p. 59 ff; Adang O, Stott C (2004) Evaluation of public order policing during EURO 2004. http://policestudies.homestead.com/Euro2004evaluation.html. Accessed 29 January 2015. According to these authors, based on empirically documented findings with regard to the EURO 2004, the choice of as many police measures related to the concrete risk as possible is key and comprehensive gathering of information during the event is inevitable (so-called low or high-profile approach).

[46]Concerning the problems with regard to the preparation of the EURO, see Steiner 2008, p. 19.

Table 8.1 3-D-Philosophy, Winter/Klob

	Dialogue	De-escalation	Drastic action
Who?	SKB/spotters	SKB uniformed force	Uniformed forces (esp. EE, WEGA)
How?	Set up contact network with the fans (information)	Communicate with fans highlighting legal consequences of actions conflict management	Consistent action
When?	Beyond the match (long-term)	Concrete situation at the match	No other approach possible
Why?	Prevention	Maintenance of public safety	Restoring public safety

8.4 Safety Management in Football

8.4.1 Police Measures

In recent years, measures implemented by the police have played a key role in safety management in Austrian stadia in relation to safety-relevant behaviour of fans.[47] In the top two leagues during 2010/11, 1,158 police reports of fan misbehaviour were recorded. More than 50 % of these reports related to administrative criminal law offences such as disturbances affecting the maintenance of law and order, and breaches of pyrotechnic law. Only a quarter of the reports related to criminal offences under the Austrian Criminal Law Act. In the first division, 46 arrests were carried out under administrative criminal law and another 32 arrests under the Criminal Procedure Act. In addition, 547 identity verifications and 92 stadium expulsions were recorded. A further 282 reports were recorded relating to offences under the Austrian Criminal Law Act and supplementary statutes, 268 of which concerned the tipp3-Bundesliga. Of these offences, more than a quarter concerned damage to property (§§ 125, 126 Austrian Criminal Code, StGB), another quarter concerned common assault (§§ 83, 84 StGB) and more than one fifth of the offences reported concerned obstructing a police officer in the course of his/her duty (§§ 169, 170 StGB). Insult made up 6 % of all cases recorded. Another 6 % of the reports related to theft or robbery (§§ 127, 128, 131, 141, 142 StGB). Other reports concerned the endangering of public safety (§ 89 StGB), affray (§ 91 StGB), duress (§ 105 StGB), threat (§ 107 StGB) and other offences. In this context, the amendment[48] of the SPG that entered into force on 01.01.2007 (BGBl I 2007/113) provided not only further measures in an effort to prevent violence at major sports events but also extended the security authorities' special powers.[49]

[47]Concerning international police work, see Baasch 2009, p. 67.

[48]Andre 2008, p. 117 f.

[49]Austrian Ministry of Interior, ordinance dated 29.05.2009, 3.

8.4.1.1 Safety Area (§ 49a Section 1 SPG)

Using this measure and independent from a stadium ban, the police are also permitted to eject individuals from a safety area surrounding a sports stadium, thereby preventing them from entering the stadium. Here SKB/spotters are also entitled to take action and take or recommend measures.[50]

8.4.1.2 Expulsion and Prohibition to Enter (§ 49a Section 2 SPG)

Expulsion is another area relevant to the work of SKB/spotters. If a safety area is established around a sports venue, the police are entitled to expel individuals and prevent them from entering the stadium.[51] Individuals can be expelled if there is the likelihood of violence or disorder in the safety area following previous incidents, in light of other indicating factors, or the registration of a spectator on the database of violent criminals. If a person violates the expulsion order, s/he can be arrested for committing an administrative offence under § 84 Sec 1 Z 5.[52] In this context, police officers are also entitled to verify identification. The individual must be informed about the duration of the prohibition to enter and s/he may be expelled using coercion. An individual violating this order may be arrested under § 35 VStG.[53]

8.4.1.3 *Gefährderansprache* (Appeal, § 49b SPG)

The biggest—and for the police most relevant—field of activity is an appeal by the police to the troublemakers' address. This is the least instructive SPG measure. It aims at teaching lawful behaviour. It is a prerequisite for § 49b SPG that the person has attracted attention for an administrative offence under §§ 81 and 82 SPG or pyrotechnic law 2010 (PyroTG 2010) in connection with major sports events and that it is likely that this individual may commit such offences in the future.[54] Here a file note has to be prepared and then passed to the SKD (SKB/spotter Coordination and unit II/11).[55] In this case, the SKD is sought to collaborate with the authority and provide an assessment of the likelihood that future offences will be committed.[56]

---

[50] See expert interview A3, Z: 102–102; Ad, Z: 373-377; A20, Z: 188-214; A21, Z: 79-81.

[51] Mayer 2009, p. 207. The author explains that a prerequisite for the power to point away persons is the existence of a safety area.

[52] For more detail on the 'Ausübung of Zwangsgewalt' in connection with expulsion and prohibition to return: Mayer 2009, p. 210.

[53] Austrian Ministry of Interior, ordinance dated 29.05.2009,10 f.

[54] Thanner and Vogl 2010, p. § 49b, 451.

[55] Austrian Ministry of Interior, ordinance dated 29.05.2009, 4 f.

[56] Austrian Ministry of Interior, ordinance dated 29.05.2009, 5.

8.4.1.4 *Meldeauflagen* (Duties to Report, § 49c SPG)

§ 49c SPG regulates the conditions and the duty to report for supporters considered to pose a risk of violence or disorder. Duties to report aim at both teaching a person lawful behaviour and keeping him/her away from the sports event. For this purpose, the person has to attend a police station. It is a prerequisite for the issuance of a duty to report that in the past two years the person has attracted attention for violent behaviour or for breach of a prohibition to enter in connection with major sports events and that this person shows potential for danger through this behaviour.[57] Duties to report are police decisions. Violent behaviour is in this case considered to be the exercising of violence in connection with a dangerous attack against life, health or someone else's property. Force may be used if necessary to make an individual served with a duty to report to fulfil their obligations in this respect.[58] The person has to be informed about his/her previous behaviour, his/her potential for danger and the legal consequences for such behaviour.[59] The duty to report must not last for more than 1 h. The individual must be invited to appear in person by official notification. The file note regarding the duty to report also has to be brought to the attention of the SKB/Spotter Coordination and unit II/11[60] and SKB/Spotter Coordination should collaborate with the authority.

8.4.1.5 Video Surveillance (§ 54 SPG)

Video surveillance may only be used by security authorities if it is necessary for securing safety in the stadium. With the help of this, dangerous situations should be detected and evaluated early on the monitors so that preventive measures can be taken.[61] In this regard, SKB/spotters can be used to support the identification of persons on the ground.

8.4.1.6 Databases

The security authorities have also made increasing use of the exchange of personal data. The centralised gathering of information is considered to be of great importance in both a national and international context. Since the introduction of § 57 Sec 1 z 11a SPG on 01.01.2006 (BGBl I 2005/158; BGBl I 2007/113) security authorities are entitled to identify:

- names, former names, gender
- nationality

[57]Mayer 2009, p. 190 ff; expert interview A22, Z: 69–71.

[58]Thanner and Vogl 2010, § 49b, 472.

[59]Austrian Ministry of Interior, ordinance dated 29.05.2009, 5.

[60]Austrian Ministry of Interior, ordinance dated 29.05.2009, 5.

[61]Hauer and Kepplinger 2011, § 54, 592.

- date of birth, place of birth and address
- name of the parents and alias data of a person

If an individual is registered as 'Gewalttäter-Sportgroßveranstaltungen' (violent offenders—major sports events) this record exists for all future events.[62] The registration is made by the security authority that is relevant for the offence committed.[63] A person is registered as 'violent offender—sport' if it is believed they are likely to engage in violence or disorder in the future. This prognosis is made by the SKB/spotter who best knows the individual. Therefore, information from the SKB/spotter and other findings can be an indicator for the future perpetration of an offence.[64] The SKB/spotter is responsible for the recording and the administration of the data during a sports event. The data has to be deleted 2 years after the last recording.[65]

8.4.2 Ground Regulations or 'House Rules'

The Bundesliga safety guidelines are binding directives aimed at protecting spectators at Bundesliga matches. They apply to both the home and the visiting club. For the maintenance of safety in the stadium, the regulations also contain sanctions that can be imposed by the Bundesliga or the ÖFB in the event of misbehaviour by fans and breaches by the club. In order to maintain safety in the stadium, football clubs mainly make use of security and order services[66] and transfer the respective ground regulations (or 'house rules') of the organiser onto these service providers. Thus, tasks relating to order around stadia are either the responsibility of club stewards or private security firms.[67] The requirements and tasks are the same for internal or external services. The number of stewards to be appointed depends on the local conditions (number of entrances and exits, emergency exits, fence-free stands), the number of expected spectators and the perceived potential danger of the event.[68] If a match is considered low risk in advance, one marshal for 100 spectators is considered to be sufficient, while at risk matches the proportion is

[62]Austrian Ministry of Interior, ordinance dated 29.05.2009, 7 ff.

[63]According to the Austrian Ministry of Interior, on 30.06.2011 311 persons were registered as 'Gewalttäter Sport' (violent sport offenders).

[64]Mayer 2009, p. 165.

[65]Austrian Ministry of Interior, ordinance dated 29.05.2009, 7 ff.

[66]Similar in the German Bundesliga, Krahm 2008, p. 77.

[67]Regarding the responsibility under adminstrative criminal law, Mayer 2009, p. 138.

[68]Bundesliga 2009: Nr. 8.4.3.2.

1:75 and at high risk matches 1:50.[69] The main tasks of a security and order service in a stadium are access control, safety in the sector and conflict management. In practice, stewards and security staff are often fans of the club that they are responsible for and this has the potential to impact upon their concentration at the expense of safety.[70]

8.4.2.1 Stadium Bans

As the owner of the stadium, the club has the legal authority to issue house rules that make access to the stadium dependent on certain conditions (behaviour, forbidden items) and that set out the consequences of not abiding by these rules.[71] In practice, it is the role of private security and order services to ensure that the stadium regulations are adhered to. According to Bundesliga regulations, spectators that have violated the house and stadium rules of the club can be sanctioned by the club. The committee for stadia and safety of the ÖFB can also issue a stadium ban for a duration of between 10 months and up to 10 years throughout Austria if their behaviour has affected or endangered safety and order. In this case, the person is denied access to the stadium. However, only if that person is registered on the database of violent offenders, or included in a list of violent offenders of another country, can s/he be expelled from a safety area by the police.[72]

Stadium bans are not police measures. They are preventive measures based on a civil law imposed solely by the organiser under the house rules.[73] Their aim is to curtail spectator violence and prevent behaviour that may risk the safety of other spectators. Local bans restricted to one stadium can be imposed for the duration of 2–6 months once a year. In the event of a recurrence (similar or identical violation) that requires a stadium ban throughout Austria imposed by the Bundesliga (senate 3), this can be imposed for between 6 months and 2 years.[74] An individual banned from all Austrian stadia can appeal to the protest committee. Should a banned supporter be found inside a stadium or a prohibited local area while serving a ban, it will be extended for an additional year.

---

[69]See News, interview with Michael Zoratti (02 April 2008) www.news.at/articles/0642/270/154351/sicherheits-experte-fußball-em-2008-nicht-hochrisiko-spiele. Accessed 12 January 2015.

[70]In more detail Zoratti 2007, p. 54.

[71]Mayer 2009, p. 263.

[72]In April 2011, 41 stadium bans imposed by the Bundesliga and 6 stadium bans for all over Austria imposed by the ÖFB were brought to the attention of the Austrian Ministry of Interior, see Austrian Ministry of Interior 2011c, 9.

[73]See also the decision of the Council of Europe dated 17.11.2003 on the bans on access to venues of football matches with an international dimension (2003/C281/01).

[74]Regarding the reform of stadium bans in Germany (effective from 31 March 2008) based on the 'Positionspapiere zur notwendigen Überarbeitung der Stadionverbots-Richtlinien' der Interessengemeinschaft der Fanorganisationen (Unsere Kurve) (07 September 2008) www.unserekurve.de/cms/pages/materialien.php. Accessed 12 January 2015.

In certain circumstances a stadium ban can be prematurely annulled if close examination involving the locally competent security authority—in particular SKB/spotters—leads to the finding that the person concerned will at future football matches behave peaceably or if the person concerned can prove his/her innocence or s/he is acquitted of the offence leading to the imposition of the ban by the courts. A record of all stadium bans is stored in a database of the Bundesliga and information on bans is shared on a regular basis with relevant clubs. Typical grounds for a stadium ban include repeated aggressive behaviour against stewards/executives (2 months), a report for common assault (6 months) or the use of fireworks and/or dangerous pyrotechnic items (e.g. 'supercobras') in the stadium (24 months).

8.4.2.2 Pyrotechnics

Alongside flags and loud chants, there is increased use of pyrotechnic items with special smoke and colour development. Pyrotechnic Law 1974 was replaced by Pyrotechnic Law 2010[75] thereby implementing European directive 2007/23/EG.[76] The heat generated from pyrotechnics has the potential to lead to crowd surges and health risks from smoke inhalation, both of which pose a risk for spectators.[77] The new law increases the range of punishments for fans setting off pyrotechnics and categorises devices according to risk. The designated use and the degree of dangerousness are now relevant in order to improve the safety of the user.[78]

A special regulation for sports events is included in the 2010 Law. Under Section 39 PyroTG 2010, pyrotechnic items may not be possessed or used at sports events[79] and a maximum fine of 4,360 Euro can be imposed on individuals who violate this prohibition (§ 39 s 2 PyroTG 2010).[80] However, this has led to significant fan resistance; the initiative "Pyrotechnic is not a Crime"[81] resulted from a union of fan clubs who have campaigned to decriminalise pyrotechnics. The initiative sought to show that pyrotechnics usually causes no damage and that contrary to the statements of the Ministry, they pose no risk for people.

According to police and representatives of the clubs interviewed in the research, pyrotechnics, mainly Bengal Fire (flares), are widely used at fan marches. However, the use of pyrotechnics inside the stadium is deemed considerably more

[75]BGBl I 131/2009.

[76]See Directive 2007/23/EG of the European Parliament and of the Council dated 23.05.2007, 2007/L 154/1; Salimi 2010, p. 88.

[77]Winter and Klob 2011, p. 52 f.

[78]Salimi 2010, p. 88.

[79]The ban starts with the first spectators entering the stadium and ends after they left the stadium after the event.

[80]PyroTG 1974, § 31 and PyroTG 2010, § 40.

[81]See Pyrotechik ist kein Verbrechen (16 December 2009) www.pyrotechnik-ist-kein-verbrechen.at. Accessed 12 January 2015.

dangerous. Research data indicated that despite inspections at entrances, fans have little problem getting pyrotechnics inside stadia, either hiding them in the stadium prior to match-day or smuggling them in on match-day. Ultra groups were considered to be especially well organised in this regard. Typically while one group held banners to block the sight line of video cameras, another group covered their faces and lit smoke pots so that yet another group in the protection of the smoke was able to set off flares. The tactics of the fans makes it extremely difficult for the police to identify individual offenders.

However, the authorities can grant exceptions for organisers of special events. Permission can be granted if the person is deemed reliable and of a certain age, and if, considering the circumstances, the planned use of the pyrotechnic items guarantees that there is no danger for life, health and property of people or public safety and that unacceptable noise is avoided (§ 39 Sec 3 PyroTG 2010).

8.5 Conclusions

This chapter provides an overview of the most important statutory laws and governing body regulations relating to fans at football matches in Austria. Mirroring national regulations and ordinances for the maintenance of safety in football stadia, five components in the field of safety can be identified, that in observing their key competences on the one hand exert themselves for the support of the fans but on the other hand limit the rights and freedom of the fans: clubs, ÖFB and Bundesliga, private security and order services, fan work and police.

Currently, the illegal use of pyrotechnic items in the stadium poses one of the main problems for the Bundesliga. For many fans, lighting up fireworks is a major part of creative fan choreography and a typical expression of fan freedom. Despite the fact that the rules in the PyroTG 2010 and possible sanctions such as stadium bans are clearly defined, there is disagreement within the clubs regarding the questions of whether pyrotechnics can/should be banned from the stadia. Furthermore, the clubs suffer a conflict of interest between generating ‘atmosphere’ in support of their team, and the safety requirements. Often they do not distance themselves from the misbehaviour of their fans.

Education and communication with fans to highlight the laws and regulations are of vital importance. A club distancing itself from fan misbehaviour does not harm the attachment of the fans to the club—on the contrary. It facilitates peaceful fans, especially families with children attending stadia and prevents the reputational damage of the club. However, those fans that have previously been involved in physical disorder or violence, and the use of pyrotechnics, can also be actively included in the club family; they do not necessarily have to be excluded. Especially with regard to young people, new ways can be found to generate positive fan atmosphere and to effectively curtail negative behaviour thereby satisfying the interests of the club and the majority of its fans.

The findings of the above-mentioned empirical studies provide information as to what extent safety strategies, plans of action and reaction from the fans and the safety field experts can influence football. The nature and the scope of the use of police powers is governed in the SPG but the majority of fans interviewed in season 2007/08 considered the relationship between the police and the fans to be poor. Police were not welcome in the stadium by many fans and amongst 'risk fans', the police were typically perceived to be an 'enemy'. The majority of those interviewed also believed that uniformed police and police dressed in heavy protective clothing provoked disorder and that there should be less visual police presence in the stadium.

The use of uniformed forces in the stadium should be as proportionate and low profile as the situation allows. Separating the police into smaller groups around the stadium instead of them converging as a total unit could also have a positive influence on the behaviour of the fans. Police action should always be proportionate to the actual danger; here professional analysis of the danger by specially trained officers on the ground (SKB/spotters) is essential. As a link between the club, fans and police, they are of particular importance in assessing the situation. However, SKB/spotters often find themselves in an ambiguous position between supporting the legitimate intentions of fans and more traditional 'police work'. It is therefore essential that these officers are provided with appropriate and substantial training. The cooperation of the SKB/spotters with uniformed forces is necessary, as is the balance between preventive and necessary repressive measures. Only in this way can the balance between guaranteeing the greatest possible freedom of fans as well as realistically securing their safety be reached.

References

Adang O, Schreiber M (2008) Intelligentes Management von Großereignissen. die "Low Profile"-Ansatz. SIAK-Journal 1:57–66

Andre P (2008) Sichere Sportgroßveranstaltungen. Öffentliche Sicherheit 3–4:117–118

Baasch S (2009) Herstellung von Sicherheit und Produktion von Kontrollräumen im Kontext von Großevents: die Fußball-Weltmeisterschaft 2006 in Hamburg. Dissertation. Hamburg

Bundesliga, österreichische (Hg.) (2007a) Sicherheitsrichtlinien für die Bewerbe der österreichischen Bundesliga, gültig ab dem Spieljahr 2007/2008. Wien

Bundesliga, österreichische (Hg.) (2008b) Sicherheitsrichtlinien für die Bewerbe der österreichischen Bundesliga, gültig ab dem Spieljahr 2008/2009. Wien

Feßl J (1993) Veranstaltungsrecht. Dissertation. Vienna

Hauer A, Keplinger R (2005) Sicherheitspolizeigesetz—Kommentar. Linde Verlag, Vienna

Horak R, Reiter W, Stocker K (1985) Soccer Hooliganism. Theoretische Überlegungen und erste empirisch-systematische Überprüfung der Fußballgewalt in Österreich. Eine Studie der Projektgruppe, Fußballrowdytum in Österreich. Vienna

Jedelsky P (2008) Der polizeiliche Einsatz bei Sportgroßveranstaltungen. In: Grundei A, Karollus M (eds) Berufssportrecht I—Schwerpunkt Fußballsport. Jan Sramek Verlag, Linz/Vienna, pp. 195–221

Krahm B (2008) Polizeiliche Maßnahmen zur Eindämmung von Hooligangewalt. Schriften zum Recht der Inneren Sicherheit 10, Richard Boorberg Verlag, Stuttgart

Limberger F (2003) Zur Struktur der österreichischen Fußball-Bundesliga. In: Karrollus M, Achatz M, Jabornegg P (eds) Aktuelle Rechtsfragen des Fußballsports III. Linde Verlag, Vienna, pp. 97–99

Mayer M (2009) Öffentliche Sicherheit und Ordnung in Sportstadien, Veranstaltungsrecht, Sicherheitspolizei, private Sicherheitsdienste. Jan Sramek Verlag, Vienna

Österreichischer Fußball-Bund (2007) Satzungen des Vereines Österreichischer Fußball-Bund, p. 1ff. Wien

Österreichischer Fußball-Bund (2008) Vorschriften für die Strafausschüsse. Wien

Österreichischer Fußball-Bund (2009) ÖFB-Rechtspflegeordnung. Wien

Sabitzer W (2005) Sicherheit bei Sportgroßveranstaltungen. Freundliche Spiele. Öffentliche Sicherheit 11–12:6–12

Salimi F (2010) Pyrotechnik- und Sprengmittelrecht. Öffentliche Sicherheit 5–6:88–89

Steiner K (2008) Das Match um die Sicherheit. GÖD-Magazin 4:18–19

Thanner T, Vogl M (2010) SPG—Sicherheitspolizeigesetz—Kommentar. Neuer Wissenschaftlicher Verlag, Vienna/Graz

Wess N (2008) Rechtliche Rahmenbedingungen bei Durchführung von Sportveranstaltungen, insbesondere Fußball. Grundei A, Karollus M (eds) Berufssportrecht I—Schwerpunkt Fußballsport. Jan Sramek Verlag, Linz/Vienna, pp. 177–193

Winter K (2007) Blitzlichter in Rot-Weiß-Rot. Egoth, Vienna

Winter IC, Klob B (2011) Fußball und Sicherheit in Österreich. Verlag für Polizeiwissenschaft, Vienna

Winter IC, Jaeger B, Geissler P (2012) Neue Ausbildung für szenekundige Beamte—zur Entwicklung von internationalen Ausbildungsstandards. SIAK Journal 3:47–57

Winter IC, Jaeger B, Geissler P (2013) New Training for Spotters—Development for Spotters. Journal for Police Science and Practice, International Edition 31–41

Zoratti M (2007) Sicher ist sicher. Sicherheit bei Veranstaltungen. WKO, Vienna

Chapter 9
Legal Responses to 'Football Hooliganism' in Ukraine

Alla Shvets

Abstract This chapter analyses the legal regulation of 'football hooliganism' in Ukraine. Euro 2012 provided an incentive to introduce wide-ranging legal regulation, inter alia in the field of ensuring public order and public safety in connection with football matches, and with respect to liability approaches of football supporters. 'Best practices' common in other countries, such as police 'spotters', an international centre for police cooperation and a National Information Football Point were implemented. Finally, football banning orders were introduced. However, while these limitations and restrictions on football supporters were designed to address football-related violence, the civil and human rights of football supporters were not always sufficiently taken into account.

Keywords Football · Hooliganism · Public safety · Public order · Offence · Crime · Fans · Ultras · Ukraine

Contents

Alla Shvets is Lead Legal Advisor, 'Direct Sight Acquisition' Ltd. (U.A. Inter Media Group), Kyiv, Ukraine and a Member of the Legal Committee of the Basketball Federation of Ukraine.

A. Shvets (✉)
Kyiv, Ukraine
e-mail: alla_shvets@mail.ru

A. Tsoukala et al. (eds.), *Legal Responses to Football "Hooliganism" in Europe*,
ASSER International Sports Law Series, DOI 10.1007/978-94-6265-108-1_9

9.1 Introduction

This chapter highlights the basic legal approaches to the management of football crowds and the prevention of football-related violence and disorder in Ukraine, and assesses the respective measures with a focus on the human rights of spectators. Legal regulation of football hooliganism aims to ensure public safety and public order in connection with football matches and imposes legal responsibility for football-related violence. Sect. 9.2 explores football 'hooliganism' as a social phenomenon in Ukraine. Sect. 9.3 analyses the development and the basic provisions of Ukrainian legislation with respect to ensuring public order and public safety in connection with football matches. Sect. 9.4 examines 'hooliganism' as an offence under administrative and criminal legislation and sports associations' regulations. Finally, Sect. 9.5 draws some conclusions and gives a number of recommendations regarding the legal regulation of football supporters. Throughout this chapter, special attention is paid to the civil rights of football spectators under the Constitution of Ukraine, and the application of the proportionality and legality principles when imposing different measures of a restrictive and prohibitive nature on football supporters.

9.2 'Football Hooliganism' as Social Phenomenon in Ukraine

Organised fan culture in Ukraine is a relatively new phenomenon. The largest fan groups appeared in the 1980s and consisted mostly of supporters of Dynamo Kyiv, the oldest Ukrainian football club. In the Soviet era the majority of violent inter-fan conflicts were between Dynamo supporters and fans of Spartak Moscow. Tensions between the supporter groups increased from 1986 onwards, following the success of Dynamo on the national and European stage. On 20 September 1987, one of the most notorious incidents between supporters in Soviet times took place. The incident occurred after the end of the match, when a mass fight involving around 400 Muscovites and 500 Kyivans occurred at Central Kyiv railway station.[1] Tensions between Ukrainian and Russian supporters have remained following Ukraine's independence.

After the collapse of the Soviet Union, domestic disorder decreased. However, at the end of the 1990s, as a result of the growing competition between Ukrainian clubs, new fan groups emerged and old rivalries were revived. Subsequently, football-related incidents of violence and disorder have become more frequent.

Football spectators are generally divided into the following categories:[2]

(a) Supporters—the largest group, which includes those who are interested in football, who wear team/club symbols, but who are not organised or familiar with fan chants and songs and who do not regularly visit away matches.
(b) Fans—actively support their team inside and outside the stadium, regularly attend both home and away matches and are sometimes involved in incidents. The majority of Ukrainian fans who call themselves Ultras support their team through bright visual, pyrotechnic and sound displays. Football clubs keep in touch with such groups and provide them with special season-passes to their matches.
(c) Football hooligans[3]—hooligans are not only interested in football, but also actively seek football-related violence. They usually dress in 'casual' clothes and do not wear club symbols. The main element of football hooligan groups is the so-called 'firm', consisting of up to 20 individuals. Firms usually consist of students or working people between 15 and 25 years of age. Hooligans participate in football-related violence, the so-called 'makhach'. The leaders of these groups typically arrange fights in advance, choosing solitary places to avoid the interference of third parties. 'Makhach' is held under an internal code of conduct, in accordance with certain rules such as the prohibition of the use of weapons and the prohibition of beating combatants when they are down. However, sometimes these rules are violated. For example, on 22 July 2012 an unplanned 'makhach' between hooligans of various Kyivan football clubs took place in the centre of Kyiv, prior to the derby between Dynamo and Arsenal, which resulted in the serious injury of a number of participants.[4]

The Ultra movement in Ukraine has the following subcultural features: Ultras are involved in the movement mainly because of friends and relatives; the choice of their preferred team is determined by regional self-identification; Ultras have their own internal hierarchy and the groups are inhomogeneous in nature; the movement is based on fans' initiatives and input and exists because of their own material support (as opposed to the official fan clubs which depend on, and are primarily financed by, the football clubs); Ultras treat the club symbols sacredly

[1] Pylypenko 2007, p. 158.

[2] See Golubovych 2009 and Borodavko 2012, pp. 413–415 and Pavelchuk 2009, p. 336.

[3] Football hooligans are also sometimes treated as a subcategory of football fans or Ultras.

[4] See www.rbc.ua/ukr/newsline/show/po-faktu-draki-fanatov-dinamo-i-arsenala-vozbuzhdeno-ugolovnoe-23072012170300. Accessed December 7, 2014.

and have their own chants, claims, slang (which is developed to such a degree, that a third person might not understand a conversation between Ultras); in many cases Ultras support extreme right-wing nationalistic ideology; and finally Ultras object to the commercialisation of football.[5]

The main tensions between Ukrainian fan groups are based on:

(a) the rivalry between teams traditionally contesting the national championship (e.g. the rivalry between Dynamo Kyiv and Shakhtar Donetsk);
(b) specific incidents (for example between Shakhtar and Metalurh Zaporizhzhia, after supporters from Donetsk were unexpectedly attacked by hooligans in Zaporizhzhia)[6];
(c) historical reasons (fans of Dynamo Kyiv, Dnipro Dnipropetrovsk and Karpaty Lviv traditionally maintain friendly relations with each other and oppose to the supporters of Arsenal Kyiv, Chornomorets Odesa and Metalurh Zaporizhzhia because of the latter's close relations with Muscovite clubs established during the Soviet era)[7];
(d) ideological reasons (the confrontation between the majority of Ukrainian football clubs' fans supporting right-wing ideology and the supporters of Arsenal Kyiv famous for their left-wing ideology and sometimes even anti-Ukrainian views);
(e) territorial reasons (Shakhtar Donetsk and Zoria Luhansk, Dynamo Kyiv and Arsenal Kyiv).

A further complicating factor relating to football-related violence in Ukraine is the relationship between football supporters and law-enforcement bodies. A number of incidents of football-related violence have occurred between fans and the militia (police). On 27 May 2007, during the final match of the Cup of Ukraine between Dynamo and Shakhtar, mass disorder between fans and the 'Berkut' (special police) left 300 individuals injured.[8] The disorder occurred when several fans lit fireworks in the stands. After the incident, a video of a member of the 'Berkut' attacking an unarmed young girl was widely shown in the media.[9] After this incident, a criminal investigation was launched into abuse of powers by members of 'Berkut'.[10]

As a result of such incidents, the maintenance of public order and security inside the stadium has gradually been transferred to private security forces. On 1 January 2012 the responsibility for public order was entrusted to the sports facility operator and event organiser, when the Law of Ukraine 'On Aspects of Ensuring

[5]See Solovyova 2012, pp. 135–142.

[6]Ibid., pp. 136–137.

[7]Pavelchuk 2009, p. 336.

[8]See Kyrylenko and Pozhydaev 2011, p. 48.

[9]See www.censor.net.ua/news/9899/izbienie_fanatov_quotorlami_tsushkoquot_na_matche_quotdinamoquot__quotshahterquot_svidetelstva_ochevidtsa. Accessed December 7, 2014.

[10]See www.pravda.com.ua/rus/articles/2007/06/14/4419903/. Accessed December 7, 2014.

Public Order and Public Safety in Connection With Preparing and Hosting Football Matches' came into force.[11]

Fans often use football matches for political expression. On 7 August 2011, during a match between Dynamo Kyiv and Karpaty Lviv, several Dynamo fans attacked a stadium worker who attempted to remove a flag of the Karpaty supporters depicting the historic leader of the Ukrainian national-patriotic movement, Roman Shukhevich. When the match was interrupted to enable medical staff to assist the injured worker, Dynamo supporters initiated a chant denouncing the new president.[12] As a result of this incident, a number of oppressive measures were taken against football fans throughout Ukraine, including stricter searches while entering the stadia, confiscation of certain symbols, a prohibition on certain traditional chants (including certain traditional Ukrainian chants, such as 'Slava Ukraini!—Geroyam Slava!'[13]), and 'preventive' questioning of fans by the militia.[14] In response to these measures in November 2011 Ultras of Shakhtar, who had always opposed their rivals Dynamo, made a statement of support by refusing to actively support their football club as a sign of protest against the measures taken by law-enforcement bodies.[15] Later, the Supreme Council accepted a Bill,[16] which included administrative liability of football fans for demonstration of banners of a political nature (the Bill will be discussed in more detail in Sect. 9.4). The Bill resulted in almost unanimous protest among the Ultras movement in Ukraine. The summary of the Bill acknowledges that some of the measures proposed as administrative offences constituted infringments upon citizens' constitutionally protected rights of freedom of thought and speech and free expression of views and beliefs.[17] These expressions therefore cannot be considered unlawful, because they do not constitute a social danger and are not sufficiently damaging in order to be treated as offences.[18] However, it is important to ensure the protection of supporters' fundamental right to freedom of speech which is extremely crucial for developing countries.

---

[11]Law of Ukraine 'On Aspects of Ensuring Public Order and Public Safety in Connection With Preparing and Hosting Football Matches' No. 3673 dated July 8, 2011.

[12]Korrespondent (2011) Thank you to Donbas inhabitants. The Dynamo fans' chant has gathered approximately a million of views in Youtube. http://korrespondent.net/sport/football/1279048-spasibo-zhitelyam-donbassa-rechevka-fanatov-dinamo-nabrala-bolee-milliona-prosmotrov-na-youtube. Accessed December 7, 2014.

[13]Translated as 'Glory to Ukraine!–Glory to Heroes!'.

[14]See www.pravda.com.ua/news/2011/10/26/6705917/. Accessed December 7, 2014.

[15]See www.champion.com.ua/football/2011/10/21/465562/. Accessed December 7, 2014.

[16]Bill on amending of certain legislative acts (in respect to ensuring public order and safety prior, during and after football matches) (Reg. No. 9662 dated December 29, 2011) http://w1.c1.rada.gov.ua/pls/zweb2/webproc4_1?pf3511=42250. Accessed December 7, 2014 (link no longer active).

[17]Ukraine is also a signatory to the European Convention on Human Rights, raising issues here under Article 10 (Freedom of Expression).

[18]See http://w1.c1.rada.gov.ua/pls/zweb2/webproc4_1?pf3511=42250. Accessed December 7, 2014 (link no longer active).

The political activity of Ukrainian ultras can also be seen in their active support of the 'Euromaidan Revolution 2014'[19] and their active voluntary entry into the Ukrainian military forces fighting in the west of Ukraine.[20]

9.3 Measures Ensuring Public Order and Public Safety in Connection with Preparing and Hosting Football Matches

9.3.1 Evolution of Legislation

An important step in regulating football-related disorder was the accession to the European Convention on Spectator Violence and Misbehaviour at Sports Events and in particular at Football Matches, which came into effect on 1 May 2002.[21] On 29 June 2004 the Cabinet of Ministers of Ukraine adopted the 'Procedure of Organisation of Activities ensuring Public Order and Safety during Football Matches', implementing the provisions of the European Convention.[22]

When Ukraine and Poland jointly secured the right to host the European Football Championship Final Tournament 2012 (Euro 2012), there was a strong incentive to adapt Ukrainian legislation on the regulation of football matches in accordance with European standards and UEFA requirements. Ukraine enacted a number of legislative and non-legislative acts aiming at ensuring public order and public safety in connection with Euro 2012 and football matches in general. On 17 September 2008, the Cabinet of Ministers of Ukraine adopted the 'Integrated Concept of Ensuring Safety and Legal Order during Preparing and Hosting Euro 2012 in Ukraine'.[23] This Concept outlines the major issues and tasks associated with organising Euro 2012 and the measures needed while preparing for the tournament. In doing so, the Cabinet in effect admitted a lack of legislative regulation of these issues. On 8 July 2011 the Supreme Council of Ukraine adopted the Law of Ukraine 'On Aspects of Ensuring Public Order and Public Safety in Connection

[19]DSNEWS.UA (2014) Why football ultras support Euromaidan even in pro-governmental regions: comments of fan and member of "Right Sector". http://www.dsnews.ua/politics/pochemu-futbolnye-ultras-podderzhivayut-evromaidan-dazhe-v-provlastnyh-regionah-kommentarii-fanata-i-radikala-iz-pravogo-sektora. Accessed December 7, 2014.

[20]See http://ua.tribuna.com/tribuna/blogs/editors/649262.html. Accessed December 7, 2014.

[21]European Convention on Spectator Violence and Misbehaviour at Sports Events and in particular at Football Matches dated August 19, 1985/Official Gazette of Ukraine as of March 15, 2006.

[22]Decree of Cabinet of Ministers of Ukraine 'On adoption of the Procedure of Organization of Activities Ensuring Public Order and Safety during the Football Matches', No. 823 dated June 29, 2004.

[23]Instruction of Cabinet of Ministers of Ukraine 'On adoption of Integrated Concept of Ensuring safety and legal order while preparation and hosting in Ukraine of European Football Championship Final Tournament in 2012', No. 1244-r dated September 17, 2008.

With Preparing and Hosting Football Matches'[24] (the 'Safety Law') which entered into force on 1 January 2012. On 25 April 2012, the Cabinet of Ministers of Ukraine enacted 'The Procedure of Organisation of Activities ensuring Public Order and Safety while Hosting Football Matches'[25] (the 'Safety Procedure') to implement the provisions of the Safety Law. The Safety Law and the Safety Procedure remain the main instruments regulating public safety and public order in connection with football matches.

9.3.2 Basic Principles of Ensuring Public Order and Public Safety at Football Matches and the Legal Status of Spectators

The Safety Law regulates the organisational and legal aspects of public order and public safety at football matches. The Safety Law is applicable to all professional football matches in the Championship, the Series, the Cup of Ukraine and the Supercup of Ukraine and other football matches under the auspices of FIFA and/or UEFA held on the territory of Ukraine.[26] It defines the term 'public safety' as the protection of 'vital interests' (material and moral values) of society from sources of danger while preparing and hosting football matches, and ensuring the prevention of damage by such sources of danger. 'Public order' is defined as a complex of social relations ensuring the 'normal conditions' of vital human activity and the activities of entities, institutions and organisations while preparing and hosting football matches by means of the imposition, adherence to, and realisation of, legal and ethical norms.[27]

Article 4 of the Safety Law states that maintaining public order and safety shall be based on the principle of legality; the prevention of spectator violence, misbehaviour, antisocial and racist expressions; the implementation of preventive measures; the establishment of beneficial relations between the various stakeholders; mutual respect; and the quest for compromise, transparency, publicity, and responsibility.

To ensure public order and public safety, a number of documents must be adopted by the organisers of football matches. One of these documents is the 'Rules of Conduct'. The Rules of Conduct are adopted by the respective sports facility operators with the approval of internal affairs bodies, the Ministry of Emergencies of Ukraine and state supervisory bodies in the field of fire and technological security. These rules need to be located at a place that is accessible and

[24] Law of Ukraine 'On Aspects of Ensuring Public Order and Public Safety in Connection With Preparing and Hosting Football Matches', No. 3673 dated July 8, 2011.

[25] Decree of Cabinet of Ministers of Ukraine No. 341 as of April 25, 2012 'On adoption of the Procedure of Organization of Activities ensuring Public Order and Safety while Hosting Football Matches'.

[26] Law of Ukraine 'On Aspects of Ensuring Public Order and Public Safety in Connection With Preparing and Hosting Football Matches' No. 3673 dated July 8, 2011, the Preamble and Article 2.

[27] Ibid., Article 1.

visible for the spectators and an extract of these Rules of Conduct are printed on the actual match ticket. The Rules of Conduct play an important role in ensuring public safety and public order at football matches. These rules specify to spectators their obligations at the stadium. However, in order to safeguard spectators' fundamental rights while specifying the limitations on their conduct, it is essential to determine their legal status legislatively.

The legislation uses the term 'Spectators', which is defined as individuals visiting football matches.[28] The Safety Law does not elaborate upon spectator rights, specifying only in Part 1 of Article 17 that spectators have the right to visit a football match, provided that they comply with the legislation and Rules of Conduct of the sports facility.

The Safety Law specifies some of the obligations of spectators. According to part 2 Article 17, spectators are obliged to:

1. adhere to the Rules of Conduct and other requirements in respect to ensuring public order and public safety;
2. follow lawful demands of stewards, volunteers, sports facility (football club) security services and law-enforcement bodies, with respect to the observance of legislation, and in an emergency situation to the requirements of the evacuation plan;
3. inform stewards, volunteers, sports facility (football club) security services and law-enforcement bodies about threats to public order and safety.

Spectators are furthermore expressly prohibited from: (a) being in the stadium in a state of intoxication; (b) having sources of open fire, and (c) bringing into the stadium weapons, ammunition, explosive substances, pyrotechnic devices, flammable substances, and other items, devices and substances prohibited by legislation and identified in the Rules of Conduct.[29]

The above-mentioned obligations and prohibitions seem legitimate in order to protect public order and public safety during football matches. However, the question arises whether these prohibitions may be extended in the Rules of Conduct of a private entity, the stadium operator. The Safety Law does not provide an answer to this question. However, the issue was addressed in the summary to the Bill.[30] Classifying a violation of the Rules of Conduct as an administrative offence is problematic, because sports facility operators do not have the necessary powers to issue documents of a regulatory character. This is a prerogative of the Cabinet of Ministers of Ukraine (Ukrainian government).[31] For this reason, there are serious questions regarding the legality of restrictive provisions in the Rules of Conduct, which are not explicitly based on the Safety Law, the Safety Procedure or other acts.

---

[28]Ibid., Article 1.

[29]Ibid., Part 3 Article 17.

[30]Bill on amending of certain legislative acts (in respect to ensuring public order and safety prior, during and after football matches) (Reg. No. 9662 dated 29.12.2011) http://w1.c1.rada.gov.ua/pls/zweb2/webproc4_1?pf3511=42250. Accessed December 7, 2014 (link no longer active).

[31]http://w1.c1.rada.gov.ua/pls/zweb2/webproc4_1?pf3511=42250. Accessed December 7, 2014 (link no longer active).

9.3.3 *Entities Responsible for Ensuring Public Order and Public Safety and Their Legal Status*

To maintain public order and public safety at football matches, it is important to involve all stakeholders in this task. Article 7 of the Safety Law charges the following entities with this task:

- the sports facility operator;
- the football match organiser;
- special subjects of ensuring public order and public safety (bodies and divisions of the Ministry of Internal Affairs of Ukraine (MIA) and the Ministry of Emergencies of Ukraine (MEU);
- the football clubs;
- the local state administration and local self-government bodies.

The most powerful entities responsible for public order and safety are bodies of the MIA and the MEU, which provide control over the arrival, accommodation and departure of spectators. These bodies can take legal measures against persons who have committed offences and these bodies can react to emergencies.[32] These bodies pursuant to Clause 21(2) of Safety Procedure, while taking into account the risk assessment regarding the specific match and the number of spectators expected, on the day of match draw up a 'plan of measures ensuring public safety and public order', specifying the strength of security forces required, their deployment on certain territory and the reserve of forces and measures to be applied in event of spectator misconduct threatening the life and health of people, including in the stadium.

In accordance with Article 15 of the Safety Law, the football match organiser, the stadium operator and the football club are responsible for ensuring public order and public safety in the stadium, while the internal affairs bodies are responsible for the territories adjacent to the stadium, on the evacuation routes, and in other public areas near where the football match is being held.

9.3.4 *Special Measures in Connection with Organising Euro 2012*

Euro 2012 demanded the full attention of all state bodies. Ukraine identified and implemented what it considered to be best practice from the experiences of other nations that had organised major sporting events, especially the World and European Football Championships. For Euro 2012, Ukraine furthermore looked at the European Union's recommendations contained in the 'Handbook with recommendations for

[32] Ibid., Article 10.

international police cooperation and measures to prevent and control violence and disturbances in connection with football matches with an international dimension, in which at least one Member State is involved'.[33]

Ukraine invited police delegations from other nations participating in Euro 2012 to help with maintaining public order and public safety. During Euro 2012 more than 130 officers of foreign police delegations from 16 countries assisted, with more than 100 officers patrolling as 'spotters' together with Ukrainian militia in places where foreign supporters were present (airports, railway stations, fan-zones, stadia etc.).[34] Such delegations worked in the cities hosting Euro 2012 pursuant to the schedule of their national teams' matches. Their main tasks were to prevent offences by the citizens of their countries and to provide practical assistance in this respect to internal affairs bodies. Almost a year later on 18 March 2013, MIA has adopted the 'Instruction on Organisation of Execution by Militia Officers of the Function of Spotter during Events related to Preparation and Staging of Football Matches',[35] which specifies the responsibilities of militia officers acting as spotters in connection with football matches of the Ukrainian national team and/or clubs of the Ukrainian Premier League.

Another important initiative during Euro 2012 was the introduction of the 'International Centre for Police Cooperation', which united the representatives of MIA, Interpol, police officers from Belorussia, the Czech Republic, Denmark, England, France, Germany, Hungary, Italy, Netherlands, Poland, Portugal, Slovakia, Spain and Sweden.[36] The main task of this Centre was to ensure the operative exchange of information with foreign partners, including information on supporter movements and the presence of individuals potentially posing a threat of violence or disorder.

9.3.5 Football Banning Orders

Euro 2012 served as an incentive to implement measures restricting supporters' access to football matches. Such Football Banning Orders are widely used in many other countries. To regulate the access to sports event of football hooligans,

[33]Council Resolution of June 3, 2010 concerning an updated handbook with recommendations for international police cooperation and measures to prevent and control violence and disturbances in connection with football matches with an international dimension, in which at least one Member State is involved (2010/C 165/01) www.eur-lex.europa.eu. Accessed December 7, 2014.

[34]http://mvs.gov.ua/mvs/control/mai@n/uk/publish/article/760971;jsessionid=9C8590903AADB4E7A19CEC91AE26FFFB. Accessed December 7, 2014 (link no longer active).

[35]Order of MIA No. 255 as of March 18, 2013 'On Approval of Instruction on Organisation of Execution by Militia Officers of the Function of Spotter during Events related to Preparation and Staging of Football Matches'.

[36]Ibid.

Ukraine joined the initiative introduced in Council Decision 2002/348/JHA,[37] and in 2010 created the National Football Information Point of Ukraine (NFIP). An important task of the NFIP is the exchange of information with respect to so-called 'problem supporters' from different countries participating in Euro 2012, and for this goal blacklists were exchanged.

During Euro 2012, this exchange was aimed at preventing the access to matches by 'football hooligans' from foreign countries. After receipt of 'blacklists' from other countries, listing potential troublemakers, the NFIP forwarded these lists to the State Border Guard Service of Ukraine (SBGS). The SBGS were then charged with denying these individuals entry into Ukraine. This procedure was first used in October 2011, for a match between Shakhtar (Donetsk) and Zenit (St. Petersburg). The NFIP received information about more than 100 risk supporters from Russia and as a result seven were denied entry into Ukraine by the SBGS.[38] Notwithstanding that the above-mentioned measures were not reflected in special legislation, their legal grounding can be found in general provisions of Law of Ukraine 'On legal status of foreign nationals and stateless persons', pursuant to which a ban on entry into the territory of Ukraine to foreign nationals may be imposed in order to ensure national safety and public order, and in cases when it is necessary for preserving health or protecting the rights and liberties of Ukrainian citizens and lawful residents.[39]

In addition, the NFIP was tasked with collecting information on Ukrainian 'problem supporters'. The MIA, by its Order No. 56 of 20.01.2011, created the database 'Problem supporters' which contained information about individuals who had committed offences at or in connection with football matches.[40] By 30 May 2012, this database contained information on 1,400 supporters.[41] The inclusion in the above-mentioned database has the following consequences: (a) this information is forwarded to other (European) countries and where such 'problem supporters' can be prevented from entering, and (b) such persons can be denied entry to the stadium.

The imposition of Football Banning Orders was not specifically provided for by legislation. Football Banning Orders are specified in the FFU Disciplinary Regulations (for acts of racism—Article 37—and for intentional destruction or damaging of property and equipment of the stadium and adjacent territory—Clause 9 of Appendix 4).[42] The Safety Law in Article 18 merely specifies that the entry to stadia is forbidden to spectators that:

---

[37]Council Decision 2002/348/JHA of 25 April 2002 concerning security in connection with football matches with an international dimension.

[38]http://zn.ua/SPORT/v_ukrainskoy_militsii_pered_evro-2012_sozdali_tsentr_kontrolya_nad_ultras.html. Accessed December 7, 2014.

[39]Law of Ukraine 'On legal status of foreign nationals and stateless persons', dated September 22, 2011, paras 2 and 3 Part 1 Article 13.

[40]Order of MIA No. 56 as of 20.01.2011, "On creation of united database of persons of record category 'Problem Supporter'".

[41]Unian (2012) Militia has calculated 1400 football hooligans in Ukraine. http://www.unian.net/sport/656479-militsiya-naschitala-1400-futbolnyih-huliganov-v-ukraine.html. Accessed December 7, 2014.

[42]Football Federation of Ukraine Disciplinary Regulations 2014. http://www.ffu.org.ua/files/ndocs_476.pdf. Accessed December 7, 2014.

- do not have an appropriate ticket;
- refuse to allow inspection by members of the militia and/or security service or representatives of the stadium, conducted according to the established procedure;
- violate the established rules in respect of bringing certain items or substances into the stadium;
- are intoxicated;
- are under 14 years of age and not accompanied by an adult.

The Football Banning Order was first introduced by the Law of Ukraine 'On the Peculiarities of Legal Proceedings on Administrative Cases during Euro 2012'. On the basis of this Law, an authorised body has an obligation to consider the administrative offences listed in this Law and to take into account the character of the relevant offence and the personality of the offender when determining whether to impose a banning order. To ensure the effectiveness of these measures, special electronic devices to identify spectators were installed at the entrance of the sports facilities.[43] However, this Law entered into force at the beginning of Euro 2012 and ceased 30 days after the tournament ended. Therefore, on what basis were such sanctions imposed on Ukrainian supporters who committed offences before Euro 2012?

According to Article 33 of the Constitution of Ukraine, everyone legally present in the territory of Ukraine has the right to freedom of movement (except for the limitations expressly provided by law).[44] The grounds for a limitation on freedom of movement are stipulated in the Law of Ukraine 'On the Right of Free Movement and Choice of Place of Residence in Ukraine',[45] which contains the following limitations: (a) limitation with regard to persons against whom preventive measures or punishment in the form of imprisonment or personal restraint have been imposed and persons who are otherwise under administrative supervision,[46] and (b) limitations on the movement on private land. In the first situation, the respective measures must be preceded by a court decision and may only be taken on the basis of serious crimes or drug- related crimes. In the second case the Safety Law does not specifically refer to limiting access to stadia to spectators included on these 'blacklists'. To a certain extent, it is possible to apply Clause 20 of Article 11 of the Law of Ukraine 'On militia' entitling militiamen to limit or forbid access within their competence to citizens on certain territories, or objects on temporary grounds with the aim of ensuring public order, public safety, and the

[43]Law of Ukraine 'On the Peculiarities of Legal Proceedings on Administrative Cases during the Final Part of European Football Championship 2012 in Ukraine', No. 3568-VI, dated 05.07.2011, Article 4.

[44]Constitution of Ukraine dated 28.06.1996.

[45]Law of Ukraine 'On the rights of free movement and choice of place of residence in Ukraine', No. 1382-IV, dated 11.12.2003 (amended and supplemented), Article 12.

[46]Law of Ukraine 'On administrative supervision after the persons set at liberty from the places of imprisonment'. No. 264/94-VR, dated 01.12.1994 (amended and supplemented), Article 1.

protection of life and health.[47] However, the issue is whether the mere presence of supporters in the database 'Problem Supporters' constitutes a real threat to public order and safety. The inclusion of the supporters on the above-mentioned database, follows on the basis of the sole criteria that they are persons who have committed offences in connection with football matches.[48] However, the database does not specify the types of offences, does not take into account the gravity of these offences, and the sentence that was imposed. This raises serious issues with regard to the proportionality of these measures and the protection of the rights of supporters. Pursuant to the opinion of Ukrainian supporters, not only real offenders were included in the database, but also supporters who were 'too active' in supporting their team.[49] In this respect, the Soviet approach, when 'every non-authorised collective expression of emotions during the football match was assessed as socially dangerous', should be noted.[50] The majority of representatives of Ukrainian Ultras were included on these blacklists, which was one of the main reasons for the Ultras boycotting Euro 2012.[51]

Another attempt to implement Football Banning Orders legally was made during the Euromaidan Revolution in Ukraine, when on 16 January 2014 among 'anti-protest laws', Law No. 722-VII[52] was adopted which (a) specified the 'football banning order' as a separate measure of administrative liability in the Code of Administrative Offences to be applied for a period from 6 months to 2 years; and (b) established presenting documents certifying the person's identity as a condition for acquisition of tickets and entering the football venue. However, this law has been treated by football fans, actively participating in political protests in the country, as an oppressive measure and has resulted in widespread protests. As a result of these protests, the law was cancelled along with the majority of other 'anti-protest laws' within two weeks of adoption.[53]

To ensure the adherence to the principles of legality and proportionality, and observe supporter rights, it is important to clearly stipulate the criteria for the inclusion of supporters on these 'blacklists' and in the database 'Problem Supporters'. Criteria that should be taken into account are the type and gravity of offence, and the statute of limitations on these offences. It is also crucial to specify the procedure for such measures to be applied.

---

[47]Law of Ukraine 'On militia' dated 20.12.1990 (amended and supplemented).

[48]Order of MIA No. 56 as of 20.01.2011. "On creation of united database of persons of record category 'Problem Supporter'", Clause 4.1.

[49]http://focus.ua/society/232805/. Accessed December 7, 2014.

[50]Almashyn 2012, p. 3.

[51]See www.wz.lviv.ua/articles/106817. Accessed December 7, 2014.

[52]Law of Ukraine 'On Amendments to Certain Legislative Acts with respect to Liability for Committing Administrative Offences during Football Matches', No. 722-VII, dated 16.01.2014.

[53]Law of Ukraine 'On Certain Laws to be Deemed to have lost their Force', No. 729-VII, dated January 28, 2014.

9.4 The Offence of 'Football Hooliganism' and Liability for 'Hooliganism'

9.4.1 General Approach to 'Football Hooliganism' as an Offence and Liability Issues

Ukrainian legislation neither separates football-related offences from other administrative and criminal offences, nor defines the term 'football hooliganism'. Such a definition, however, can be found in certain non-binding act of internal character, such as the MIA 'Methodological recommendations on prevention of crimes committed by radical youth gangs during football matches', which defines 'football hooligans' as individuals who violate public order in association with their affinity for football.[54]

An attempt to introduce special football-related offences and liability for such offences was made prior to Euro 2012.[55] This Bill proposed to supplement the Code of Administrative Offences[56] (CAO) by introducing the following football-related offences:

Article 173-3—violations of the Rules of Conduct in stadiums and violations of public order and safety of citizens before, during and after sports events (which criminalised the participation in fights, moving between the sectors in the stadium and infringing public order and safety);

Article 173-4— xenophobic, racial, anti- semitic, and discriminatory chants and other demonstrations (including of a political content);

Article 174-1—the use of pyrotechnic devices.

The Chief Scientific-and-Expert Authority of Supreme Council of Ukraine in its Summary to this Bill emphasised that the majority of proposed offences are either already covered in the CAO and the Criminal Code, or may not be considered as offences due to their conflict with certain civil rights provisions. At the time of writing, this Bill had not been adopted by Supreme Council of Ukraine. Thus, in accordance with the legislation currently in force, illegal actions of football supporters, depending on their severity, are determined either as existing administrative offences or as crimes.

---

[54]Cherniavsky et al. 2010, p. 16.

[55]Bill on amending of certain legislative acts (in respect to ensuring public order and safety prior, during and after football matches) (Reg. No. 9662 dated 29.12.2011) http://w1.c1.rada.gov.ua/pls/zweb2/webproc4_1?pf3511=42250. Accessed December 7, 2014 (link no longer active).

[56]Code on Administrative Offences No. 8073-X, dated 07.12.1984 (amended and supplemented).

9.4.2 'Football Hooliganism' as an Administrative Offence

Most football-related incidents are classified as 'disorderly conduct',[57] defined by Article 173 of the CAO as foul expressions in public places, offensive harassment to citizens, and other similar actions infringing public order and a citizen's peace. The penalty for disorderly conduct specifies the imposition of a fine from three to seven TFA,[58] community service for a period of 40 to 60 h, correctional works for 1 or 2 months with a salary deduction of 20 %, or administrative detention for up to 15 days. The definition of disorderly conduct is broad and therefore offers the possibility to encompass any action capable of infringing public order. An analysis of judicial practice demonstrates, for example, that courts in the majority of cases define the use of pyrotechnical devices as disorderly conduct.

During Euro 2012, a special law 'On the Peculiarities of Legal Proceedings on Administrative Cases during the Final Part of European Championship 2012 in Ukraine' was enacted.[59] This law introduced a fast-track procedure for settling cases for a number of administrative offences committed during Euro 2012, including disorderly conduct, drug-related offences (Article 44 CAO), the consumption of alcoholic beverages in areas where it is forbidden and public intoxication (Article 178 CAO), using pyrotechnic devices (Article 195-6 CAO) and holding prohibited demonstrations (Article 185-1 CAO). These offences are dealt with in administrative proceedings and foreigners and stateless persons can be deported when they have committed such offences.

9.4.3 'Football Hooliganism' as a Crime

In more serious cases, the actions of football hooligans are classified as crimes pursuant to the Criminal Code of Ukraine[60] (hereinafter—'CC'). According to Part 1 of Article 296 of CC, 'hooliganism' is defined as a gross violation of public order, motivated by obvious disrespect for society, accompanied by particular imprudence or exceptional cynicism. The Supreme Court of Ukraine has clarified that 'particular imprudence' implies particularly gross violations of public order, such as violence which inflicts bodily injury and the destruction or damaging of property. 'Exceptional cynicism' acts are defined as those displaying disrespect for

[57]This can be translated as 'minor hooliganism'.

[58]Tax-free allowance which as of December 7, 2014 amounts to 17 (seventeen) hryvnia (except during determination of administrative and criminal offences).

[59]Law of Ukraine 'On the Peculiarities of Legal Proceedings on Administrative Cases during the Final Part of European Football Championship 2012 in Ukraine', No. 3568-VI, dated 05.07.2011 (amended and supplemented).

[60]Criminal Code of Ukraine No. 2341-III, dated 05.04.2001 (amended and supplemented).

universal moral principles, which demonstrate carelessness, or acts which target individuals who are in a vulnerable position.[61] In cases where the respective offence is not accompanied with particular imprudence or exceptional cynicism, the acts shall be classified as disorderly conduct under CAO.

The penalty for 'hooliganism' can be a fine from 500 to 1000 TFA, detention of up to 6 months, or personal restraint for up to 5 years. The same actions, if they are committed by a group of persons (Part 2 Article 296 CC), can be penalised by personal restraint for up to 5 years or imprisonment for up to 4 years. If such actions are committed by a supporter previously convicted for hooliganism, or are accompanied by resistance to the authorities (Part 3 Article 296 CC), the punishment can be imprisonment for 2 to 5 years. If such actions are conducted using firearms or other weapons (Part 4 Article 296 CC), they can be punished with imprisonment for 3 to 7 years.

The Supreme Court has also held that with regard to criminal cases on 'hooliganism', the courts shall establish all factual circumstances of the case, including the intent, motives, goals, and specific actions of each participant. The court must establish whether the actions of the accused actually violated public order and whether they were motivated by obvious disrespect for society and accompanied by particular imprudence or exceptional cynicism.[62] Otherwise the actions cannot be classified as acts of 'hooliganism'. The courts shall determine the fault of the accused individuals, impose a justified punishment, enforce measures for the full indemnification of material and moral damages, and establish the reasons and conditions for the commission of the 'hooligan' acts.[63]

9.4.4 'Football Hooliganism' as a Violation of the Rules of Football Associations and the Liability of Football Fans

Spectator misbehaviour is categorised among football offences under Article 8 of the FFU Disciplinary Regulations (FFU DR). In addition, Appendices to the FFU DR contain the following offences that can be committed by spectators prior, during and after a match: intentional destruction or damage to the stadium; supporters misconduct; collective or mass actions violating the Rules of Conduct; setting off fireworks inside the stadium; throwing pyrotechnic devices and other items on the pitch; pitch invasions; and the termination of a match because of third person (including spectators) interference.

The FFU follows the general approach introduced by FIFA and UEFA of imposing liability for the actions of spectators on football clubs (or associations).

[61] Resolution of Plenum of Supreme Court of Ukraine 'On judicial practice in cases on hooliganism', No. 10, dated 22.12.2006, Clause 5.

[62] Ibid., Clause 1.

[63] Ibid., Clauses 1 and 4.

According to Article 21 of the FFU DR, clubs, irrespective of fault, bear liability for the conduct of their supporters. At the same time, the club hosting the match is responsible for public order and security in the stadium and the adjacent territory prior to, during and after the match (Article 21 FFU DR). These provisions reflect the rules contained in the UEFA Disciplinary Regulations. The difference however is that the FFU DR directly stipulate that liability is imposed 'irrespective of fault', implementing in this way the principle of strict liability. Thus, spectator misbehaviour leads to the imposition of various sanctions (including financial penalties up to 125,000 Hryvnias) on clubs by the FFU.[64]

However, in recent times a trend has emerged where Ukrainian clubs who have received fines from the associations because of supporter misconduct, have filed lawsuits against supporters to claim back the fines.[65] The courts have usually satisfied such claims in favour of the clubs. One of the first cases was the decision of the Zhovtnevyi regional court of Zaporizhzhia, on 04 October 2007, granting the claim of Metalurh Zaporizhia for material damages against a supporter who fired a pyrotechnic device during a UEFA Cup 2006 qualifying match between Metalurh and Panathinaikos. The UEFA Control and Disciplinary Body had imposed a fine of 3,000 CHF against Metalurh and the Court ruled that the above-mentioned amount in full, plus court costs, had to be reimbursed to the club by the supporter.[66] In another case, Metalist Kharkiv claimed indemnification for material damages against a spectator who ran on the pitch on 18 August 2011 during a UEFA Europe League play-off match between Metalist and Sochaux. Because of this incident, the match had to be stopped for 2 min and the UEFA Control and Disciplinary Body imposed a penalty of 15,000 Euro on Metalist. On 18 June 2012, the Kominternisvsky Regional Court of Kharkiv ruled that Metalist should receive the full fine of 15,000 Euro (plus court costs) from the supporter.[67]

This practice of lawsuits against spectators is problematic. First, in these cases the provisions of the Civil Code of Ukraine[68] on non-contractual compensation for damages (tortious liability) apply. However, tortious liability in these cases has to arise on the basis of a violation of an absolute subjective right (such as a right to life, a right to health, a right to honesty and dignity, property right, authorship right, etc.).[69] However, it is not quite clear which absolute subjective rights were violated by the spectators in these cases. It is unclear whether the right to public

[64]As of December 5, 2014 the currency exchange rates of hrivnya under National Bank of Ukraine are as follows: $100 = 1541,55 Hrivnyas; 100 Euro = 1897,80 Hryvnias.

[65]A similar practice is noted in Chap. 4 in this Volume in respect of fines levied against German clubs.

[66]See Case No. 2-1197/2007. http://reyestr.court.gov.ua/Review/2139192. Accessed December 7, 2014.

[67]See Case No. 2020/4580/2012 http://reyestr.court.gov.ua/Review/24865900. Accessed December 7, 2014.

[68]Civil Code of Ukraine No. 435-IV dated 16.01.2003 (amended and supplemented), Chapter 82.

[69]Bobrova D 2002.

order and public safety can be viewed as an absolute subjective right. Second, in these cases it is important to consider the legal relations between the club and the association on the one side and the supporters/spectators on the other side, and the legal nature of penalties imposed. These penalties are imposed by the association against the clubs on the basis of their membership in the respective association and therefore are more likely to arise from a contractual relationship than in tort. Furthermore, the goal of the imposition of these penalties by the associations is to stimulate the clubs to duly perform their obligations with respect to ensuring public order and safety during the matches, a duty which is imposed on them by enforcement of the Disciplinary Regulations of the respective association. Thus acts like setting off fireworks or pitch invasions are the actions of spectators, breaching certain rules of conduct. However, at the same time, they are the result of improper performance by the club of its obligations *vis-à-vis* the association, in ensuring public order and safety inside the stadium. Accordingly, the reason for the imposition of sanctions was not only the spectator's misbehaviour, but also the failure of the club in the performance of its obligations. Finally, the obligatory elements of tort liability are the presence of unlawful behaviour, the harmful effect of the underlying acts, the relation of cause-and-effect between the act and its result, and the fault of the respondent.[70] However, the presence of fault with regard to the spectator's violation of the Disciplinary Regulations of the respective association seems doubtful, because the spectator is not a member of the association and can therefore not be considered to be aware of the disciplinary sanctions imposed by the football association against its members. Thus, this practice of compensation by spectators of very heavy financial penalties imposed against clubs, based on a broad interpretation of the provisions of the civil law, needs a more thorough examination by courts, with due consideration for the rights of the spectators.

9.5 Conclusions

The expanded and improved legal regulation of football-related disorder, while taking into account the experiences of other European countries, is a positive trend. However, when introducing measures to address football-related disorder, and especially those of a restrictive and prohibitive nature, it is crucial to keep in mind the civil rights of supporters under the Constitution of Ukraine and their human rights under the ECHR. With regard to these rights of supporters, it is important to take into account social and political tensions in society, subcultural peculiarities of football fans, existing threats to public safety and order, and the possibility of achieving the same result by less-restrictive measures.

Some practices which aim at addressing the problem of football-related disorder and violence in Ukraine still need a more profound assessment with respect to

[70]Resolution of Supreme Court of Ukraine 'On practice of settlement by courts of civil cases on indemnification claims', No. 6, dated 27.03.1992 (amended and supplemented), para 1 Clause 2.

the protection of supporters' civil and human rights. Accordingly, football banning orders require that the procedure for the imposition of such a measure is clearly laid down. Furthermore, the criteria for inclusion of supporters on 'blacklists' or on the 'Problem Supporter' database should only follow on the basis of clear criteria and in accordance with a valid legal procedure, which takes into account considerations regarding the gravity of the committed offence and the Statute of Limitations of those offences.

The introduction of separate offences for football-related incidents and strengthening the liability of football supporters therefore seems unnecessary at the moment. Most of the incidents categorised as football-related disorder are already covered by the CAO and the CC. However, if future legislation is implemented to address football-related disorder, such legislation needs to take possible infringements on the fundamental civil and human rights and freedoms of supporters into account. The practice of holding spectators liable for penalties imposed against clubs by football associations also needs a more thorough examination by the courts in relation to consideration and protection of spectator rights, and with due consideration for the legal relations between the football associations and supporters.

References

Almashyn V (2012) More than game. Tales, myths and legends of reactional obscurantism. Kyiv

Bobrova D (2002) Undertakings arisen of infliction of damages. In: Dzera O (ed) Civil Law. Urincom, Kyiv, T.2, pp. 505–566

Borodavko D (2012) Classification and criminological characteristic of representatives of football-related subculture. Customs Affairs, No. 2(80), part 2, book 1, pp. 413–415

Cherniavskyi S, Kopotun I, Lupalo O and others/edited by Dgiugia O (2010) Prevention of crimes committed by radical youth gangs during football matches: methodological recommendations. Kyiv National Internal Affairs Univercity, Kyiv

Golubovych A (2009) Moral problems of modern football. Physical culture, sport and nation health, 8th edn, vol.1.-No. 19

Kyrylenko V, Pozhydaev A (2011) Analysis of participation of forces of law enforcement in ensuring hosting football matches and summary of potential dangers during hosting in Ukraine of Final part Euro-2012. Honor and Law, No. 2, pp. 45–50

Pavelchuk E (2009) Football hooliganism as a phenomenon and its possible influence on the hosting of Euro-2012. Scoentific buletin of Lesia Ukrainka Volun National University, International relations, No. 4, pp. 334–337

Pylypenko D (2007) Crimes in sport. Geleos, Moscow

Solovyova Y (2012) The subculture of Ukrainian football fans (on the example of the fans of Ukrainian Premier League clubs). Bulletin Taras Shevchenko Lviv National University, 2(237):133–143

Cases

Case No. 2020/4580/2012. http://reyestr.court.gov.ua/Review/24865900. Accessed December 7, 2014.

Case No. 2-1197/2007. http://reyestr.court.gov.ua/Review/2139192. Accessed December 7, 2014.

Other documents referred to

Bill on amending of certain legislative acts (in respect to ensuring public order and safety prior, during and after the football matches) (Reg. No. 9662 dated 29.12.2011) http://w1.c1.rada.gov.ua/pls/zweb2/webproc4_1?pf3511=42250. Accessed December 7, 2014 (link no longer active).

Civil Code of Ukraine No. 435-IV dated 16.01.2003 (amended and supplemented) http://zakon1.rada.gov.ua/laws/show/435-15. Accessed December 7, 2014.

Code on administrative offences No. 8073-X dated 07.12.1984 (amended and supplemented) http://zakon2.rada.gov.ua/laws/show/80731-10. Accessed December 7, 2014.

Constitution of Ukraine dated 28.06.1996/Official Bulletin of the Supreme Council of Ukraine as of 23.07.1996, 1996, No. 30, Article 141.

Council Decision 2002/348/JHA of 25 April 2002 concerning security in connection with football matches with an international dimension/Official Journal L 121, 08/05/2002 pp. 0001–0003.

Council Resolution of 3 June 2010 concerning an updated handbook with recommendations for international police cooperation and measures to prevent and control violence and disturbances in connection with football matches with an international dimension, in which at least one Member State is involved (2010/C 165/01) www.eur-lex.europa.eu. Accessed December 7, 2014.

Criminal Code of Ukraine No. 2341-III dated 05.04.2001 (amended and supplemented) http://zakon2.rada.gov.ua/laws/show/2341-14/card2#Card. Accessed December 7, 2014.

Decree of Cabinet of Ministers of Ukraine 'On Adoption of the Procedure of Organization of Activities Ensuring Public Order and Safety during the Football Matches', No. 823, dated June 29, 2004/Official Gazette of Ukraine as of 16.07.2004, 2004, No. 26, p.36, Article 1707, Code of Act 29282/2004.

Decree of Cabinet of Ministers of Ukraine No. 341 as of April 25, 2012 'On Adoption of the Procedure of Organization of Activities ensuring Public Order and Safety while Hosting Football Matches'/ Official Gazette of Ukraine dated 04.05.2012/2012, No. 32, p.300, Article 1198., Code of Act 29282/2004.

European Convention on Spectator Violence and Misbehavior at Sports Events and in particular at Football Matches dated August 19, 1985/Official Gazette of Ukraine as of 15.03.2006/2006, No. 9, p. 235, Article 589, Code of Act 35382/2006.

Football Federation of Ukraine Disciplinary Regulations (2014). www.ffu.org.ua/files/ndocs_476.pdf. Accessed December 7, 2014.

Instruction of Cabinet of Ministers of Ukraine 'On Adoption of Integrated Concept of Ensuring Safety and Legal Order while Preparation and Hosting in Ukraine of European Football Championship Final Tournament in 2012', No. 1244-r, dated September 17, 2008 (amended and supplemented) http://zakon2.rada.gov.ua/laws/show/1244-2008-%D1%80. Accessed December 7, 2014.

Law of Ukraine 'On administrative supervision after the persons set at liberty from the places of imprisonment', No. 264/94-VR, dated 01.12.1994 (amended and supplemented) http://zakon2.rada.gov.ua/laws/show/264/94-%D0%B2%D1%80. Accessed December 7, 2014.

Law of Ukraine 'On Amendments to Certain Legislative Acts with respect to Liability for Committing Administrative Offences during Football Matches', No. 722-VII, dated 16.01.2014 http://zakon4.rada.gov.ua/laws/show/722-18. Accessed December 7, 2014.

Law of Ukraine 'On Aspects of Ensuring Public Order and Public Safety in Connection With Preparing and Hosting Football Matches', No. 3673, dated July 8, 2011/Official Bulletin of the Supreme Council of Ukraine, 2012, No. 9, Article 64.

Law of Ukraine 'On Certain Laws to be Deemed to have lost their Force', No. 729-VII, dated 28.01.2014 http://zakon4.rada.gov.ua/laws/show/732-18/paran2#n2. Accessed December 7, 2014.

Law of Ukraine 'On legal status of foreign nationals and stateless persons' dated 22.09.2011/ Official Bulletin of the Supreme Council of Ukraine dated 18.05.2012, 2012, No. 19-20, p.833, Article 179.

Law of Ukraine 'On the Peculiarities of Legal Proceedings on Administrative Cases during the Final Part of European Football Championship 2012 in Ukraine', No. 3568-VI, dated 05.07.2011 (amended and supplemented) http://zakon2.rada.gov.ua/laws/show/3568-17. Accessed December 7, 2014.

Law of Ukraine 'On the rights of free movement and choice of place of residence in Ukraine', No. 1382-IV, dated 11.12.2003 (amended and supplemented) http://zakon2.rada.gov.ua/laws/show?nreg=1382-15&find=1&text=%F1%EF%EE%F0%F2&x=0&y=0. Accessed December 7, 2014.

Law of Ukraine, No. 565-XII, 'On militia', dated 20.12.1990 (amended and supplemented) http://zakon2.rada.gov.ua/laws/show/565-12. Accessed December 7, 2014.

Order of MIA No. 255 as of 18.03.2013 'On Approval of Instruction on Organisation of Execution by Militia Officers of the Function of Spotter during Events related to Preparation and Staging of Football Matches'. http://zakon4.rada.gov.ua/laws/show/z0567-13. Accessed December 7, 2014.

Order of MIA, No. 56 as of 20.01.2011, 'On creation of united database of persons of record category 'Problem Supporter'. www.umdpl.info/files/docs/1319482923.rtf. Accessed December 7, 2014.

Chapter 10
Conclusions: Social Control at the Expense of Civil Liberties and Human Rights

Anastassia Tsoukala, Geoff Pearson and Peter T.M. Coenen

Abstract Despite significant differences in both fan culture and the problems of violence and disorder in connection with football, there has been a convergence of legal and policing tools designed to manage football crowds across Europe. Set in a wider neoliberal political context, where there is an increasing emphasis on prevention and security at the expense of more traditional modes of criminal justice, the management of football crowds across Europe has seen the introduction and development of pre-emptive policing powers, administrative 'control orders', and the gathering and sharing of personal information on suspected 'hooligans'. This increasing social control of football crowds has been at the expense of both traditional state civil liberties and also human rights under the ECHR. These security-centric approaches to football crowd management are disproportionate to their human rights infringements given the actual extent and severity of the problem of football disorder and violence, and the existence of less restrictive—and more effective—alternatives.

Keywords Football · Hooliganism · Europe · Comparative law · Human rights · Social control

Dr. Anastassia Tsoukala is tenured Associate Professor at the University of Paris XI. Dr. Geoff Pearson is Senior Lecturer in Criminal Law at the University of Manchester's Law School. When editing this book, Peter Coenen (deceased) was Assistant Professor of Law at Maastricht University in the Netherlands.

A. Tsoukala (✉)
University of Paris XI, Orsay, France
e-mail: tsoukala.anastassia@gmail.com

G. Pearson
University of Manchester, School of Law, Manchester, UK
e-mail: geoff.pearson@manchester.ac.uk

A. Tsoukala et al. (eds.), *Legal Responses to Football "Hooliganism" in Europe*,
ASSER International Sports Law Series, DOI 10.1007/978-94-6265-108-1_10

Contents

10.1 Introduction

Our comparative analysis of the legal responses adopted in eight European countries to combat football-related violence and disorder has uncovered a growing erosion of football supporters' civil rights, civil liberties and in many cases human rights. One of the striking features of the individual chapters in this collection is that despite the varied approaches to criminal law and policing, the varied political outlook of the legislators, and the differing nature of the problem, approaches to football crowd regulation have converged. It is now possible to discern a pan-European philosophy in legal and policing responses to 'hooliganism'. The following measures are now typical throughout Europe:

- An absence of any legal definition of football 'hooliganism'.
- A focus on introducing sporting or football-specific laws rather than relying on existing criminal provisions.
- An increased use of powers introduced to control football gang violence against supporters engaging in lesser 'anti-social behaviour'.
- Prohibitions on pyrotechnics in stadia.
- Restrictions on alcohol consumption in stadia.
- Increasing custodial sentences for offences considered to be 'football-related'.
- Video camera surveillance of football crowds by police/football authorities.
- Compilation of databases of 'risk' supporters and exchange of that information with various parties (public/private), both domestically and internationally.
- Exchange of 'best practice' in policing and security throughout the EU and Council of Europe nations.
- Administrative or civil orders banning convicted and suspected 'hooligans' from attending matches.

Another feature that has united the approaches outlined in this collection is the lack of scientific analysis of the success or otherwise of these measures in reducing disorder and violence in connection with football. 'Best practice' in both legislative and policing terms is shared across Europe, often without any evidence that it has achieved its stated aims.

Notwithstanding national specificities, the widespread decline of previously prevailing procedural safeguards stems from an array of correlated factors that, in turn, reflect worldwide shifts in the political and economic realm following the expansion of neoliberal modes of governance. The impact of these broader shifts on the legal regulation and policing of football crowd disorder can be seen through the changes generated within the criminal justice system by the rise in risk-oriented rationalities and the ensuing decline of democratic modes of governance. These effects have been greatly enhanced by the ongoing politicisation of internal security issues and the concomitant strengthening of the position of law enforcement agencies in the security field, thereby reducing the spectrum of possible alternative approaches.

10.2 Risk-Led Rationalities and the Decline of Democratic Modes of Governance

In each of the countries analysed in this volume, we can see that the previously prevailing legal order has been overturned, as both lawmakers and law enforcers have departed from the rehabilitative crime control model to support a risk-oriented one that focuses on threat and suspicion rather than utilising the formal mechanisms of the criminal legal system to punish offenders for breaches of criminal law. The wide introduction and further legitimisation of proactive policing methods that are based upon profiling and social sorting techniques have thus institutionalised control and punishment of deviance, thereby calling into question the value of the rule of law and the effective protection of civil rights, civil liberties and pan-European Human Rights in twenty-first century liberal democracies.

In an ever-expanding surveillance and intelligence-gathering nexus, the presumption of innocence and the principles of legality and proportionality are being increasingly marginalised; their offence-rooted nature simply renders them inappropriate, if not counter-productive, to the current suspicion-based modes of policing. In most of the countries analysed here the personal data of football supporters may be registered on a police database even without a criminal offence having taken place. This targeting of the allegedly 'threatening' football supporter blurs the borders between criminal and deviant behaviour both in the gathering and the further use of relevant intelligence. Football supporters may be arrested and listed on databases on the basis of vaguely-defined criteria, thereby leaving the police a broad margin of discretionary power to define what is 'social order' and what poses a threat to it. The blurring of the legal grounding of the police activity is mirrored by that of both the assessment and the limits of this activity. While the Ukrainian police databases make no distinction between types and gravity of offences committed by football supporters, in the Netherlands surveillance seems to be open-ended, as police officers track football supporters even in their everyday life activities. The subsequent weakening of the protection of the football supporters' rights becomes even more worrisome in Germany, where football supporters' personal data may also be registered for minor incidents, and may remain registered even if ensuing investigation leads to a dismissal of the case.

The position of German football supporters in the criminal justice system is further deteriorated because they cannot defend themselves by appealing this registration as they are not informed of their having been registered.

Similarly, the informal registration of fans as 'risk supporters' in England and Wales takes place without the suspect or their peers being informed. However, should other fans 'associate' with those labelled as risk supporters, this association can be used as evidence that these third parties should be served with football banning orders. The vagueness of the levels of deviancy deemed necessary to lead to action by police and other security organisations is not helped by the current EU definition of 'risk supporter', which includes reference to supporters that are 'posing a possible risk to public order or antisocial behaviour'.[1] This is an incredibly low threshold when much European supporter culture is based on activities which in other contexts may be seen as 'anti social', such as heavy drinking, drug use or engagement in indecent chanting.

Such a radical transformation of the principles lying beneath the dominant crime control model could not possibly take place without its being reinforced by correlated shifts in the classic democratic balance of powers. Quite unsurprisingly then, all the countries analysed in this volume share a common feature: the legislative and judicial powers are being eroded to the benefit of the executive and/or the market-driven private sector. In the absence of any domestic or European legal definition of football-related violence, lawmakers and the judiciary are circumvented by the executive and, to a lesser extent, by sports authorities that seek to impose their own definition of the phenomenon and, consequently, their own way of addressing public order and safety issues. Entangled in a mutually reinforcing process that involves law enforcers, private stakeholders and the media, police knowledge and authority is often overvalued, to the extent that police threat assessments are taken for granted even when they are refuted by other evidence, while critical voices denouncing the inefficiency of these policies are being marginalised.

One of the methods that best illustrates these trends is the expanding use of extra-judicial football bans. Bans following conviction for 'football-related' offences were first seen in England and Wales in 1986, but other European states have taken this further with the introduction of extra-judicial bans. Initially introduced in Italy in 1989, extra-judicial bans exemplify the pervasiveness of the risk-focused mindset in managing football-related violence. In contrast with England and Wales, where football bans on complaint remain within the judicial system, albeit with diminished procedural safeguards, in most of the countries analysed here, football supporters' freedom of movement is being restricted by the police on the basis of a mere suspicion. In all cases, it is clear that these bans do not target just offenders but also supporters who are believed to pose a risk of engaging in future violence or disorder, sometimes on the flimsiest of evidence. Providing

[1]Council Resolution OJC 322/1, 04.12.2006. The current definition does not make grammatical sense. The authors assume what the resolution is intended to mean is that risk supporters pose a risk *of causing or engaging in* anti-social behaviour.

such a broad discretionary power to the police is all the more problematic when we take into account the fact that, whenever appealed, domestic judges have ruled that standard principles of criminal due process do not apply because these bans are deemed to be preventive and not punitive measures. This is in spite of the significant and onerous punitive effect that the conditions attached to these bans have upon those subjected to them. The judicial legitimisation of extra-judicial modes of controlling people has led to the increased use of a measure which has, in effect, normalised the state of exception. French law enforcers regularly resort to administrative football bans to an abusive extent, while police in England and Wales increasingly use dispersal orders designed to manage antisocial and alcohol-related disorder, and in Italy football-related disorder is assimilated with mafia-related crime in practice, and football supporters may be subject to measures restricting personal freedom that are provided by anti-mafia law.

10.3 Restructuring Governance Around Security

The abovementioned tendencies, which arguably reflect the rise in neoliberal modes of governance, were boosted by the rapid politicisation of internal security issues from the late twentieth century onwards and especially in the aftermath of the 2001 New York terrorist attacks. The expanding presence of security-related concerns in all political discourses and policies across Europe cannot be only attributed to the rise in insecurity and the subsequent need of the political elites to legitimise their role by reassuring their electorate of their capacity to maintain order in a rapidly disintegrating socioeconomic and geopolitical context. The powerful ascendency of (ultra) conservative political parties and movements, and the ensuing twist to authoritarianism in many different European countries suggest that the interests lying behind the protection of internal security go beyond the legitimate role of the mainstream political parties to reshape the relationship between state and individual by providing the executive with a hegemonic position within the political field.

When it comes to addressing football-related violence, post-September 11 security policies reinforced and legitimised prior trends in policing football supporters. The move towards securitisation started in the mid-1980s in the UK, and in the 1990s in continental Europe. From then on, the effects of the upgrading of the executive at the expense of the legislative and the judiciary on the regulation of football crowd disorder have been to some extent established and further developed due to the incorporation of internal security-related issues into the political field, be it domestic or EU-wide, and the subsequent production of bureaucratic dynamics within law enforcement agencies that often also seek to promote corporatist interests in an increasingly insecure risk-obsessed environment.

Under these combined influences, all the legal frameworks compared in this volume tend to converge in both their key guiding principles and specific crowd-management tactics, ranging from the privatisation of control inside stadia to the expanding recourse to technology by the social control apparatus. Domestic regulation of football crowds is becoming increasingly common from one country to another because it is elaborated in line with the 'European Convention on Spectator Violence and Misbehaviour at Sports Events and in particular at Football Matches', as well as in accordance with UEFA requirements and relevant EU-planning of regulatory and police action.

This standardisation of domestic responses to football-related violence has been greatly facilitated by the regular organisation of international tournaments that, from the mid-1980s on, were seen as laboratories providing an incentive to test and update forms of police cooperation and modes of policing sports crowds. While international police cooperation is strengthened through intense police networking prior to the tournament and the establishment of international centres for police cooperation during the tournament, policing football supporters also evolves out of the exchange of what is considered 'best practice'.

The impact of this process is most visible in countries that host international tournaments for the first time. For example, prior to its co-hosting of Euro 2012, Ukraine enacted an array of regulations aimed at ensuring public order and safety during the tournament. At the same time, the Ukrainian authorities looked at the experiences of other countries in organising similar sports mega events. As the exchange of 'best practice' also aims at preventing football-related violence on a permanent basis, international cooperation on the occasion of tournaments goes well beyond the law-enforcement realm to involve both lawmakers and sports authorities. For example, the Ukrainian authorities became aware of the German strategy of holding fans accountable for fines levied against football clubs and introduced the administrative liability of football supporters. It is too early to see whether this measure will be applied across Europe but its conformity to the civil laws of many European countries is highly questionable because individual spectators are not a part of the disciplinary proceedings that result in the imposition of such club sanctions.

In countries that have experience of hosting international tournaments, the security-related preliminaries of the organisation of a sports mega event reshape domestic control of football crowds on a permanent basis by updating and reinforcing pre-existing legal frameworks and police strategies. The German example shows clearly how the preparation of the 2006 FIFA World Cup led to an extension of pre-existing security measures, the introduction of new ones and the legitimisation of further restrictions on civil rights. After the tournament, there was no significant de-escalation of the new security pattern. Thus the regulative creep is a one-way process; there are pitifully few examples of outdated or ineffective regulations and laws being scrapped anywhere in Europe.

The growing quest for hegemony stands no opposition. In many of the countries analysed in this collection, representatives of football supporters' organisations are excluded from negotiation processes and strategic meetings regarding football crowd management strategies. The fact that government and police unwillingness to engage in negotiations with football supporters is dissociated from the (in) efficiency of preventive policies is clearly evidenced in the German case where football supporters are excluded from the decision-making process despite the undeniable longstanding success of the Fan Projekts. Of the countries evaluated in this collection, only in England and Wales do we see an apparent move towards increasing supporter influence on policing strategy, but even here supporter voices are largely silent—or silenced—in the legislative process.

In the rare cases of institutional opposition to these liberty-restricting patterns of managing sports crowds, the contesting of existing policies is typically a response to bureaucratic interests rather than the protection of the rule of law or higher principles of human rights. This prevalence of security-oriented policies, be they coercive or proactive, is clearly illustrated in the Netherlands, where many municipalities did not adopt extensive proactive powers provided to authorities by the Football Law. They chose not to do so not just because it was thought that the efficiency of the new provisions was not clearly evidenced, but also because the conditions for imposing the law were too demanding and required rigorous administrative efforts.

10.4 An Alternative Approach: Is It Possible?

At first blush, considering alternative approaches to what is an application of broader worldwide patterns of social control in a rapidly changing political and economic environment may be seen as naïve. Until now, the only approach that has sought to replace coercive security-focused practices with more engaging models of crowd management has been the so-called 'friendly but firm' policing that was utilised at Euro 2000 (in the Netherlands but not Belgium), Euro 2004 in Portugal and in some German states during the 2006 FIFA World Cup. However, as we saw with regard to Austria, even some manifestations of this approach can be criticised as overly reliant on extensive surveillance and intelligence-gathering practices that may be a disproportionate violation of football supporters' rights and liberties.

10.4.1 Judicial Scrutiny of the Executive

Although the gradual escalation of security measures around football matches has led to a certain 'normalisation' of security mechanisms, members of some political parties have shared fans' criticisms of excessive control methods regarding, for example, travel arrangements. Such political reactions remain, however, relatively scarce. In the absence of any clear, linear approach that is likely to guarantee effective protection of the rule of law and human rights inside and around football stadia, the democratic foundations of European legal systems can potentially be preserved by the judiciary. The fact is that the executive power, be it government officials or law enforcers, fails in many cases in its duty to maintain law and order around football matches in ways that conform to the protection of civil liberties and human rights; here, checks and balances can only be sought by the judiciary. It is the responsibility of the judiciary to limit police arbitrariness and to prevent social control mechanisms from encroaching on the citizens' rights and liberties.

Judicial engagement in halting the gradual dismantling of the human rights-based criminal justice systems across Europe cannot possibly be efficient if it is not supported by the active involvement of football supporters in the defense of their rights. As has been seen in the UK, for example, where the FSF play an important role in representing football supporters, fans should be engaged in more organised forms of protest in order to establish themselves as part of the domestic and EU policy-making process, while managing their image in the mass media. Football supporters should assume their responsibility in what, by definition, must become a collective struggle to restore declining democratic governance in Europe.

10.4.2 A Human Rights-Based Approach to Football Policing and Regulation

The nations analysed in this collection all formally share similar human rights protections and are all signatories to the European Convention on Human Rights. This means that not only do football spectators across these nations share the same rights not to have their liberty arbitrarily curtailed, their privacy unnecessarily or disproportionately invaded and their right to a fair trial restricted, but the states regulating them have a duty to protect their positive rights to Free Expression and Free Assembly and Association. These state obligations point to a genuine alternative approach to the regulation and policing of football spectators.

Instead of regulating and policing crowds with the focus primarily on preventing antisocial behaviour and crime, the state should be placing the positive human rights of supporters at the forefront of its considerations. The state should be careful not to criminalise, or otherwise limit through various proactive mechanisms, activities that form part of supporter culture but which do not severely restrict the rights of others where these activities are associated with rights to free expression and assembly. Similarly, policing responses should not be focused merely on preventing crime or nuisance but should primarily look to support these human rights. Obviously, where activities connected to fan culture are infringing the rights of others then a balance between the rights of spectator groups and/or members of the public needs to be struck; where spectators are engaging in violence, disorder or crime that is having an impact on the rights of others, then obviously the police have a duty to intervene. However, the mere risk of potential disorder or the committal of minor offences by individuals in a larger crowd should not lead to interventions that infringe the rights to Free Expression or Assembly for a crowd of football supporters. Nor should they lead to interventions that infringe the rule of law, regarding presumption of innocence and (for the civil law systems that dominate this collection) the principle of proportionality, or that which restrict freedom of movement. As we saw in Chap. 3, it should also not be forgotten that these policing styles have been proven to reduce the chance of disorder involving 'non risk' fans escalating, with policing approaches that prioritise the rights of spectators more likely to be seen as legitimate and less likely to lead to resistance and the risk of disorder. It is therefore not the case that a less confrontational policing style will necessarily lead to more violence or disorder; the evidence suggests the opposite.

10.5 Concluding Remarks

Across Europe it is clear that football supporters are still considered a threat to public order, and a social group that requires both innovative new laws and policing strategies to prevent them from engaging in violence or disorder. This is despite the fact that in most states football-related incidents and arrests are on the decline, and football stadia are generally seen to be more orderly and safer places than in the past. In this collection we have seen that this approach has severely limited the civil and human rights of supporters, the vast majority of whom do not attend matches with the intention of engaging in violence or disorder.

Our contention is that European states need to approach the management of football crowds from a different perspective. Football supporters should first and foremost be seen as a peaceful social group whose rights to free expression and assembly should be actively protected by the state, from both restrictive laws and policing methods and also the actions of any violent 'risk' groups present. Increasingly onerous sporting or football-specific laws are not needed in addition to normal state criminal laws that apply to all citizens, and when it comes to criminal penalties for offences, football supporters should be treated in the same way as those committing the same offences in different contexts. Databases and intelligence-sharing on suspected 'hooligans' should only occur where there is genuine evidence of an individual posing a risk of violence in a football context, and as part of an ongoing investigation aimed at taking criminal action against that individual. While banning orders as part of a punishment following conviction for a football-related offence are a sensible approach to containing the risk posed by that minority who engage in violence in connection with football matches, the current move towards administrative banning orders for those merely suspected of such involvement is disproportionate, particularly in the absence of any evidence such bans are effective in reducing 'hooliganism'. Moreover, they contribute to reinforcing authoritarian trends in current liberal democracies as, in circumventing the judicial to the benefit of the executive, they marginalise the rule of law thereby disturbing the traditional balance of powers in the polity.

As we put together the concluding chapter for this book in late winter of 2015, football supporters were once again in the media and political spotlight. Feyenoord Rotterdam and AS Roma supporters were involved in serious disorder in Rome prior to the first-leg of a Europa League fixture and at the return fixture a plastic banana was thrown onto the pitch causing the game to be briefly halted. In the same week in the Champions League, footage of a group of Chelsea supporters racially abusing a black Paris Metro passenger went viral on the Internet. Once again football supporters generally were castigated as violent and racist in certain sections of the media. However, the aim of this collection is not to make a judgment on the behaviour of football supporters. Too many times the discussion in the media and other public forums has focused on judging 'right and wrong' or 'good and bad', on who are 'hooligans' and how they can be controlled. It is, of course, essential to successful crowd management to identify the varying subcultures within football support, the different motivations and behaviours of these groups, and the relationships between them, and between them and football authorities, as well as between them and law enforcers. However, we do not seek to engage in the 'blame game' regarding incidents such as those in Rome, Rotterdam and Paris. We do not even set out to provide an answer to the question of why football-related disorder occurs, although many of the authors in this collection have criticised the exaggeration of the power possessed by 'hooligan' groups and have pointed towards the influence that police tactics have in terms of reducing or exacerbating the risk of wide-scale football violence.

Our aim in this collection is to take stock of the level of protection of the civil and human rights of football supporters across Europe. These rights should be indiscriminate; they form a barrier for ordinary citizens against unfettered executive power and apply to everyone. Human rights thus apply to *all* football supporters, not merely those that government, police, judges, football authorities or the media define as deserving of protection. In challenging the often taken-for-granted assumption that certain categories of citizens are not worthy of full protection of their rights and liberties, the authors hope that this book can contribute to accomplishing two goals. First, to support the principle that all football supporters have certain basic human rights, which must be protected and which can be defended through the courts. Secondly, this collection shows the ways in which these rights are being violated all over Europe. In all of the jurisdictions studied in this edited volume the state is encroaching upon these rights and, in many, football supporters are being prevented from exercising their rights. Such state responses are often untested in terms of their utility, and disproportionate in their effect. The civil and human rights of football supporters look more and more fragile in the face of increasing legal and quasi-legal powers and restrictions which are being rolled out across Europe in an almost unified fashion. From this standpoint, the scope of this book goes beyond football and football supporters to illustrate both the shifts of, and the threats posed to, the political and judicial foundations of twenty-first century legal systems in Europe.

FSC
www.fsc.org
MIX
Papier aus verantwortungsvollen Quellen
Paper from responsible sources
FSC® C105338

If you have any concerns about our products,
you can contact us on
ProductSafety@springernature.com

In case Publisher is established outside the EU,
the EU authorized representative is:
Springer Nature Customer Service Center GmbH
Europaplatz 3, 69115 Heidelberg, Germany

Printed by Libri Plureos GmbH
in Hamburg, Germany